# MEMOIRS OF THE LIFE AND WRITINGS OF THE ABATE METASTASIO

## VOLUME III

Da Capo Press Music Reprint Series

GENERAL EDITOR

FREDERICK FREEDMAN

VASSAR COLLEGE

# MEMOIRS OF THE LIFE AND WRITINGS OF THE ABATE METASTASIO

*Including Translations of His Principal Letters*

By Charles Burney

VOLUME III

 DA CAPO PRESS • NEW YORK • 1971

A Da Capo Press Reprint Edition

This Da Capo Press edition of the
*Memoirs of the Life and Writings
of the Abate Metastasio* is an unabridged
republication of the first edition published
in London in 1796.

For purposes of convenient reference, the table
of contents for each volume has been moved from
the end of the volume to the front.

Library of Congress Catalog Card Number 76-162295

SBN 306-71110-9

Published by Da Capo Press, Inc.
A Subsidiary of Plenum Publishing Corporation
227 West 17th Street, New York, N.Y. 10011
All Rights Reserved

Manufactured in the United States of America

# MEMOIRS OF THE LIFE AND WRITINGS OF THE ABATE METASTASIO

## VOLUME III

# MEMOIRS

OF THE

## LIFE AND WRITINGS

OF THE

## ABATE METASTASIO.

IN WHICH ARE INCORPORATED,

## TRANSLATIONS

OF HIS

## PRINCIPAL LETTERS.

---

By CHARLES BURNEY, Mus. D. F. R. S.

Omniaque ejus non folum facta, fed etiam dicta meminiffet.

CIC. SOMN. SCIP.

IN THREE VOLUMES.

## VOL. III.

LONDON:

PRINTED FOR G. G. AND J. ROBINSON,
PATERNOSTER-ROW.

M.DCC.XCVI.

## ERRATA TO VOL. III.

Page 8, note *, *for* feventy-four, *read* feventy-two. P. **10**, laſt line but five, *r.* haſtily. P. 11, laſt line but four, *for* remonſtrances, *r.* remembrances. P. 14, l. 17, *r.* 1774. P. 26, l. 14, *r.* brethren. P. 30, note (*d*) *for* above, *r.* Vol. II. P. 33, l. 15, *r.* extremely. Ibid. l. 21, *r. cangiar.* P. 40, Letter XIV. has, by miſtake, been tranſlated and inſerted here a ſecond time. P. 54, title of Let. II. *r.* ONOFRI. P. 71, l. 10, *r.* always. P. 102, l. 4, et alia, *r.* Eryſipelas. P. 178, l. 20, *dele* of. P. 242, l. 15, *r.* occaſions. P. 283, l. penult, *r.* fulfilling ; and laſt line, *r.* acquiring. P. 284, l. 3, *r.* meed. P. 297, l. 20, *for* elegant, *r.* ingenious. P. 298, l. 21, *r.* delineates. P. 301, l. 17, *r. Vinci.* P. 302, l. 16, *r.* the Olympiade. P. 303, l. 8, *r.* hiſtorical. P. 323, l. 18, *r. Vertu.* P. 324, l. 20, *r.* Scenes. P. 362, note (*k*) for theſe extracts, *r.* this abſtract. P. 378, l. 11. *r.* commiſeration. P. 380, note (*r*) l. 4, *r.* Rauzzini. P. 399, l. 21, *r.* Clytemneſtra.

## CONTENTS.

# CONTENTS

OF THE

## THIRD VOLUME.

------------

### SECTION I.

INTRODUCTION to the Poet's correfpondence with the Abate *Vincenzo Camillo Alberti*, of Bologna. Thanks for a Cantata from this Abate; and for a Sonnet, which, however, he declines accepting in the form of a dedication—Thanks Signor Alberti for his indignation at the alterations made in his dramas by Compofers, Singers, and opera Poets—Pleafantry on the Abate breaking in upon him, when he wifhed to feclude himfelf from all commerce with his correfpondents, while he was writing a new drama—Metaftafio's opinion of Blank Verfe—On the Countefs Bianchi's partiality to him—On the Emperor Jofeph's Tour, incognito, to Rome—Thanks for, and encomiums on, the works which the Abate had fent him—Account of the Opera of *Siface*, an old mufical Drama, corrected by Metaftafio —On the report of his being appointed Imperial Librarian.
Introduction to his correfpondence with the *Abate Fabroni*, at Florence.

LETTER

# CONTENTS.

Extracts

# CONTENTS.

# CONTENTS.

## SECTION II.

Introduction to Metastasio's correspondence with literary, and musical ladies.

LETTER

# CONTENTS.

E E 2                    Grand

# CONTENTS.

The notice with which the two Mifs Davies's were
honoured at Vienna, by the Emprefs Queen.

I             contrary

# CONTENTS.

built

# CONTENTS.

LETTER

# CONTENTS.

# CONTENTS.

## SECTION III.

# CONTENTS.

LETTER

# CONTENTS.

# CONTENTS.

# CONTENTS.

# C O N T E N T S.

# CONTENTS.

SECTION,

# CONTENTS.

## SECTION IV.

# CONTENTS.

Character of this Princefs—Anecdotes concerning her private life. - - 254

F F acceptance

# CONTENTS.

Further

# CONTENTS.

Reflections

# CONTENTS.

# CONTENTS,

# APPENDIX.

# MEMOIRS

OF THE

## LIFE AND WRITINGS

OF THE ABATE

## PIETRO METASTASIO.

———

## SECTION I.

About the time that Signor Mattei opened a correfpondence with our bard, he had many letters to write of mere compliment to authors who fent him their works, and of civility to others who had praifed his own. Except the letters to the *Romanina* and his brother, thofe to *Farinelli, Saverio Mattei,* and his old friend Sig. *Filipponi* of Turin, are the moft confidential. However, there are frequently paffages in his letters to others, which merit prefervation, either for their wit, ingenuity, politenefs, or, for the fentiments they contain on fubjects of literature; and of thefe we fhall felect a few, previous to refuming his correfpondence with his more particular friends.

In 1766, the Abate *Vincenzo Camillo Alberti* began a correfpondence with our poet, which continued till 1773; of which correfpondence near thirty letters have been inferted in the printed collection. But as they are fhort, and contain little more than expreffions of thanks and politenefs for his offers of friendfhip and prefents of his works, but little can be extracted from them, that can either amufe or intereft an Englifh reader; particularly, when deprived of the fafcinating elegance with which they are expreffed in their native language.

The firft letter from Sig. *Alberti* to which the anfwer of Metaftafio is preferved, inclofed a Cantata—" I cannot but be much flattered and obliged by your voluntary offer of friendfhip, with fuch partial expreffions in my favour; and as a demonftration of its value, you communicate to me a Cantata of your own writing, which is truly happy, affecting, and graceful. But how can a man at my time of life, tired with his indifpenfible occupations, fupport a regular correfpondence? Unlefs you could remove a number of Olympiads from my fhoulders, and

give

give me a little of your own leifure, I fhould certainly merit only your compaffion for my inability to avail myfelf of the honour which you fo generoufly offer me."

When Sig. *Alberti* fent Metaftafio a Sonnet which he had written with an intention of prefixing it as a dedication of his Cantatas to the poet, he fays: " I am extremely grateful for your affectionate partiality, and congratulate you on the production of fo beautiful a Sonnet; but at the fame time, muft entreat you moft earneftly, to relinquifh your obliging defign: as fuch incenfe has ever, from time immemorial, been devoted to the favourites of fortune, not to us poor inhabitants of Parnaffus. And this reafon has, hitherto, fufficed in defending me from others who have had a fimilar defign: and I promife to myfelf the fame complacence from you, which I fhall regard as a proof of your friendfhip, and a ftimulus to the continuance of that efteem with which I have the honour to be, &c."

This Abate feems, with great friendfhip and zeal, to have complained to Metaftafio of the liberties then taking by fome opera botchers with his dramas; to which the poet replies: " Spare your virtuous indignation, my moft obliging Sig. Alberti, for occafions

more

more worthy of your wrath, than the alterations of fome of my dramas. If the corrections are juſt, I ought to be grateful to thoſe who ſhall enlighten me ; and if otherwiſe, I ſhall not be forry that the public, occupied with the faults of others, ſhall have the leſs leiſure for reflecting upon mine. Let not my averſion to the writing long letters diminiſh your eſteem : on the contrary, believe me ever, in ſpite of this infirmity, invariably yours."

Metaſtaſio having, in ſport, told the Abate, that he ſhould be unable to write for fome time, as he was ordered by his imperial miſtreſs to take a journey to Parnaſſus ; Signor Alberti, not underſtanding that the poet meant to ſhut out all interruption, and devote his whole time to the muſes, broke in upon him with an unexpected letter, to which he pleaſantly makes the following reply. " Long life to my moſt officious Sig. Alberti! who for the ſake of his friends, in imitation of Hercules and Theſeus, does not decline having a commerce with the other world. Upon my having told you that I had made my laſt voyage to the Elyſian fields, you went thither by letter to feek me : folicitous to know the truth from myſelf. For once, I have the pleaſure to thank you from Vienna.

Vienna. But if I had been found in that remote region, I know not whether my anfwer would have come fo foon. However, after this convincing proof, I am fure that the inexorable fates may rob me of what they pleafe; but they will never place me beyond the power of your compafs."

The following extract from a letter to the Abate *Alberti* will communicate to the reader Metaftafio's opinion of blank verfe.

" I am much obliged to you for the new poetical compofition which you were fo kind as to inclofe in your laft letter, and which I fhould rather call an epiftle, than a poem. It appears to me learned, the thoughts feem noble and well digefted, and the ftyle as poetical and harmonious as is poffible in our endicafyllable meafure, ftript of rhyme. Whether from reafon or habit, I know not; but my ear cannot eafily accommodate itfelf to this convenient liberty, which perhaps, idlenefs has recommended to fome of our illuftrious Italian bards. It is true, that rhyme fometimes tyrannically impedes the expreffion of our thoughts : but it is likewife true, that it often fuggefts to us ideas that are more luminous and fublime, to which our minds would never have foared, but for the violent efforts to which this troublefome

B 3              ftimulatrx

ftimulatrix has obliged us to have recourfe in our diftrefs. And it is certain, that there is as much difference in the force of the fame thought happily expreffed in rhyme and in blank verfe, as in that of a ftone thrown with the hand, and with a fling. Not that I difapprove of this liberty in the epiftolary or didactic ftyle. In thefe, it feems as if the poet may difpenfe a little with this mufic, which is always effential to true poetry."

" I know not what can poffibly have feduced the worthy Countefs Bianchi in my favour. I am fo proud of fuch an enviable partiality, that I pray to heaven fhe may never be undeceived. Pray prefent her my moft humble thanks, and try to keep her in this miftake."——

Speaking of the Emperor's Tour through Italy, incognito, in 1769, he fays : " we know nothing more of the auguft pilgrim here, than that he quitted Vienna the 3d of this inftant March, in the evening ; that there is no doubt but that he intends to vifit Rome in this manner to avoid ceremony, of which he is an irreconcileable enemy; and that he pro-pofes to pafs unknown wherever he goes ; but his ftar is thought too luminous to be conccaled concealed by any cloud which he can get behind."——

" My moſt obliging Sig. Alberti, ever eager to confer favours on me, has been the firſt to inform me of the happy delivery of the little niece of my dear Gemello : pray accept of my beſt thanks for the courteous diligence with which you have quieted my ſolicitude *."

Metaſtaſio's correſpondent, the Abate Alberti, had been long confined to his bed by a broken ancle. When he ſent him ſome works which he had produced during that ſtate—The Imperial Laureat ſays : " I ſhall read the book whenever I can get time for that gratification ; but, at preſent, I have hardly leiſure ſufficient to thank, you for it. I have, however, peruſed the little Cantata that was incloſed in your letter, by which I find, that though lame, you have either been able to clamber mount Parnaſſus, or are ſo well with the muſes, that they ſcruple not to viſit you in bed. Get up, for heaven's ſake, that you may no longer oblige them to

* This was the little fractious homely child, of which Farinelli was ſo fond, when I viſited him at Bologna, in 1770.

ſuch

fuch practices as, to thofe who envy you, may
appear fcandalous."——

" In your laft letter, you wifh me to be
diffufe in my anfwer, and point out an opportunity for me to difcufs certain queftions in
the Afiatic manner. Ah, my dear Abate,
you fuppofe me young, robuft, and idle.
Would to heaven you were not miftaken!
But, for my misfortune, neither youth,
ftrength, nor leifure, are allowed me. The
mere duties of my office are now a grievous
burthen to me : think then how unfit I muft
be, to fcrawl whole fheets, merely to fhew
my eloquence and genius ; I leave all this to
you, who are in the prime of life *."——

" The laft Sonnet with which you have
been pleafed to favour me, leaves all the
other poetical compofitions which the mufes
have hitherto dictated to you, far behind. I
congratulate you upon it : but am unable to
comprehend how, in your painful fituation, it
is poffible for you to have an inclination to
tune the lyre. Though I can plead no fuch
painful impediment, yet I can never brufh
the duft off mine, unlefs from abfolute neceffity. In the enfuing nuptial celebration

* Metaftafio was now feventy four.

there

there will be no theatrical exhibition. I obtained not this information, till I had almoſt finiſhed a drama which I was ordered to write : ſo that I have not been ſpared, as I might have been, a labour which is now become heavy and ungrateful *.———

" Your ſonnet ſhall be enjoyed by the few palates that are able to taſte it."———

" I know not whether I ought to congratulate you on the huge purchaſe you have made of Italian dramas. You will find, as formerly happened to myſelf, in an immenſe quantity of ſtraw, but very little grain, and that of a bad quality. *Siface* will not compenſate for the bad harveſt. I am extremely grateful to you for the obliging offer of it, which you make me ; but having, ſome years ago, met with a copy of this old opera, I gave it a peruſal, and am by no means tempted to acknowledge it as my legitimate offspring. It is a drama compoſed againſt my will : the idea was to reform an old opera at the requeſt of *Porpora* : and in reforming, it was entirely changed; as the original materials

* This drama (*Ruggiero*) was, however, completed, ſet to muſic by Haſſe, and proformed at Milan, in 1771, upon the marriage of the Arch-duke Ferdinand, with the princeſs of Modena.

were

were so totally different from the additional, and so discordant, as to form a contrast that was insupportable and monstrous. And yet, it is not mine, though I believe there remains not one verse as it was written by the first author. In order to be truly mine, the first design should have been of my invention; but my intention was merely to rectify some particular parts; and though I have left none untouched, I have never regarded them as members of a whole fabric of my construction. Therefore the connexion must necessarily remain imperfect. Make, however, what use you please of *Siface*; only do not let it pass for a child of mine, as 1 cannot conscientiously regard it as such.

Writing is always an inconvenient business to me; but to-day, on account of the excessive heat, which dissolves me, it is insupportable, so that being totally unable to lengthen my letter, I haly conclude."

Vienna, June 29, 1772.

There are two more short letters to the *Abate Alberti* in the collection; but they contain nothing very piquant or interesting. It had been reported about this time, all over Europe,

Europe, that the poet had been appointed Imperial Librarian, in the room of Baron *Van Swieten* deceafed; and upon being congratulated by the Abate Alberti on this promotion, he fays, " the report is entirely without foundation ; nor do I imagine that my auguft fovereigns ever thought of me, when the vacancy happened. Indeed if, from excefs of clemency, they had, I fhould have been obliged to implore their difpenfation from a weight fuperior to my phyfical force, which would not have enabled me to perform the duties of fuch an appointment."—

In the laft letter to the Abate, he thanks him for a neat and elegant edition of his Italian poetry. He denies the writing a Canzonetta in praife of the immortal Marefhal Daun, which Alberti had afcribed to him : " take care not to defraud the real author of thofe praifes which are his due— Pray return with my refpeĉts, due thanks to the moft obliging Lord Huntingdon for the courteous remonftrances with which he honours me,"

Vienna, April 29, 1773.

---

A correfpondence feems to have been begun about the year 1767, between our poet and

the

the Abate FABRONI, afterwards Bifhop of
Pifa ; a perfon of literary abilities, for whom
Metaftafio manifefts great refpect.　His
Lives and Eloges of illuftrious men of his own
country, which he began to publifh at this
time in decades, feem undertaken with a
patriotic view, during the difputes between
the French and Italians for literary and
fcientific pre-eminence.　The title of his
biographical work is certainly the fame as
that of *Perrault*, in the laft century (*a*); but
then the Italians have to boaft of many works
on the fame plan, and under the fame title,
which are much more ancient than that of
Perrault.　Signor Fabroni having expreffed
an intention to write the life of Metaftafio,
in order to infert it among his lives of eminent men, the following letter contains the
poet's modeft diffuafion from that enterprize.

(*a*) *Eloges des Hommes illuftres de ce Siecle* (the xvii.)
*Elogi d'alcuni illuftri Italiani.*

# LETTER I.

## TO THE ABATE FABRONI, AT FLORENCE.

WITHOUT framing excufes for the flow arrival of my anfwer to your very obliging letter of the 9th of laft May, the well-known confufion in which we have been thrown, by the lofs of a moft amiable Emprefs; by our fears of being deprived of our maternal and revered Sovereign; and, at prefent, the univerfal, and tumultuous joy, for having miraculoufly preferved her, will have already made my defence, and procured your pardon. Therefore, after rendering the fincere and due thanks which I ought, for your moft conftant voluntary partiality, I congratulate your royal Sovereign, who, in having promoted you, has given fuch an indubitable teftimony of his enlightened mind, and generous heart; always ready to fee merit and reward it.

But, notwithftanding your partiality, I perceive, that you have a defign to injure me very ferioufly. The perfifting in your idea of writing my life, is an evident proof, that my repugnance, in confenting to it, has been regarded by you as a kind of female modefty, which

which a little entreaty would overcome. No, my dear Abate, you are very much deceived. Whether from reafon, or weaknefs, I cannot think of any one writing my life, without the utmoft difquietude. From this fincere and candid confeffion, I hope that you will have the friendly condefcenfion to relinquifh the enterprize; a favour which I moft earneftly fupplicate, and fhall receive with all due gratitude.

Vienna, June 11, 1767.

This requeft was complied with, during the poet's life; but two years after his deceafe, his eloge, by this author, appeared, with thofe of *Galileo Galilei, Mich. Angelo Giacomelli, Tommafo Perelli, Card. Leopoldo de' Medici,* and *Carlo Innocenzio Frugoni.* Pifa. 1754.

## LETTER II.

### TO THE SAME.

From your obliging letter, reverend Sir, dated July 6th. I was induced to hope, that I fhould foon receive the firft decade, of your *Lives of Illuftrious Italians,* which I have expected

pected with the utmost impatience. Occupied at prefent in the exercife of my employment, it was my intention to defer
anfwering your kind letter, till the arrival of
the gift. But as it has not yet reached my
hands (by one of thofe innumerable accidents
which ufually difturb the courfe of fimilar
prefentations) I fhall not fuffer a longer
filence, now my inevitable duties are fulfilled, to injure me in your good opinion.
Know then, moft reverend Prior, that in the
perufal of your letters, my mind is filled with
all the gratitude, confufion, and affection,
which are due to your friendly and unfolicited partiality, for one who has neither the
opportunity, nor the power, of meriting it.
But being in poffeffion of this ineftimable
acquifition, I am, and ever fhall remain, extremely proud of it.

But why, with fuch difpofitions in my
favour, do you imbitter my fatisfaction, by
publifhing fuch frivolous letters as thefe,
written without the leaft reflection, in the
full confidence that they would never fee the
light? Good God! You eftimate the public
indulgence by your own, and are deceived.
The public is a moft fevere judge; and if it
made the father of Roman eloquence tremble

ble (which he was not afhamed to confefs) at a time when he had fully prepared him-felf for its tribunal, with what confcience can it be called excefs of modefty in me, to dread prefenting myfelf before it, with four miferable little letters, written in hafte to confidential friends, without ever perufing them? No, moft reverend Prior, I have not the courage, or rather arrogance, requifite for fuch an exhibition. And whether my fears are reafonable, as I really think them, or conftitutional errors, I have no hopes of ever vanquifhing them. If you ftill regard them as infirmities, the pardoning fmall defects is one of the moft facred duties of friendfhip. Treat them, therefore, as fuch, moft worthy Prior, and indulge me in this petition, as you obligingly did, in renouncing the defign of writing my life. The literary world abounds with fubjects much more worthy of your pen, and I have, in my former letter, honeftly confeffed how much I am difturbed by the mere idea of ufurping fuch incenfe as is by no means my due.

Vienna, September 24, 1767.

LET-

# LETTER III.

## TO THE SAME.

THE firft volume of the lives of illuftrious men, of which you have been pleafed, moft reverend Sir, to make me a prefent, has been obligingly delivered to me, by Count *Strafoldo*. The names of perfons with whom, during childhood and adolefcence, I lived, or at leaft was acquainted, and who compofe the chief part of this firft decade, ftimulated immediate perufal ; and the infinuating flow and elegance of ftyle, would not fuffer me to lay the book down, till I was arrived at the laft page, and had perufed the additional commentary on the life of my dear fellow ftudent, Count *Dandini.* Having now gratified the firft hafty curiofity, I fhall give the work a fecond and more deliberate perufal; not paffing by, as was the cafe before, the two lives written by *Morgagni,* which treating of perfons with whom I have but little acquaintance, had not excited the fame curiofity as the reft. The rapidity of my perufal, however, did not prevent my feeing the merits of the writer ; befides the ftyle, which manifefts long ftudy and experience,

c the

the laborious tafk of collecting materials fo
difperfed and obfcure, the prudent and laudable dexterity of uniting truth with difcretion, and the various and deep learning and
fcience, neceffary for the accurate difplay of
whatever faculties the fubject prefented,
juftly entitle the author of fo folid a work, to
the praife and gratitude of the public.

Vienna, October 8, 1767.

## LETTER IV.

### TO THE SAME.

You wifh me, Sir, to give you my opinion
of the dramatic works of my predeceffor,
APOSTOLO ZENO, as if your own judgment
were not lefs likely to be warped by prejudice, than that of a man who has run the
fame career, and who feduced by that too
common and vicious emulation, fometimes
even without knowing it, to which *Figulus
Figulo* is very feldom favourable. For
my own part, I am far from certain that I
fhould be able in a minute examination of
thefe dramas to fteer with fafety between
the rocks of envy and affectation; however,
if no other poetical merit were allowed to

Apoftolo

Apoftolo Zeno, it muſt be granted that he
fuccefsfully demonſtrated, that our melodrama
is not incompatible with reaſon (as was long
thought by the public and the poets whom he
found in poſſeſſion of the theatre when he
began to write) that it was not exempt from
the laws of probability, that it could ſubſiſt
without the wild and bombaſt ſtile which
then reigned; and, laſtly, that the buſkin
might be freed from the comic ſcurrility of
the ſock, with which it was miſerably mixed
and polluted; theſe are merits fully ſufficient
to entitle him to our gratitude, and the
eſteem of poſterity.

Vienna, December 7, 1767.

## LETTER V.

### TO THE SAME.

THE ſtudying to be uſeful to our fellow
creatures, and ſeconding the zeal of a worthy
and partial friend, like yourſelf, are duties
which procure blame if negleſted, yet have
little right to praiſe if performed. Hence
thoſe with which you have entruſted me,
moſt reverend Sir, refleſt more honour on the

good-

goodnefs of your own heart, ever eager to fulfil the duties of humanity, than on mine.

I very much wifh that our traveller may continue to enjoy that attention and politenefs, during his refidence in Poland, which our recommendation had procured him on his arrival : where, according to the accounts which I have received, his reception was extremely flattering; but that kingdom, at prefent convulfed by Confederations, is all arms and tumult : circumftances very unfavourable to the fine arts. But a ftate of fuch violence cannot be durable. The humours, decompounded, muft find their equilibrium, and that tranquillity return which is fo indifpenfibly neceffary to national as well as individual happinefs.

The well-merited teftimonies of efteem with which you have been honoured by the amiable Queen of Naples, manifeft the mature judgment of that incomparable princefs, at fo early an age. Hence, I have a double reafon for exultation.

Materials for the *Index* which you defire are wanting (*b*). The manufcripts which remain, are fuch as have been already pub-

(*b*) Sig. Fabroni had requefted of Metaftafio, a complete fift of all the inedited works of his patron Gravina.

lifhed,

lifhed, or fketches and fragments of tracts, begun for amufement, and chiefly left unfinifhed; the author himfelf having judged them
unequal to the public expectations excited by
his high reputation. There may have been
works of more importance; but foon after
his deceafe, all his writings were demanded,
and retained for fome time, by thofe who
had legitimate authority for fo doing; and
were afterwards returned in the exact number and ftate in which they now remain. So
that it feems as if this article fhould be
wholly omitted in your work.

Permit me to enjoy that enviable place
which you have been pleafed to affign me in
your good heart, and believe me to be always
unalterably with due refpect, &c.

Vienna, June 13, 1768.

## LETTER VI.

### TO THE SAME.

AT length the cuftom-houfe officers, after
condemning and rejecting all my demands
and enquiries, have produced the little parcel
with the dialogues of Phocion fo long de-
tained; and convicted of their irregularity

C 3

and negligence, have fent it to my houfe when I defpaired of ever receiving it; but accompanied with fuch childifh excufes, as were much worfe than the fault.

I indulged my impatience by the immediate perufal of the book, and have ran over five of the dialogues and the greateft part of the notes. I would not poftpone writing till I had finifhed reading the whole work, becaufe I was unwilling to let a poft depart ere I had acknowledged the receipt of your valuable prefent, in order to prevent you from kindly beftowing upon me another copy, on the fuppofition that the firft was loft. I fhall not now enter on the merit of the original (c); I muft confefs that the great truths which thefe dialogues enforce are well known; but befides their being fuch as cannot be too often repeated, elegance and learning give them the graces of novelty, I cannot help admiring the excellent difpofition of the happy tranflator's mind and heart, who though able to produce architypes of his own, tranfported by the love of hu-

(c) *Entretiens de Phocion fur le rapport de la morale avec la politique,* publifhed by the Abbé Mably, 1763, in which work, though not written by PHOCION, the fentiments of this illuftrious Greek are well fupported.

manity,

manity, could not refrain from undertaking a labour fo much below his faculties, for the love of truth, and the defire of communicating it. I congratulate you on the accomplifhment of this work, and full of that affection which you ftudy to propagate among mankind, I remain refpectfully, &c.

Vienna, June 23, 1768,

## LETTER VII.

### TO THE SAME.

I PERCEIVE, moft reverend Sir, from the effects of your laft letter, which announces to me the honour which the members of the academy *della Crufca* have deigned to confer upon me, by admitting me of their body, how little I knew myfelf, and that my former power of fuppreffing all ambitious views had loft its efficacy. It feems now, that inftead of contracting my wifhes and hopes, that I may venture to extend them ; finding myfelf fortunately decked with the participation of that fplendor, with which this illuftrious inftitution has not only dignified its members, but all Italy. Having had the power, by the force of your friendfhip and affection

C 4         unfolicited

unfolicited to procure me this diftinguifhed
honour, I muft entreat you to paint to my
venerated colleagues, in all the warm colouring of your native eloquence, not only my
joy on this occafion, but my moft fincere
fentiments of refpect and gratitude : nor muft
you forget to reprefent to yourfelf how much
my debts of gratitude to you are encreafed
by this recent and moft obliging manifefta-
tion of your friendly zeal.

To judge with chriftian charity of our
neighbour, as it is my duty and intereft to
do, I have the pleafure to believe, that the
frequent calls for my laft production are
fymptoms of affection and partiality ; but if
I fhould derive this eagernefs from a lefs
flattering fource, I fhould ftill have the fatif-
faction of afcribing it to that friendfhip with
which I am honoured, and have authority to
boaft,

Vienna, September 19, 1768.

There are feveral other letters to Monfignor
Fabroni after he was Bifhop of Pifa, which
though full of that urbanity and politenefs
with which the poet treated men of letters
in general with whom he correfponded ; yet,
as

as they contain no fentiments or criticifm of importance to literature, their infertion here feems unneceffary.

The following correfpondence was obtruded upon our bard, by a perfon whofe name feems never to have reached his eyes or ears, before the arrival of the letter which produced the fubfequent reply.

# LETTER VIII.

## TO THE ABATE D. GIUSEPPE AURELIO MORANI.

BEING perfectly ignorant of the fituation of the perfon with whom I correfpond, he is intreated to affure himfelf, that it will not be from difrefpect, but want of information, if I fhould omit any of the *formala* due to his rank and circumftances.

After the perufal of Sig. *Giufeppe Aurelio Morani's* moft elegant letter, I cannot be miftaken in regarding him as a young man of great application, genius, and learning; and poffeffed of that knowledge in the Greek and Roman claffics, at which few arrive in riper years. I congratulate my delightful Parthenope (Naples) in the having given you birth;

birth: an honour in which by the right of long
refidence, and a thoufand ties of gratitude, I
take a part. But the courteous D. Giufeppe
is extremely miftaken in the too partial opinion which he has conceived of me. My
talents are much more limited than he imagines: never having arrived at fuch profound
learning or merit of other kinds as to be able
to entertain *convivas cultores,* or claim a place
*in lauto hofpitio.* With refpect to genius,
father Apollo has treated me with a generofity not above the common, and, in other
refpects, has not diftinguifhed me from my
brethern. Senfible, however, of the merit of
D. Giufeppe, I gratefully thank him for his
obliging wifhes for my profperity, and am
with true efteem, &c.

Vienna, 1766,

## LETTER IX,

### TO THE SAME.

As your firft letter infpired me with ideas
of your genius and cultivated talents, the
fecond, which I now anfwer, convinces me
of the candour, moderation, and other uncommon virtues with which your heart is
furnifhed ;

furnifhed : internal qualities which I regard
as more worthy of being honoured, than the
fplendor of external circumftances, which
are the mere capricious gifts of fortune. If
I had not in common your ideal parent
*(Penia)* I fhould give you very different
proofs of my efteem, than thefe vain officious
expreffions. And as you think you have not
exaggerated this metaphorical confanguinity,
I wifh you to reflect, that the *wretched man* is
he to whom the neceffary fupports of life are
wanting, *quibus doleat natura negatis.* The
*poor,* he who procures thefe neceffaries from
the generofity of others, He who poffeffes
a *competency,* is able to provide for his own
wants. And he whofe means exceed that
power, is *opulent.* If you wifh to find my
place, it muft be in the fecond of thefe four
claffes, where I fhould fuffer with ftill greater
refignation the rigourous juftice which providence renders to moderate abilities, if I did
not frequently feel the privation of the
greateft pleafure granted to mortals, the
power of conferring benefits on the worthy.
Add to this, that living in a climate where
literature is not reckoned among the merchandife of fociety, my infufficiency is likewife

wife extended to thofe kind offices, which elfewhere perhaps would not be ufelefs.

With refpect to my immortal mafter, Gravina, he publifhed before his deceafe, all thofe works which he thought would contribute to his fame. The reft were never defigned for the prefs, though fordid editors, have counteracted his intentions : fo that inquiries after them are as vain, as the affaults of his detractors, from whofe fangs he is as fafe as every man muft be, who like him is *totus teres, atque rotundus.*

Notwithftanding the narrow limits of my fituation, if you could fuggeft to me an opportunity of manifefting my zeal for your fervice, I fhall do it with that fincere and cordial efteem with which I am, and ever fhall continue, &c.

Vienna, September 24, 1766,

## LETTER X.

### TO THE SAME.

You muft not wonder, my dear Sig. *Morani*, at the tardinefs or brevity of my anfwer to your moft obliging letter of laft

December.

December. A great number of indifpenfible letters, together with the capricious ftate of my health, oblige me to defer, and fometimes entirely deprive me of the pleafure I fhould have in correfponding with perfons whom I efteem and love, and from whofe forbearance I promife myfelf the greateft indulgence. But this involuntary negligence, efpecially when there is no bufinefs in queftion, ought not to diminifh the credit of a perfect correfpondence, with thofe who have a mutual affection for each other. Do me the juftice to believe, in fpite of circumftances, that impreffed with a partiality for your talents and character, I fhall ever remain invariably yours.

Metaftafio begins every fubfequent letter to this Abate, by an apology for not writing to him more frequently; which though reafonable, ingenious, and well-turned, in the original, would appear monotonous and infipid in another language. I fhall therefore extract from thefe letters, the moft interefting paffages on other fubjects than his own delinquency as an irregular correfpondent.

In

In 1769, Sig. *Morani* wifhed him to enter the lifts among the champions for Italian literature, in oppofition to the French, who on all occafions arrogantly claimed the fupremacy. After excufing himfelf for inability to keep up a regular correfpondence with his friends, he fays—" from thefe involuntary omiffions, you may judge whether I fhould be able to apply myfelf to the parallel which you propofe between the French and Italian literature : a work of great labour, for any one who fhould not wifh to decide impertinently, without furnifhing folid reafons on both fides. Nor am I more able to obey you, in tranfmitting the MSS. you requeft, which being merely intended to affift my own memory, merit not tranfcription, or the honour of appearing before the public ; nor will they ever fee the light, though curiofity has been awakened by Sig. *Diodati* publifhing the letter in which I inconfiderately mentioned them (*d*)."

In the next letter to the Abate *Morani*, in anfwer to a queftion, whether a French tranflation of Metaftafio's works was pub-

(*d*) See the letter to *Diodati* above, p. 306.

lifhed

lifhed at Vienna, he fays : "It is not at
Vienna but at Paris, that a tranflation of
my works in the French language has
appeared ; but having had an unfavourable
account of this verfion by thofe who have
feen it, I have carefully avoided the perufal,
in order to fhun the rifk of becoming
ungrateful to him who has given fuch a public proof of partiality to my writings by
tranflating them. It would by no means
become me arrogantly to decide, as you
wifh me, whether *Corneille* or *Racine* has
the primacy on the French theatre. The
natives find all the grandeur of Sophocles in
the firft, and all the truth of Euripides in
the fecond. The one filling the mind of
the fpectator with the moft magnificent
ideas, and the other agitating the heart
with the moft tender affections : hence thefe
two artifts have arrived at equal excellence,
but by different roads. However, *Corneille*
cannot be denied the great merit of having
pointed out the path which his rival
purfued." 1770.

"If you would read without fcruple,
*Pope's Effay on Man*, I recommend to you
the excellent tranflation *in terza rima*, lately
publifhed by Count *Giuf. Maria Ferrero di
Lauriano.*

*Lauriano.* In the judicious, christian, and learned notes with which he has illustrated the work, you will see the innocence of the original evidently proved. You will find in Pope a great poet, and a deep philosopher; but not such axioms as are necessary to support his own system. "

Though it has been said that Metastasio, unwilling to hear of death, permitted no one even to mention it before him; yet he frequently complains to his correspondents of his having too many Olympiads on his shoulders. And in a letter to the Abate *Morani,* in 1771, when he was in his 74th year, he says: " The state of my health, though not exactly what I wish it, is much better than I have a right to expect. As to my occupations, when the commands of my sovereign allow me to choose them, I, like your favourite Cicero, have recourse *ad Litterulas*; not with the hopes of fame or profit, but to keep off the *tædium vitæ*, and to march to the end of my journey as flow as possible. "

In a subsequent letter to the same Abate, in answer to his enquiries concerning the poet's translation of Horace's *Ars Poetica,* he says: " Not only my translation in Italian verse verfe of the Poetics of Horace, with the notes which feemed neceffary, but an extract of that of Ariftotle, with obfervations, which rendered the tafk more tedious and laborious, have been entirely finifhed a confiderable time. And I have exacted the premium of my fatiguing occupation in imagining, that there was fome merit in having employed my leifure without remorfe. However, it has never been my intention to trouble the public with thefe labours : and if even temptation fhould take me by furprife, it would be neceffary, ere they appeared, rigouroufly to examine what I have written : a work to me entremely difagreeable. At prefent, both fleep in my portfolio, fecure, at leaft, from infult, while they are unknown. You fee, that to comply with your requeft, I muft vanquifh my irrefolute and perverfe difpofition ; and you know that

*Che cangiai di natura*
*E'imprefa troppo dura.*

The tafk is hard for human creature
To change propenfities of nature.

" The tragedies of my immortal beneficent mafter, are fufficient to prove what philofophy and immenfe learning the writer poffeffed.

poffeffed. He has executed what he propofed: that is, to give us an idea of the
Greek theatre. If, in after-times, the enormous change of manners renders them in-
confiftent with the prefent reigning tafte, it
cannot be afcribed to him as a fault, becaufe
to flatter it was not his intention."

The particular occafion of the following
letter does not appear; there feems, however,
to be fome degree of vaticination in it,
which reminds us more of the prefent times,
than of the period when it was written.

# LETTER XI.

### TO A ROMAN PRINCE. (PRINCE GHIGI.)

THE ftrange and univerfal ferment in
which facred and profane things are now
thrown, throughout the known world, affords
little hope that the crifis of its termination
is near at hand. The fire has long been
burning in fecret, but the fuel is weak, and
the humours are too heterogeneous to produce
an equilibrium. The object of thofe who
might give us repofe, is innovation, not
tranquillity. Hence, to regulate and reduce
to order the enormous confufion of fo dark a
chaos,

chaos, feems to want nothing lefs than omnipotence, which needs only fay, *fiat lux,*
for light to appear. I hope thefe gloomy
thoughts proceed from the vice of my own
temperament, and a natural propenfity to
deplore the prefent, and exalt the paft.
But it is very certain, that all great revolutions and changes of ancient fyftems, (even
if it were certain that pofterity would be
benefitted by them) are ever fatal to the unhappy mortals, who are condemned to be
fpectators of the conflict.

Vienna, 1767.

In the following letters, he defcribes his diftrefs at the imminent danger into which his
Patronefs, the Emprefs Queen, was thrown
by the fmall-pox, with which fhe was feized
at the fame time as the Emperor Jofeph's
firft confort, to whom the difeafe was fatal.

## LETTER XII.

### TO A FRIEND AT MILAN.

From the defcription which I have given
you of the premature death of this fovereign,

an

and of the extreme danger into which my
Patronefs was thrown at the fame time, you
may conceive how pungent muft have been
my affliction, at thefe mournful events. It was
eafy to read in my countenance, the internal agitation of my mind ; nor was there a
fingle perfon from whom I could conceal
it. My confufion, my tears, the being con-
tinually in the gallery of the imperial palace,
and perpetually making enquiries of the
phyficians and ladies of the court, concerning the ftate of my Patronefs's health, too
plainly difcovered to the crowd of cour-
tiers, my confufion and excefs of grief. I
fincerely affure you, my dear friend, that
among the many fad cataftrophes to which
I have been fubject during fixty-nine years,
this would have been the moft terrible, if it
had not pleafed divine providence to hear
the fervent prayers of her fubjects.

Vienna, 1767.

LET-

## LETTER XIII.

TO PADRE PAZZONI, MAESTRO DI
CAPELLA, IN SIENA.

THOUGH I cannot, without manifeſt
ingratitude, doubt of your affection, yet
every confirmation of it which you kindly
give me, has all the grace and efficacy of
novelty. I ſhould be totally infenſible, not
to be pleaſed with the peruſal of your laſt
letter, in which is diſplayed at once, all the
candour and openneſs of your good heart, and
the honoured and enviable place which I
occupy in it : a place of which I have great
reaſon to be jealous and proud. With this
confidence, not doubting of the fimilarity of
our ſentiments, I muſt entreat you to come
to an explanation with this generous, and
worthy lady, by whoſe partiality I am no
leſs confuſed than pleaſed. Firſt begin by
aſſerting my infinite gratitude and reſpect ;
and then proceed to implore her to ſpare me
the mortification of ſeeing in print, as ſhe
intends, any of my familiar letters. The
public merits reſpect from all, and particularly from myſelf ; nor can I have the

courage

courage to expect from it that indulgence
with which I am honoured by my friends.
The major part of my letters having been
written in hafte, were never read by myfelf,
and God knows how many repetitions, trivi-
alities, and negligences, I fhould be condemned to blufh for. I have fufficient motives to fear for my moft laboured works ; and
I beg of her not to encreafe the number of
thofe fears unneceffarily. Unite, therefore,
your friendly folicitations with my own, to
prevail on this lady, my protectrefs, not to
put her defign in practice, — tell her that it
would be an infult, not a favour, to oblige an
honeft man to quit his bed-room, and
expofe himfelf publicly, in his night-gown
and flippers.

Adieu, my dear friend. I abfolutely depend on your friendfhip, to prevent this
dreaded publication. But at the fame time,
do not conceal the gratitude with which I
am impreffed by the obliging, and favourable, though ill-founded opinion, which has
given birth to this idea.

Vienna, January 29, 1767.

———————————

There is no date to the following letter ;
but it feems to have been written about this
time,

time, when the poet was oppreffed by *forced loans* of his time and opinions, to authors, whofe works

    " With fad civility, he fat, and read
    With honeft anguifh, and an aching head."—
    Befet by wits, an undiftinguifh'd race,
    Who firft his judgment afk, and then a place."—
                    POPE.

But the Italian bard more patient and lefs peevifh than the Englifh, brufhes off his tormentors gently, and difmiffes them in good humour. His reputation, however, muft fometimes have fuffered on the fide of fincerity, or good tafte, where his praifes of obfcure authors, which were always inftantly publifhed by thofe on whom they were beftowed, bordered on hyperbole. Whether the fonnets, mentioned in the following letter, deferved the encomiums beftowed upon them by the Imperial Laureat, we know not, as they, and even the name of their author, feem equally unknown in the literary world.

LET-

# LETTER XIV.

## TO THE CAVALIER ANTON-FILIPPO ADAMI.

I SHALL not dwell long on the exceffive expreffions of efteem with which you honour me, in order to efcape the difagreeable tafk of defending myfelf from the affaults of vanity, which might infiduoufly feduce me, coming from fuch high authority. I am abafhed by your too favourable opinion; yet I fhall not attempt to undeceive you, fearing to fhake the foundation of the friendfhip which you offer me, and which I wifh to deferve.

I have perufed, and re-perufed, the fonnets which you have been pleafed, Sir, to communicate to me, and always with juft admiration. I have found in them all, force, dignity of ftyle, deep learning, lively fancy, and above all, that unity, proportion, and correfpondence of the feveral parts, which diftinguifh an inhabitant of Parnaffus from a paffenger. Though I am pleafed with them all, the fonnets upon providence have ftruck me the moft. Perhaps the countenance of

thefe

thefe being lefs auftere, diftinguifhes them,
when compared with their companions.
Your highly polifhed productions, wheneve.
you fhall be pleafed to communicate them to
me, will always be received with pleafure.
And if you accompany them with any commands, you will greatly gratify my impatience to convince you of the refpect and
obedience with which you have infpired me.

The following letters to an author, who
forced the poet into a correfpondence, by
prefenting to him his works without previous acquaintance or introduction, will perhaps make the reader wonder that he never
heard of fo accomplifhed a writer.

## LETTER XV.

### TO THE ABATE SILVIO BALBIS OF SALUZZO.

You muft not imagine that the juft tribute of praife which I fincerely beftow on
the magnificent poetical epiftle which you
have been pleafed to fend me, is the effect
of the gratitude due to you for your exceffive
partiality, Its own merit has no occafion to
be fupported or exalted by the fecret influence of my felf-love. Therefore, feparate
the

the debts of the one from the other, and
affure yourfelf, that truth and juftice
oblige me to confefs, what I could not without remorfe deny, that I have not for a
long time feen a compofition which has
given me equal pleafure. The clear, noble,
harmonious felicity of ftyle, and the connexion and choice of your thoughts, make
me regard as portentous, the maturity of the
productions of fo young a writer. If your
circumftances and fituation, of which I am
ignorant, allow you with prudence to chufe
a ftudy among the ufeful and glorious, unite
yourfelf in the ftrict bonds of friendfhip with
the mufes, and I will be anfwerable for the
diftinguifhed and elevated rank at which you
will foon arrive in Parnaffus. Having
afforded me fo fair an occafion for admiring your talents, afford me likewife that of
ferving you, and believe me to be, with juft
efteem and acknowledgment, &c.

Vienna, March 12, 1761.

---

The fubfequent letters to the fame correfpondent, contain further encomiums on
his writings. Metaftafio fent this Abate a
copy of his feveral dramas, previous to
general publication ; and he feems to have
merited

merited this diftinction, not only as his admirer, but champion; as the poet in one of
his letters, "thanks him and the ladies and
gentlemen of Saluzzo for defending his poor
dramas from the injuries which they daily fuffer in all the theatres of Europe, from thofe
ignorant and vain vocal heroes and heroines,
who having fubftituted the imitation of
flageolets and nightingales to human affections, render the Italian ftage a national
difgrace, in the opinion of thofe countries
which have been obliged to us for all their
knowledge of the art."

This alludes to the abridging and changing the fcenes and airs of his dramas, to
humour the caprice of fingers, who difre-
garding character, place, and propriety, not
only in *Pafticcio* operas, but in every other,
where no fcruple is made to introduce an
*Aria d'abilità*, or *di bravura*, which has been
applauded in a former drama, without the
leaft attention to the preceding recitative, or
bufinefs of the fcene. Thefe airs taken out of
their original niche, when tranflated in the
books of the opera, continue to incline the good
people of England to imagine the words of
an opera to be *all nonfenfe*; and that even
the mufical dramas of Metaftafio are as abfurd

furd and fubject to ridicule, as thofe which Addifon has defcribed with fo much pleafantry, in the *Spectator*.

Reciprocation of compliments of the higheft kind, feems, about this time, to have paffed between the poet and Signor D. *Baldaffarre Papadia*. Though we have never feen the letters of this correfpondent, we may judge of his reverence and partiality for Metaftafio, by the anfwers to them, which for elegance and urbanity, appear to merit tranflation and infertion, as much as any letters of the kind in the collection.

## L E T T E R  XVI.

### TO SIGNOR D. BALDASSARRE PAPADIA.

It would be neceffary to poffefs all the ftoical infenfibility of *Zeno* and *Cleanthes*, long to refift the temptations of vanity, with which you affail the moderation which I ought to poffefs, in fpeaking of my dear Parthenope. (Naples.) But you, Sir, by an obliging impulfe of affection, have endeavoured to give it a great fhock. God forgive you. All that you defcribe in your elegant letter, and all you imagine in your

2        fublime

fublime Sonnet, not only exceed the narrow limits of my merit, but confpire to deprive me of the true knowledge of myfelf. Heaven knows what will be the confequence of fuch feducing praifes, addreffed to a poet! However, amidft all this danger, I cannot help congratulating myfelf for the good fortune which has procured me fuch valuable friends ; whofe judgment, however partial, will help to fupport my credit. I wifh your great poetical vigour and noble imagination, which have appeared fo manifeft in the narrow compafs of fourteen lines, materials more proportioned to their powers than the gratuitous praifes beftowed on me. And fhall be anxious to fecure your efteem by the gratitude and refpectful affection with which you have infpired, your, &c.

Vienna, December 12, 1768.

## LETTER XVII.

### TO THE SAME.

THE juftice which I render your poetical talents, does not deferve the exceffive gratitude which you have expreffed in your laft obliging letter. But it has ferved to dif-

cover

cover that laudable and uncommon moderation, which is more frequently found in
thofe who have atchieved honourable and
difficult enterprifes, than in fuch as twang
the ufelefs lyre.

I am pleafed at your having chofen a
fpecies of poetry, which precifely requires
that clear, harmonious fweetnefs, facility,
and elegant fimplicity, to which you were by
nature at firft, vifibly inclined. I wifh with
folicitude for the arrival of the complete
edition of your works; and am, in fpite of
the laconic brevity to which my laborious
bufinefs of writing condemns me, &c.

Vienna, February 20, 1769.

## LETTER XVIII.

### TO THE SAME.

TRULY fenfible of the partiality with which
you honour me, by the communication of the
two paftoral Eclogues which you have laudably undertaken to write on the illuftrious
model of the Sicilian and Mantuan bards, I
beg your acceptance of my moft grateful
acknowledgments. But your obliging partiality exceeds all bounds, if you fuppofe me

to

to be fufficiently qualified, or courageous, to affume the office of corrector. I am not fo deplorably ignorant of myfelf; and if, unfortunately, I were, nature would oppofe me in fuch an ill-advifed undertaking. If your virtuous modefty requires criticifm, and counfel, in your poetical labours, how can you ever fail to find them in your native city, the nurfe of fo many rare and fublime geniufes, and in which the mufes have eftablifhed their favourite refidence? I forgive, however, this courteous infult, as it manifefts your blindnefs to my inability.

Vienna, May 11, 1769.

Signor Papadia having folicited Metaftafio to confide to him fome of his profe writings, mentioned in his Letter to *Diodati*, particularly his extracts and remarks on the Poetics of Ariftotle, he declines complying with this requeft, on account of the confufed and incorrect ftate in which thefe papers had long remained. But in anfwer to another application from the fame correfpondent, we have in the following letter, the difcuffion of a curious queftion in ancient Mythology.

L E T

## LETTER XIX.

### TO SIG. PAPADIA.

AFTER having confulted the oracle of our times, the learned Sig. *Martorelli*, to whom I have recourfe myfelf, for the folution of literary difficulties, with what confcience could you expect from me, deep information concerning the facrifices of the ancients to their divinity Cupid? Do you wifh to tempt me to be guilty of temerity? If that was your motive, you committed a great mif- take: as my ruling defect militates moft powerfully againft fuch feduction. After you have applied to my dear and much refpected Sig. *Martorelli*, what can I do but repeat what he has faid; that I remember no treatife *ex profeffo* on the fubject propofed. If it be afked what were the offerings and facrifices of the ancients to Venus; you muft yourfelf recollect, that they were innu- merable rofes, myrtles, incenfe, fifh, fhells, doves, and I know not what. Nor can it have efcaped you, that Lucian, in one of his meretricious dialogues, will have it, that a white female kid (of goat) was facrificed

to

to the popular Venus; and to the celeſtial,
a female calf; but if you aſk the ſame
queſtion with regard to Cupid, it will be
more difficult for me to anſwer.  In that
moſt abundant mythological prompter of
*Natalis Comes*, where the flowers, trees,
and animals dedicated to each particular
deity of the Pagans, are carefully ſpecified,
Cupid is omitted.  But what is ſtill worſe, I
am not ſure that this God, ſo univerſally
adored, ever had a Temple in any place
dedicated ſolely to his ſervice.  I never
remember to have heard or read that he had
one in Rome; and *Nardini*, 'the moſt diligent inveſtigator and illuſtrator of the ſmalleſt ſtone in that city, gives us no information on this ſubject.  We might indeed ſuſ-
ſpect, that there was one in Greece, in the
city of *Theſpia*, as Pauſanias in *Bœoticis*,
aſſerts, that Cupid was there adored with
peculiar veneration; but he makes no mention of any particular edifice there that was
conſecrated to him: nor where that wonderful work of *Praxitiles*, the celebrated marble ſtatue of Cupid, was placed, that *Cajus*
cauſed to be tranſported from Theſpia to Rome,
which *Claudius* ſent back to Greece; and
which being laſtly reconducted to Rome by

order of Nero, perished there afterwards, in the flames. Perhaps some of the historians who treat of the actions of this Emperor may inform us where it was placed at Rome, and with what sacred ceremonies the Romans had received it. But as such amorous researches are more analogous to your time of life than mine, to you I shall abandon the enterprise.

The present of your *Theocritus* which you kindly intend me, will be most gratefully received; and I hope you will soon find a rapid conveyance for it, which will second my impatience. In the mean time, put my obedience to any test you please, within the limited sphere of my activity, and believe me constantly, &c.

Vienna, March 12, 1770.

---

In a subsequent letter to Sig. *Papadia*, Metastasio acknowledges the receipt of his pastoral Eclogues; of which he says: "I am highly pleased to hear again the ancient sweet pipe of the amorous shepherd of Siracuse, managed by your lips: and the facility with which you play upon it, thanks to the analogy between you, authorizes me

to

to hope, that you will not let it again long remain mute, dufty, and ufelefs."

He afterwards fpeaks of other paftorals received from this author: "full of innocence, and yet noble, replete with fmiling images, and nourifhed by the Bucolic genius of the Greeks and Romans, of which even the language is become familiar to you." This correfpondence continued till the year 1781.

END OF THE FIRST SECTION.

SEC-

## SECTION II.

Among Metaſtaſio's correſpondents, to whom his letters are preſerved, there are many female writers, and women of talents; who ambitious of his counſel, or, at leaſt of his praiſe, ſent him their works. Though he did not ſeem to aſpire at theſe honours, yet he received them with due politeneſs and gallantry. We have already given ſpecimens of the tenderneſs with which he peruſed and reviſed the writings of Signora Accarigi (*e*).

The following letter to a lady who had ſent him a copy of verſes under the feigned academical name of *Iſidèa Egirena*, or challenge to a poetical intercourſe, is ſo polite, ſportive, and gallant, that it is difficult to imagine it to have been written, even by a poet, at the age of ſixty-nine.

(*e*) This alludes to a letter written in 1774; 'but the correſpondence continued to 1776.

L E T-

## LETTER I.

TO SIGNORA MARIA FORTUNA.

WHETHER the beautiful Stanzas addreſſed to me, and delivered by the common poſt, are the production of a ſhepherd or ſhepherdeſs, they will always excite my wonder and gratitude. They are ſo replete with good ſenſe and candour, and ſupported by ſuch a ſweet, noble, clear and harmonious facility, that the writer has no occaſion to mitigate critical rigour by the reſpect due to the fair ſex. I profeſs myſelf infinitely obliged to whomever is the author. But if, as my ſelf-love inclines me to believe, it is truly the production of a female pen, I beg the ingenious, obliging ſhepherdeſs, who has done me ſuch honour, to forgive my doubts, and not to treat them with diſdain, as they ariſe from that uncommon merit which exalts her above her peers.. Nor let her condemn my diſcourteſy, if I decline ſoliciting my jaded muſe to furniſh me with a reply—In the firſt place, ſhe is not now ſo ready at the call of an old huſband, as formerly, at that of a young lover. And beſides

this,

this, fate having placed me, though unworthy, at the foot of the Imperial throne, has procured me, and ftill procures, fuch frequent poetical challenges, that the duty of anfwering them, would have robbed me of the time neceffary to my employment, if I had not from the beginning, though fometimes unwillingly, declined reciprocation.—— And if at prefent I were to change my fyftem, I fhould incur the juft indignation of all thofe whom I have hitherto involuntarily neglected. Suffer me therefore, if not in the language of the Gods, at leaft in one more familiar to truth, to affure you, that I have the honour to be, with the moft grateful and perfect efteem, &c.

Vienna, November , 1767.


## LETTER II.

### TO SIGNORA GIACINTA BETTI ONOFEI, AT BOLOGNA.

For many folid reafons too long to be detailed here, it will not be in my power to fecond your ardent wifhes in the work you mention. Receive at leaft kindly, my dear Signora Giacinta, the counfel that I fhall venture

I

venture to give you. The merit of the fubject which you have to celebrate in your
native language, cannot be expreffed with
due energy by any one whofe mind is not
impreffed with it in the lively manner which
you feem to feel. Boldly, therefore, take
your pen, and be affured, that your extraordinary talents, animated by that ardour which
reigns throughout your letter, will fuggeft
ideas to you; which can never prefent themfelves to the cold imagination, even of a
great poet. Nothing is impoffible to your
abilities; and I feel myfelf already difpofed
to admire them, even in this new enterprife.

Vienna, September 26, 1768.

## LETTER III.

### TO THE SAME.

THE obliging manner in which you have
informed me of the new ftate into which
you will have entered when this letter
arrives, is an amiable inftance of your
regard. The laudable qualities, with which
you are well acquainted, of the fpoufe
whom providence has deftined for you, are
the moft certain means of tranfmuting your,

E 4                          perhaps,

perhaps too lively quickfilver into gold, and to conftitute all the felicity of which we are capable. This is not only what I wifh, but boldly predict: certain that you will co-operate on your part in procuring it, and not draw on yourfelf 'all 'the blame of a failure.

A long letter would ill correfpond with your prefent gay occupations: affure your-felf therefore of my fincere wifhes for your happinefs, and believe me invariably yours.

Vienna, February 2, 1769.

## LETTER IV.

### TO THE SAME.

YOUR acquaintance, moft amiable Sig-nora Giacinta, with my dear Gemello, the Cavalier Brofchi, is a new motive for the encreafe of that efteem which I have always had for you: as his excellent difcernment affures me of the merit of thofe perfons with whom he is in habits of intimacy. And I envy you both that mutual enjoyment of each other's company, at which I can never afpire. Though *Dido* is my eldeft daughter, I fhall never pardon her for having been the

occafion

occasion of any danger to my beloved Cavalier Broschi (*f*). This undutiful daughter has but ill seconded the inclinations of her sire, by incommoding persons that are so dear to me. I flatter myself, however, by your account, that the accident had no serious consequences: and I beg you to be the bearer of my most affectionate wishes to this worthy friend.

March 30, 1771.

––––––––––

Metastasio's correspondence with this lady, who was a poetess, a musician, and an electrician, continued till the year 1779. But what still seems more to have contributed to her favour with the Imperial Laureat, was her residence at Bologna, and being in friendship with Farinelli; of whom he takes occasion to speak with the warmest and most cordial affection, in almost all the letters which he addressed to her.

" You have obliged me extremely (says he in 1771) my dear *Signora Giacinta*, by honouring me with the continuance of your correspondence, and assuring me of the af-

––––––––––

(*f*) Alluding to a fall at the opera-house in Bologna, at a rehearsal of *Didone abbandonata*.

fectionate

fectionate remembrance which my dear and
refpected friend Sig. *Carlo Brofchi* retains for
me, which I return with a mutual and moft
conftant reciprocation. I love and efteem
him as much as it is poffible for a man to be
loved and efteemed, who has fo far furpaffed
all his peers, not only by his excellence in the
charming art which he profeffed, but by the
uncommon virtuous qualities of his mind,
which have rendered him amiable, and admirable, in every fituation into which fortune
has thrown him.  Deliver to him in my
name, I entreat you, my moft affectionate
compliments ; and if the Doctor, your fpoufe
(whom I devoutly reverence) has no objec-
tion to the commiffion, give him for me a
thoufand moft cordial embraces."

In another letter to this lady, fpeaking of
Farinelli's magnificent manfion (called a
palace) at Bologna, he fays : " my imagination has conveyed me to the habitation of
my dear Gemello, where I have feen the
fplendid decorations of *Nitetti* (g) in all the
perfection which he fuggefted to the ingenious artifts he employed ; and in fpite of the

(g) This opera was performed in Farinelli's houfe, with
the fame decorations with which it was originally reprefented at the court of Spain.

distance,

diftance, and without the affiftance of a pencil, poetical fancy has prefented to me the
amiable figure of *Signora Giacinta*, of which
fhe muft doubtlefs be poffeffed, in order to
bear any proportion with the ferenity, grace,
and vivacity of her mind. Figure to yourfelf
the pleafure I muft have received from the
falutations of my beloved friend, procured by
your means. But I beg you to complete the
work, and render him, in my ftead, a modeft
but affectionate embrace. I have interefted
myfelf as I ought, in all the joys and forrows
which you have been pleafed to communicate
to me ; and I pray, and hope, that in future,
fortune may not fo frequently change from
the firft to the fecond. Take care, my much
refpected Signora Giacinta, not to truft too
much to the falacious magic of poetry, when
you wifh to vanquifh the chilnefs of philofophy. The inchantments of Parnaffus have
fome efficacy in the theatre, fupported by
the harmony of the lyre or trumpet ; but are
totally impotent when we dare to try their
power beyond the limits of fiction. The
magic which feldom fails, and which moft
infallibly governs the human heart, is that
with which nature gratuitoufly furnifhes you
females, who without poring over books,
with

with a fmile, a glance, a word, a ftudied negligence, perform daily fuch wonders, as the
grafs-hoppers of Helicon never have nor
never will atchieve. Seek, therefore, among
the veffels of your own difpenfary, and you
will certainly find a fpecific adapted to your
wants."

Such politenefs and gallantry from a man
in his eightieth year, to a female whom he
had never feen, and at a period of time fo
near the total extinction of all *chivalry*, will
furprife the prefent age, and perhaps offend
the next.

This lady, a fmatterer in natural philofophy and electricity, in a letter to Metaftafio,
having expreffed her terrors at a flight fhock
of an earthquake at Bologna, in ftrong
and violent terms, and her tranfports of joy
on the opportunity which it had afforded for
electrical experiments to illuftrate the fyftem
which afcribes to that power this tremendous effect; the poet fays: " I know not
whether I ought to condole or congratulate
you on this event. In chriftian charity, I
ought to pray againft earthquakes, but am
afraid of offending you by wifhing to deprive
you of the pleafure of making experiments
to demonftrate your favourite fyftem. It
would

would be a curious problem, that by its folution fhould prove, how your happinefs could
depend on earthquakes; but then we muft
have recourfe to philofophy: a name which
you profcribe, abhor, and deteft. So that in
this dilemma, I perceive with what caution
my form of prayer muft be made, when, at
the fame time, I implore the extirpation of
earthquakes, and the folid and daily encreafe
of that electrical power to which you declare
yourfelf indebted for all your felicity."

The next literary female correfpondent
who fought the oracular opinion of the poet,
in his old age, concerning her works, found
him ftill more aufpicious to her talents, or,
at leaft, her vanity, than to thofe of any one
of the Sappho family already mentioned, as
the following letters will manifeft.

## LETTER V.

### TO SIGNORA DONNA ELEONORA DI FONSECA PIMENTEL.

THE poetical effays, particularly the epithalamium, of which you have obligingly
favoured me with a copy, for the noble and
harmonious facility of the verfification, the
lively

lively images which animate and colour
them, as well as for the abundant hiſtorical
and mythological alluſions with which they
are enriched, would be extremely worthy of
praiſe in themſelves, apart from all other
conſiderations ; but when we reflect on theſe
being the firſt productions of a lady who has
ſcarcely begun her fourth luſtre (26th year)
their merit is encreaſed to ſuch a degree, as
to become marvellous. You have very wiſely
foreſeen, that ſuch a uſurpation of the rights
of our ſex, at my age, might perhaps have
excited in me ſome degree of jealouſy ; but
with equal ingenuity and courteſy, you have
adminiſtered the antidote, by aſſuring me,
that you owe all the fermentation of your
native poetical fire, to the aſſiduous peruſal of
my writings. I readily give credit, without
examination, to this obliging aſſertion ; being
extremely glad to unite to the duty of that
juſtice which I render you, the intereſt of
ſelf-love. Continue to be the honour and
envy of your ſex, by advancing in a way correſpondent to theſe wonderful beginnings,
and believe me, &c.

Vienna, October 9, 1770.

Two

Two years after, this young lady fends him more of her poetical compofitions, which are praifed by the veteran Laureat with equal warmth and gallantry. Indeed he adds to his encomiums the encouraging affurance, that fhe has greatly furpaffed his expectations.

This correfpondence continued till the year 1776; and he not only perfeveres in praifing her productions, but, at her earneft requeft, revifes, and, corrects fmall grammatical errors and poetical inaccuracies ; a tafk to which he had always great repugnance, well knowing how much eafier it is to praife a bad poem, than correct it.

But this lady not only confulted the bard, as the oracle of Apollo, with refpect to her poetical compofitions, but as the oracle of Delphos, in other important concerns ; particularly on the fubject of travelling, which is big with fuch inconvenience and danger to females, that fhe feems in the letter, to which the following is an anfwer, to have wifhed herfelf of the other fex.

L E T-

# LETTER VI.

## TO SIGNORA PIMENTEL.

At the firſt ſight of your laſt moſt obliging letter, I wiſhed (in ſpite of my pacific
diſpoſition) for a good doſe of Archilochean
bile, to furniſh me with a torrent of vene-
mous Iambics againſt that evil genius, which
having ſo long exerciſed his wicked power
over the innocent hand of the gentle *Donna
Eleonora*, has maliciouſly defrauded me of the
pleaſure of her correſpondence. But upon a
ſecond peruſal, and maturely conſidering this
very lively letter, I find it abound with ſuch
excellent ideas, and ſeducing expreſſions,
which, being unable in conſcience to apply to
myſelf, I am obliged to aſcribe my happineſs
to that inconvenient and painful accident *,
which like the banks of a river, had doubled
the force of your uſual eloquence. This
true induction, indeed narrows the limits of
my vanity, but not of my gratitude ; of
which the partiality of a courteous inhabitant

* The lady had hurt her hand by a fall, which had occaſioned her long ſilence.

of

of Parnaſſus, who chuſes me for the object of
her poetical flights, exacts a very large portion. But remember, moſt amiable *Donna
Eleonora*, that it is not always ſafe to truſt to
the light ſuggeſtions of fancy in your poetical
paroxiſms. What an unjuſt and ungrateful
cenſure has it dictated againſt the poor innocent gown (female garb, petticoat) which
inveſts the fair-ſex with ſuch convenience,
pre-eminence, ornament and decorum! and
what are its crimes and defects! Becauſe it
is an impediment to travelling? and whither
would you go? and what to ſee? would you
fly from the warm *Sebeto* (*b*) to the frozen
*Danube*, merely to have a near view of a
miſerable Roman ruin, placed there by accident, and with which, notwithſtanding its
diſtance, you are already ſufficiently acquainted; or would you traverſe Aſia and
Africa, as far as the icy regions of Lapland,
in order, philoſophically, to combine the various inclinations and cuſtoms of the earth's
inhabitants: and thus making a minute
analyſis of humanity, enable yourſelf (as you
vainly hope) to form, in the Carteſian manner, a clear and diſtinct idea of it? Both theſe

(*b*) A river in the neighbourhood of Naples.

F enter-

enterprifes are equally ufelefs; fince the mouldering ruins, which excite in you fuch curiofity, are certainly not worth the trouble of fo long a journey; on the contrary, they would be of infinitely lefs value to you, when feen, than at a diftance : as your imagination has the happy power of embellifhing, unfeen, whatever prefents itfelf to your mind. And the undertaking to qualify yourfelf, accurately to define that ftrange compound of contradiction, called *man*, fhould be ranked in the number of impoffibilities. As I hold it for certain, that there exifts not an individual of the fpecies, who does not every inftant differ from himfelf; and we may inform ourfelves of thofe peculiarities, which are univerfally allowed, without quitting our country; for though the cornice may be infinitely varied, the building is always the fame. In every corner of the earth, men are equally the fport of their own paffions. A tafte for pleafure every where prevails : hence the indifpenfible want of fociety; yet every one is confpiring againft thofe reftraints, without which fociety cannot fubfift. All regard reafon as the neceffary attribute of human nature; and all take her for their guide in the tranfactions of life; but each moulds her to his own fancy

and

and convenience. So that I advife you, my much refpected *Donna Eleonora*, to make peace with your gown, detaching your thoughts wholly from voyages fo ufelefs, and big with hardfhips and misfortunes ; and to encourage no other wifh or ambition, than that of diftinguifhing yourfelf among your peers, in the manner you have fo happily begun. Cultivate your dramatic talents, and from the fpecimens which you have already given of your abilities, I not only hope, but venture to predict, your complete fuccefs.

Vienna, March 8, 1776.

Metaftafio having unfolded and difplayed in his dramas all the affections of the human heart, feems in his letters to female authors, to have exhaufted the language of courtefy and politenefs. The following letter, the only one in the collection to the fame lady, feems in a different key, and higher pitch of of refpect and elegance, than any of thofe to his other female correfpondents, already inferted.

LET-

# LETTER VII.

## TO SIGNORA DONNA CATTERINA MAGGI DE CALVI.

IF the beneficent feducer, who has been able to infpire you, madam, with fo much partiality in my favour, were known to me, I certainly fhould moft devoutly addrefs every fpecies of prayer and fupplication, to engage him to eftablifh me in the poffeffion of a bleffing, which I have great reafon to fear I fhall be unable to preferve. The efteem of a perfon who voluntarily adds to fo many excellent qualities of her fex, merely as accomplifhments, thofe ftudies and laborious occupations which are our duties, is an acquifition, which, however ufurped, might tempt the moft mature philofophical moderation with vanity.

I have great reafon to fufpect that Signor *Hippolito*, your moft worthy confort, has been guilty of the whole, or the chief part, of this feduction—I know not whether it would be for my advantage to exprefs my fentiments of gratitude and devotion in perfon ; but am certain, that in fpite of the rifk I fhould run of undeceiv-

undeceiving you, I cannot help wifhing it moft ardently. Continue to honour me with this favourable propenfity, thus voluntarily beftowed: afford me an opportunity of meriting it, and believe me always, with due refpect and efteem, &c.

Vienna, December 9, 1772.

---

In order to finifh the poet's correfpondence with literary Ladies, and Females of talents, we fhall deviate a little from regular chronology. The following letters, like the preceding to females of this clafs, were extorted from him by perfons whom he never faw, or by their friends. He feems, however, to have received all thefe applications, not only with patience, but to have anfwered them with good breeding, and even kindnefs; and if the correfpondence is continued, his philanthropy vifibly matures into friendfhip.

## LETTER VIII.

### TO SIGNORA MARIA ROSA COCCIA.

A FORTNIGHT ago, I received a courteous letter from Monfignor RATTI, in which

Signora

Signora MARIA ROSA COCCIA was recommended to me. I anfwered this prelate, that when I knew in what way I could be of ufe to the perfon recommended, I fhould not fail feconding the wifh of fuch a mediator. A few days after I had fent my anfwer to the poft, a parcel was announced to me from the cuftom-houfe ; which, when examined, was found to contain, not only a very elegant letter from the faid Signora MARIA ROSA, but three excellent pieces of her mufical compofition, which I faw, and refpected ; but was not able to judge of their worth. I therefore inftantly called a perfon extremely fkillful in the art, who, after carefully examining them in my prefence, and with great pleafure, affured me, that they were written, not only in a correct, but mafterly, manner. I rejoiced at this, and was flattered to find, that my dear country produced young ladies of fuch uncommon abilities. But I was mortified, at finding myfelf unable to procure fuch rewards, as are due to their merit. The princes of this court having, many years fince, made a rule, never to receive a prefent, or dedication of any book, efpecially of poetry, or mufic; to fave themfelves from the indifcreet torrent of fuch homages as they were

formerly

formerly inundated with. Here muſic is, at preſent, in the laſt ſtage of decline; and in order to know the merit of ſuch a compoſition as yours, ſuch knowledge is neceſſary as is poſſeſſed by very few people: hence all, but particularly thoſe who may aſſume the character of Mecænas, can only appreciate muſical merit by the report of profeſſors; who being likewiſe men, and ſubject to human paſſions, do not alway deliver their opinions with ſincerity. So that not knowing what uſe I can ultimately make of the elegant copies of your harmonical labours, I ſhall carefully preſerve them till I have your inſtructions. I beg you will not regard my inability, (at which on this occaſion I feel infinite concern) as a crime; but believe me to be, with ſincere wiſhes for more ſucceſs in the execution of your future commands, yours, &c.

Vienna, December 29, 1777.

## LETTER IX.

### TO THE SAME.

Your former letters, moſt reſpected Signora Rosa, have informed me of your extrordi-

nary

nary abilities in mufic; but the laft has convinced me of the uncommon goodnefs of
your heart : full of docility, modefty, and
propriety : virtues which feldom abound in
perfons who, like you, can afford fuch pleafure by the laudable fruits of their application. With thefe wonderful talents, with fuch
enviable, and rare difpofitions of the mind,
and with the fervor which animates your
exertions, you will encreafe the glory of our
country; of which, as a fellow citizen, I fhall
imagine myfelf entitled to a fhare. The
generous gift with which you have favoured
me, of your neat manufcript, for which I
am very grateful, fhall be kept facred for the
pleafure of communicating it to fuch only as
may know its true value ; and at all times
fhall be carefully preferved, and ready for
reftoration, whenever an opportunity may
occur of making a better ufe of it. Your partiality towards me, I regard as a precious acquifition ; and long for an opportunity of
meriting it, by the execution of your commands.

Vienna, February 12, 1778,

---

The chief fubject of the next letter to this
lady, (1779) is the poet's favourite cenfure
of

of the *compliments of the feafon,* which he denounces to almoft all his correfpondents.

In 1780, Signora COCCIA fent him a print engraved from her picture, for which the following letter contains his acknowledg-ments.

## LETTER X.

### TO THE SAME.

YOUR obliging attention, in furnifhing me with an impreffion of the engraving made from your picture, has given me infinite pleafure: as it has helped me to form an idea of a perfon fo eftimable, in fpite of the libe-rality of the engraver, who has beftowed upon you more years than really belong to you. I can, however, confole myfelf for this defect, by the other moft faithful intellectual pictures which you have fent me, in your wonderful mufical effays, by which you have fo far outftript your peers. I regard my verfes with the more partiality, for having incited you to make fo laudable a ufe of your talents. I am very glad that you have been informed of the juftice which I render you at Vienna, and you would have had more

3                                     frequent

frequent confirmations of it in my own letters, if my age did not make the bufinefs of
writing fo inconvenient to me. Furnifh
me, however, occafions for doing it with
more effect.

Vienna, February 14, 1780.

## L E T T E R  XI.

### TO THE SAME.

YOUR commands, moſt obliging Signora
ROSA, convince me how erroneous an opinion
you have formed of me and my way of life,
in believing me alert and robuſt, and in the
practice of frequenting the court and perfons
of high rank. It is a long while fince my
great age and infirmities have permitted me
to quit the afylum of my own houfe, except
to perform the duties of religion, and even
that, not conftantly. I have fmall hopes of
feeing the Grand Duke and Dutchefs of Muf-
covy, who are expected here. But if by an
accident, hardly poffible, fuch an event fhould
happen, and I had the prefumption, unfolicited,
to propofe to them an account of the fingular
merit of my admirable country-woman, how
is it poffible to hope, that after the million of
objects

objects which will have taken poſſeſſion of the mind of this prince and princeſs in their long voyage ; among the innumerable homages that will be rendered them at Rome ; amidſt the feaſts with which their preſence will be celebrated, and the curioſity which they ſhall have excited, they ſhould ever find the leaſt trace in their memories, of an humble petition made to them in paſſing through Vienna? Your wiſh ſhould have been ſeconded at Rome, by perſons dextrous in ſuch matters, who know how to avail themſelves of daily circumſtances. I wiſh moſt ardently, that your fortune were equal to your merit; and am extremely afflicted to be able at preſent to offer nothing better, than uſeleſs, though cordial, wiſhes, for your proſperity.

Vienna, September 6, 1781.

We muſt now reſume the correſpondence with his old friend Signor Filipponi, in which we had only advanced to the end of 1767.

The poet had ſuch frequent applications from bookſellers, who were perpetually multiplying editions of his works in all the great cities of Italy, particularly Turin, that he

ſeems

feems to have treated Sig. *Rabj* with a little
lefs politenefs in the following letter, than,
when a young author, he had beftowed on
*Bettinelli.*

## L E T T E R   XII.

### TO SIGNOR FILIPPONI.

Our Sig. *Rabj* does his duty in thinking
of his own intereft: but he is much miftaken,
if he imagines that I am unmindful of mine.
It is my bufinefs to judge of the refpect and
delicacy due from me to princes and princeffes,
who have rewarded my labours with fuch
fplendid magnificence. The oracles and examples produced, are not fufficient to authorize me to difpofe of things that are not my
own; hence, my dear Sig. Filipponi, advife
him to imitate my refignation.

I participate fincerely in your affliction, at
the unexpected refolution which your exemplary fon has taken; but who knows, whether
in his new ftate of perfection, he will not
afford you fuch caufe to rejoice, as will repay
you for your prefent grief with intereft? I
both wifh and hope it fincerely.

The

The Gazettes muſt have informed you of our earthquake and inundations. The firſt, which happened in Vienna, was only tremendous threats, without the leaſt fatal effeƈt ; but in the neighbourhood of the city of *Neuſtadt*, the conſequences have been very ſerious. Yet the furious over-flowing of the Danube, thanks to the paternal goodneſs of our moſt auguſt ſovereign, who with hand and heart has aſſiſted the wretched inhabitants of the deluged ſuburbs, has not produced thoſe tragical effeƈts which were juſtly apprehended: ſo that the evil has been infinitely leſs than the fright, from which we have not yet recovered. Adieu, my dear friend ; take care of your health, and believe me, &c.

Vienna, March 7, 1768.

## LETTER XIII.

### TO THE SAME.

You have done wiſely, my dear Sig. *Filipponi,* to ſpare yourſelf in writing. I ſhall venture to take the ſame liberty, as I feel too plainly, that though ours is the beſt time of life for prating, it is very unfavourable to writing ; but, in this country, an Italian ama-

amanuenſis, to whom a man can ſafely dictate, who wiſhes that his letters may not diſgrace him, is a fiſh very difficult to catch; ſo that I prefer ſhort letters, or ſilence, to the greater evil of loſing my credit or my patience.

My poor Pegaſus has trotted and galloped ſo much, that being now full of ſpavins, he ought to eat his corn in quiet. My moſt indulgent patroneſs will, I hope, conſider his crippled ſtate, and not ſoon oblige him to crawl up the mountain. At preſent, I have no orders to obey; and I have reaſon to rejoice at my eſcape.

I had almoſt inadvertently let my pen be guilty of wiſhing you a happy new year; ſuch is the force of bad habits; but thank heaven, I ſtopt juſt at the inſtant I was going to ſlip. So that I ſhall not only avoid this ſtale and injurious formality, but am certain, that you will forgive me for the averſion I have to ſo ſilly and troubleſome a cuſtom.

Count *Canale*, with all his ample and flouriſhing family, have received your teſtimonies of eſteem, with the higheſt pleaſure; and beg, reciprocally, to interchange good wiſhes; permit me likewiſe to offer up vows for every branch of your family, ſacred, and

profane,

profane, whom I love, reverence, and honour, with all my ancient entire, and incorruptible affection.

Vienna, December 31, 1768.

## LETTER XIV.

### TO THE SAME.

God forgive you ! my dear friend, for predicting the neceſſity of my clambering again up mount Parnaſſus. After ſo many journeys, ſtumbles, and falls, does not it yet ſeem time for my poor jaded Pegaſus to eat his laſt feed in peace? Inſtead of taking new ſteps (as you ſay) towards immortality, the progreſs already made on the road, is loſt, when we dare to tranſcend the bounds which nature has preſcribed to miſerable humanity. I already, but too well, know this melancholy truth, and wiſh to profit from my knowledge; but how am I to reſiſt the conſtant and benignant clemency, which overlooking my inſufficiency, ſtill wiſhes to confer benefits upon me.——

Vienna, July 3, 1769

LET-

# LETTER XV.

I SHOULD not know how to account, my deareſt friend, for the admiration with which you have honoured my letter concerning this Imperial family, if I did not reflect, that it contained nothing but plain truth, which, appears moſt beautiful, when the leaſt imbelliſhed (*i*); my vanity, therefore, will allow me to take to myſelf no part of the praiſes you beſtow on this fortunate letter. They have, however, ſo far excited my curioſity, as to make me wiſh to ſee its contents. I therefore applied to a young man, who uſed to tranſcribe ſome of my letters previous to their departure, as an exerciſe in the Italian language, which he ſtudies with great diligence ; but it was not to be found in his bundle. Whether he

---

(*i*) Notwithſtanding the democratic clamour againſt the tyranny of the Houſe of Auſtria, in later times, the inhabitants of Vienna, during the life of the Empreſs Queen, *Maria Thereſa*, who died 1780, ſeemed the happieſt, and the moſt contented with their Sovereign and her government, of any people in Europe. For inſtances of this Princeſs's virtues and benevolence, ſee *Dict. Biogr.* art. MARIE.

omitted

omitted giving it a place there for want of time or inclination, I know not. I fhould have the fame temptation to juftify your favourable reception of the trifle I wrote on the Englifh Armonica (*k*); but it is moft prudent not to enter too deeply into this ufelefs and perilous examination. Indeed if you had convinced me (as you might too eafily have done) that this little production, is unwörthy of applaufe, I fhould ftill have reafon for fome confolation; as the havıng already obtained it without defert, would be a comforting proof of the numerous band of friends and defenders which my good fortune has procured me ; and I am much more fenfible of this enviable acquifition, than of the choiceft laurels of Parnaffus.

Adieu, my dear Sig. *Filipponi*; I return you the compliments of the feafon, in revenge; finging in pure fpite, this ftale and ufelefs cant among real friends.

Vienna, November 16, 1769.

---

The talents of our two countrywomen, the Mifs Davis's, who refided a confiderable time at Vienna, in the fame houfe as Haffe and

---

(*k*) The *Glaffes*, carried to Vienna, and performed upon by the eldeft Mifs Davis.

       G        Fauftina,

Fauſtina *, have been celebrated by our bard; the eldeſt, for her performance on the *Glaſſes*, at that time a new inſtrument; and the youngeſt, for her vocal abilities. The Empreſs Queen had been ſo pleaſed by their ſeveral talents, that in the year 1769, on the marriage of the Infant Duke of Parma with the Arch-dutcheſs Maria Amelia, ſhe deſired Metaſtaſio to write a Cantata, which was ſet by Haſſe, in order to diſplay their ſeveral talents. This Cantata has been publiſhed in late editions of the poet's works, under the title of *l'Armonica*, the name of the new inſtrument on which the eldeſt Miſs Davis accompanied her ſiſter, in the performance of the Cantata.

A letter written by the poet to the princeſs di Belmonte, at Naples, recommending theſe performers to her protection, will ſerve as a comment to the Cantata juſt mentioned.


## L E T T E R   XVI.

### TO THE PRINCESS DI BELMONTE.

'THE bearers of this moſt reverential addreſs, are two Engliſh young perſons, travelling under the conduct of their worthy pa-

* See *Preſent State of Muſ. in Germany.* &c, Art. Vienna.

rents,

rents, in order to give teſtimonies at Naples
of their ſeveral abilities in muſic; their
names are Miſs Mary, and Miſs Cecilia
Davis: the firſt performs with admirable
ſkill on an inſtrument of new invention,
called the *Armonica*. It is compoſed of
glaſſes of different ſizes, revolving, by means
of a pedal, on a ſpindle. Theſe glaſſes, forming a regular ſcale of tones and ſemi-tones,
being delicately touched with wet fingers,
during their revolution, produce the moſt un-
commonly ſweet, and celeſtial tones, imagin-
able; particularly in pathetic ſtrains, for
which the inſtrument is eminently calculat-
ed. The other ſiſter, who is poſſeſſed of a
very pleaſing and flexible voice, ſings extremely well, with much art and natural
expreſſion; and when accompanied by her
ſiſter on the *Armonica*, ſhe has the power of
uniting her voice with the inſtrument, and
of imitating its tones, ſo exactly, that it is
ſometimes impoſſible to diſtinguiſh one from
the other. They have been here univerſally
admired, and applauded: and my moſt auguſt
Patroneſs, who has deigned to hear them frequently, has honoured them with munificent
teſtimonies of imperial approbation.

Vienna, January 16, 1772.

G 2　　　　　Miſs

Miſs Cecilia Davis performed in the theatre of San Carlo at Naples, the part of *Bra-
damante*, in Metaſtaſio's new opera of RUG-
GIERO.

## LETTER XVII.

### TO SIGNOR FILIPPONI.

YOUR letters, my moſt dear Sig. *Filipponi*,
always afford me the greateſt comfort, in
reviving the idea of our long, ſincere, and
diſintereſted friendſhip, and of that honourable character, ſo worthy of yourſelf, which I
have always found ſo irreproachable ; and
this certain knowledge renders every thing
dear that comes from you, even to the in-
ſult of a merry Chriſtmas ; I therefore thank
you for it, and in revenge, join the ſame
wiſh for you, with others which ought not to
be profaned by being coupled with ſuch
ſtupid and vulgar companions.

I am overwhelmed with confuſion and
gratitude, at the partial and generous diſpoſition of your obliging and learned friend,
in wiſhing to honour me with the dedication
of his *Luſiad* (*l*). I therefore beg of you to

(*l*) *Or the Diſcovery of India*, an epic poem, by LUIS
DI CAMÖENS. It does not appear who was the tranſlator
of this poem into Italian, who ſo much wiſhed to dedicate
his verſion to Metaſtaſio.

expreſs

exprefs to him the lively and fincere fentiments of my grateful heart, and my impatience to fee transfufed into our language by
a mafterly hand, a work which has juftly
merited univerfal approbation; but after
this true and candid affurance, ufe all your
eloquence, I entreat you, to convince him,
that neither the nature of the gift, nor his
own intereft or mine, can permit me to
accept of it. The oppulent fons of fortune,
among whom it has not pleafed providence
to rank me, have acquired a right by immemorable prefcription, to all dedications;
and both the work and the author (by fub-
ftituting to fome great name, that of a poor
inhabitant of Parnaffus) would be deprived
of the well founded hopes of thofe folid advantages which he might promife himfelf
from riches and power. An honour fo little
my due, would provoke the malevolent to
examine my titles; and God defend me
from fuch a dangerous enquiry! In fhort,
having hitherto, for this invincible reafon,
always refufed the acceptance of fuch incenfe, I have loft the power of compliance,
if I would not moft defervedly incur the indignation of thofe by whom it has heretofore been offered: Do you, my dear Sig.

G 3                              *Filipponi,*

*Filipponi,* endeavour to prevent this moſt reaſonable repugnance from diminiſhing the partiality of this worthy man of letters, which I would not loſe for the world.

Sig. *Canale* is very ſenſible of the intereſt you take in the recovery of his ſon-in-law ; and has conſigned to me, on your account, a thouſand grateful and affectionate expreſ-ſions. Contrive to let the venerable prieſt-eſs know how much I love, eſteem, and honour her, as well as your numerous off-ſpring, ſacred and prophane, *et nati natorum, et qui naſcentur ab illis* ; and never ceaſe to believe me invariably yours.

Vienna, December 17, 1770.

## L E T T E R  XVIII.

### TO THE SAME.

AMONG the many flattering receptions of my RUGGIERO in Italy (*m*), who was not

(*m*) The opera of RUGGIERO, the laſt of the poet's dra-matic productions, was written by order of the Empreſs Queen, and publiſhed under his own eye, in a moſt cor-rect and ſplendid edition in quarto, at Vienna. It was ſet by Haſſe, and performed at Milan, on the marriage of the Archduke Ferdinand of Auſtria, with Maria Beatrice of Eſte, Princeſs of Modena, 1771.

brought

brought up by his old fire with very fan-
guine hopes, yours, my dear Sig. *Filipponi*,
has been the moſt grateful. I am pleaſed
that you have ſtill found in this late production of my tired and exhauſted genius, ſome
features of the old countenance of your
friend ; and I have reflected with the higheſt pleaſure, on the effect of this recognition
upon your good heart. Theſe kind ſymptoms
of ſincere friendſhip, have carried me back
with infinite delight to our juvenile days,
renovating the pleaſing beginnings of
our affection, and its conſtant ſucceſ-
ſive progreſſion My lively imagination
has taken a new walk with you through the
*ſtrada Giulia*, and the dark *Parraſio* upon the
*Gianicolo*, at Rome; we have breathed
together the chearful and ſalubrious air of
the *Vomero*, at Naples; and it has repreſented to me our private feſtivities, innocent
ſympoſiacs, and poetical confabulations.
You ſee for how many gay ideas I am
indebted to your letter; I now ought to be
particularly grateful for them, as I have
great occaſion for ſuch ſpecifics againſt the
obſtinate perſecution of my hypochondriac
complaints, which tinge with darkneſs every
thought,

Without

Without the leaft fhadow of affectation, I am truly grateful to thofe who have had the partiality to wifh to dedicate to me their works; but have never had the courage to accept of an incenfe which from time immemorial has appertained to the oppulent fons of fortune. We poor inhabitants of Parnaffus are born to offer, and not to receive it; and I ought not to be condemned for refuling to become a ufurper. I entreat you to become my advocate, and to plead my gratitude and reafonable felf-denial.

Vienna, December 26, 1771.

---

We quitted the poet's correfpondence with his beloved *Gemello*, Farinelli, July, 1768, after fettling him at Bologna, and after feveral confolatory letters, and admonitions to fortitude and refignation (not very fuccefsful indeed) had been fent to him by our bard. We fhall now refume this correfpondence, and continue it, uninterruptedly, till May 1769; from which period there is a chafm of feven years in the printed edition of Metaftafio's letters to this celebrated finger, without any reafon being affigned by the editor.

L E T-

# LETTER XIX.

## TO THE CAVALIER FARINELLI.

THE kind care which my beloved *Carluccio* (*n*) took to acquaint me, in preference to fo many others, of the new form which your domeftic fociety takes, in confequence of your generofity, and the fuggeftions of your heart and benevolent mind, is a precious emanation of our affectionate and indiffoluble Twinfhip. I cannot exprefs to you the pleafure which this confidence has given me, nor fufficiently congratulate you on the occafion. In the firft place, it is a great comfort to me to find in this action, the conftant and admirable character of my dear Gemello, always like himfelf, and always determined to diftinguifh himfelf from common men by beneficence, which is one of the greateft attributes of the divinity. I hope, in the fecond place, or rather promife myfelf, that

(*n*) The diminutives and augmentatives of the Italian language are fo delicate and numerous, that it is in vain to attempt finding equivalents for them all, in any other tongue. *Carlo*, for inftance, is Charles; *Carlino*, little Charles; *Carluccio*, dear fweet Charles—*Carlone*, great Charles; *Carlaccio*, nafty filthy great Charles.

the

the neceſſary and delightful occupations
which the regulating this riſing generation
furniſhes, will, by degrees, baniſh all thoſe
gloomy and hypochondriac thoughts, which
inceſſantly haunted and governed you, day
and night; threatening your deſtruction, to
the profound, but unavailing affliction of
your friends, unable to afford you any aſſiſt-
ance.

At preſent, inſtead of theſe melancholy
imaginations, I cannot tell how many pleaſing
and happy ideas croud into my mind. I ſee
you healthy, ſerene, and making your whole
happineſs conſiſt, as uſual, in procuring that
of others : You are now full in my view,
with your dear nephew at your ſide ; I
now ſee you at the harpſichord with your
noble little niece. And very very often (only
mind how the fancy of poets runs away with
them) I ſeem to ſee you ſkipping round
your flouriſhing beds of peas, beans, and
other fortunate tender plants, which will
certainly thrive in proportion to the care of
ſo honeſt, prudent, and friendly a cultivator.
Now, my beloved Gemello, there only remains for me to thank you, as I ſincerely do,
for your particular attention to me ; and to
rejoice with you at your having diſcovered
a better

a better mode of reading my heart, where you have so long been an inhabitant, than I of explaining it, by scribbling or prating.——

Adieu, my dearest Gemello : may heaven render you happy in proportion to my wishes, and administer to you new motives of consolation,

Vienna September 1, 1768.

## LETTER XX.

### TO THE SAME.

SIGNOR *Mancini* (o) a few days ago, and Sig. *Tibaldi* yesterday, have faithfully consigned to me the affectionate remembrances of my beloved Gemello ; and have patiently answered all my numerous interrogatories, concerning the present state of your humour, as well as health. Some of the information I have obtained has consoled me, particularly that which represents you so much satisfied with the new domestic

(o) A singer of the Bologna school, educated under the celebrated Bernacchi. His voice a *soprano*; but having quitted the stage, he was now engaged as singing-master to the Arch-dutchesses, which place he filled in 1772, when I saw him at Vienna. See *Germ. Tour*, vol. I. *Art.* Vienna.

society

society which you have acquired, and the
pleasing occupation which it affords you :
but, on the contrary, the account which I
have had of the obstinate continuance of
your impertinent tertian ague, afflicts me
extremely. And finding that your niece is
not exempt from this wearing malady, has
made me reasonably conclude, that some
external cause, common to you both, has
occasioned your indisposition. If this
should have been the case, it would not be
be difficult to discover and remove it. My
fond *twinism* has suggested to me, that you
pass the chief part of your time in the open
air ; that the autumnal exhalations, and the
poisonous vapours of a great part of our
country, is not breathed with impunity ; that
the air of paved cities is much less im-
pregnated with this poison, not only from the
exhalations of the earth being impeded, but
from the numerous and constant fires, as well
as the motion of the inhabitants, which agi-
tate and correct the air. And I beg that the
necessary care of your health, may set you a
thinking of these matters which friendship
has suggested to me. Take them into con-
sideration, my dear Gemello, and examine
my suspicions : If you find them at all probable,

bable, avoid expofing yourfelf, at leaſt during the perilous feaſon. I well know that
your conduct has been fuch hitherto, as to
prove that you are in no want of tutors, and
that I pretend to no fuch employment ; but
this doubt torments me, and if I did not
communicate it to you, I ſhould be ten
times more tormented with remorfe.

I congratulate your amiable niece on her
happy maternal ſtate, and her fpoufe on the
graduation of his paternal proximity. Recommend me to them both, and infpire
them with a proportion of your affection for
me : as they are already extremely dear to
me from the love which my Gemello bears
them, whom I tenderly embrace, and of
whom I ſhall ever be moſt faithfully, &c.

Vienna, November 30, 1768.

## L E T T E R  XXI.

### TO THE SAME.

OUR extreme cloſe attachment to each
other is fo public, that every one believes, if
he is dear to one of us, that he is fure to
poffefs the friendſhip of both. Signora
Marianna *Bianchi Tozzi* (*p*), who afpires at

(*p*) A celebrated opera ſinger, who at this time ranked
very high in the favour of the public, both in Italy and
Germany.

the

the acquisition of your favour, which she has no doubt of obtaining, if I only assure you, that she is already in possession of mine: and I cannot refuse her the confession of this truth. When, not long ago, she represented in this theatre, the part of *Clelia* in my opera of that name, I was extremely pleased with her ; not only on account of her excellent performance, and blameless conduct, but for her attention and indefatigable application to fulfil all her duties. She returns to Italy, at present, through Brunswick; where, according to my accounts, she has justly received universal applause. If you will but let her know that her supposition is not entirely unfounded, I shall be extremely grateful, provided she does not fail in executing punctually all the commissions to you, with which I have charged her. Adieu, my dear Gemello. I devoutly reverence all your amiable domestic committee, and am as usual, yours.

Vienna, December 14, 1768.

LET-

# L E T T E R  XXI*.

Your laſt letter of the 9th inſtant, occaſions a mixture of pleaſure, anxiety, and affliction, which I am unable to deſcribe. The obſtinacy of your diabolical fever, the pathetic picture of the ſtate of your perhaps too good heart, and the affectionate thoughts which ſtimulated you to add new ties of friendſhip to thoſe which have hitherto ſo indiſſolubly united us, are ideas well worthy of the ſweet and bitter tumult with which I am by turns internally agitated. It was impoſſible for you to give me a ſtronger proof of your conſtant affection, than by inviting me to a ſacred alliance, in preference to ſo many diſtinguiſhed perſons to whom you might apply. You muſt therefore imagine how much I feel myſelf obliged; and how I am flattered by this new inſtance of the place I hold in your heart. But as there is no perfect happineſs in this valley of tears, the pleaſure of finding myſelf thus diſtinguiſhed by you from the croud of your

3                                    friends,

friends is difturbed by an invincible impediment, which oppofes itfelf to the execution
of your defign. The never having reprefented
the perfonage of whofe office you kindly
think me worthy, during my long life,
would be a fmall obftacle in treating with
my Gemello; but the misfortune is, that
befides the number of perfons to whom I
have excufed myfelf, it is not two months
fince I refifted the folicitations of a perfon
much connected at court, and who would
have a reafonable caufe for being offended,
if after refufing him, I complied with the
requeft of another ; and the refentment of
this perfon would not only be unpleafant,
but might be mifchievous. Nor is it poffible for me to flatter myfelf with keeping it
a fecret ; the hoping to conceal any of
our actions, who are as well known as the
North ftar, would be a Platonic dea. So
that your part, my dear Gemello, is not
only to pardon, but pity me, the lofs being
wholly mine ; and my part will be gratefully
to remember, as long as I live, what you
thought and wifhed.

In fpite of the hurry with which I am
obliged to write a heap of ufelefs letters, I
cannot forget to prefent my refpects to the
fruitful

fruitful lady who honours me with her notice, and to affure her, that by anxioufly attending to your health, fhe will add to that of yours moft faithfully.

Vienna, January 23, 1769.

## L E T T E R XXII.

### TO THE SAME.

THOUGH your moft welcome remembrance of the 12th of laft February, was only an an-fwer to my preceding prolix letter, I cannot poftpone my reply to it, nor reftrain my abufe, which your inhumanity well merits, for the manner with which you have treated my folicitude. You know in what a ftate of mind the account of your obftinate fever muft have left me; and without affuring me that you had at length fent it to the devil, you content yourfelf with merely faying, that your health is capricious. But in fpite of you, I find motives of confolation in the fteadinefs of your hand-writing; in your filence itfelf; and, above all, in the vivacity of your letter, which is not tinctured with a febrile humour. But it is not out of character for a marine monster to reduce a Gemello to confole himfelf, by having recourfe to conjecture. Thank heaven, in thefe days of penitence (Lent) I remember, like a good chriftian, that' anger muft be fubdued, otherwife I fhould not let you off fo eafily; but mind! and keep yourfelf well, if you wifh my rage fhould not be renewed.

If, at this time of our lives, you could doubt of my fincerity, or I of yours, we fhould be unpardonable. I have feen your invitation in no other light, than as a tender proof of your friendfhip; and you would be extremely unjuft and ungrateful, if you could fuppofe I had any other latent reafon for declining the offer, than that which I have candidly ftated. So that you have not the leaft occafion to repent of the friendly eagernefs with which you have fo much obliged me; nor I to blufh at my involuntary backwardnefs, in accepting of your twinly offer. Therefore, in fpite of wild and unworthy conjectures, let me enjoy in peace, the pleafure which this new proof of kindnefs has afforded me, of knowing how I ftand in your good heart.

I envy Signora *Bianchi*, and Monfieur *Lofier*, who have ere now feen and embraced

.my

my dear Gemello.  O that I could do the fame! But though I cannot fee the leaft probability of it ever happening, I cannot relinquifh the hope.

Vienna, March 2, 1769.

## L E T T E R  XXIII.

### TO THE SAME.

*Muger paridera, hija la primera* (q)  I therefore congratulate you, my deareft Gemello, on the fafe and certain fecundity of your amiable niece, and of the prowefs with which fhe has happily accomplifhed her firft maternal expedition.  Accuftomed to live among the Graces and the Mufes, You ought to be pleafed, that, under your aufpices, their chorus is going to be augmented, and that fortune has dextroufly afforded you an apportunity of manifefting your gratitude, by rendering them a due return for that education which you are fo publicly known to have 'had from them.  I entreat you to exprefs my fincere joy to the mother, in the moft fignificant words which you can think

(q) The woman is a good breeder, who begins by bringing forth a girl.  *Span. Prov.*

of ;

of ; and my tender affection for the child, by a hundred kisses at least : as this right which I claim from our twinship, cannot, at present, be susceptible of any malignant interpretation.

A friend, well knowing, like all living mortals, my affectionate eagerness to be acquainted with every thing that concerns you, has anticipated your information, and obliged me extremely by his diligence; but that has not, however, inclined me to blame your delay. To insist on a rigorous exactitude of ceremonial from a poor gentleman just brought to bed, would be unreasonable to the last degree; particularly, from one whom, from long experience, I know to be possessed of such a mind and heart, that it would be difficult to decide, during the throes of child-birth, whether the sufferings of the niece, or those of the uncle would be the greatest. But now you have vanquished the difficulty of this first apprenticeship, I hope you will have frequent occasions for exercising your courage, with much greater ease : and am, as I have ever been, and ever shall be, your most faithful, &c.

Vienna, May 1, 1769.

L E T-

# LETTER XXIV.

## TO THE SAME.

On Monday evening, the firſt of the preſent month, I ſent my ſervant Joſia to the
poſt-houſe, with my letter of congratulation
for your happy *labour*, when he brought me
back, in exchange, a confirmation of the good
tidings in your own hand-writing, dated 21ſt
of laſt April; I found, after the pleaſure which
the peruſal afforded me, another pleaſure, in
perceiving, that your affectionate and impatient twinſhip had ſeduced you to take the pen,
during the firſt myſterious days of your par-
turition: I am extremely grateful, for the
juſtice which you have done my ſolicitude on
your account; and accept, with all due gratitude, the enviable friendſhip, and patronage,
of Signora *Maria, Carlotta, Anna, Tereſa, Pe-
tronilla,* to whom I beg of you to quintuple,
on my account, in proportion to her names,
the embraces, which I conſign to you for
her uſe, by virtue of our moſt cloſe (becauſe
elective) affinity: promiſing to reimburſe
you in current coin, whenever it ſhall pleaſe

God

God to permit us to fee each other; a hope,
which notwithſtanding all the difficulties, I
do not mean to renounce. There wanted
but a little Erefypulus to try your patience,
which for a long time has certainly not been
idle. O my poor Gemello!—but I recal
this exclamation : fuch mortals as you are
in no want of compaffion. Your virtue has
afforded fufficient proofs of your knowing,
not only how to fail before the wind, but
how to tack in contrary, winds, without
loofing your ſteerage. And yet, though I
will not degrade you by my pity, I cannot
help praying for your tranquillity. I live in
the greateſt intimacy with my moſt conſtant
complaints : What would you have me do?
It is keeping bad company, but I might
have worfe. Prefent a million of kind compliments from me to your dear niece, but
qualified with the refpect due to her fublime
rank among matrons : and never ceafe, on
your own part, to return the affection of
your, &c.

Vienna, May 4, 1769.

---

Though the poet's letters to the learned
and worthy *Padre Martini*, contain nothing
of

of importance to general literature ; yet to lovers of Mufic and its hiftory, nothing that concerns this venerable *Maeftro di Capella*, can be indifferent. For fuch, therefore, we fhall give a tranflation of the following fhort letters; to whom they will probably afford fome pleafure, from the mere circumftance of two fuch men being in friendfhip, and correfpondence, with each other.

## L ᵌ T T E R  XXV.

### TO PADRE MARTINI.

THE unexpe&ted misfortune which has happened to the worthy Abate *del Monte*, which muft already have arrived at your knowledge, is univerfally lamented; it has retarded many days the pleafure of receiving your moft obliging letter of the 7th of laft January, which was delivered to me only laft week. I fent a fervant to him immediately, with fincere offers of my fervices in any way in which it was poffible for me to be ufeful; and he brings me back the comfortable news, that he was as well as it was poffible for a perfon to be, with a

broken

broken leg : which feems to fay, that the cure will not be flow, nor be attended with any inconvenient confequences. As foon as ever he is vifible, I fhall vifit him in perfon, in fpite of near two hundred fteps, which it will be neceffary to afcend, in order to attain his aerial habitation.

I am extremely impatient, not only for the fecond volume of your moft learned *Hiftory*, but for the *Duets* and *Trios*, which you make us hope : and I fhould be extremely proud, if I were able to furnifh you with any thing inedited towards your laudable undertaking ; but whatever I write, being by order and for the ufe of the court, is performed and printed immediately ; or, if fufpended by fome accident, the production is laid by for a future occafion ; and I am not at liberty to publifh it.

Take care of yourfelf, for the honour of our dear Italy ; and believe me always, with the moft juft and refpectful efteem.

Vienna, February 22, 1768.

# LETTER XXVI

## TO THE SAME.

I FOUND on my table, a few days ago, the fecond volume of the moft learned work of my very worthy *Padre Martini*; and this morning, an admirable letter from him, without knowing who was the benevolent bearer. But as I could not be ignorant of the friendly and generous hand from which fuch a precious gift, and fuch an obliging letter, came, I haften to acknowledge the inftruction I receive from the one, and the pleafure afforded me by the other. I fhall profit from this work, as much as the narrow limits of my mufical knowledge extend; and fhall procure that juftice to be rendered to it, which is due to the oracle of harmony. After thefe effufions of gratitude, my next bufinefs is to entreat the continuance of your partiality, as if I could ftill doubt of it, after the teftimonies which I have received. But it is my duty to affure the illuftrious donor, of the high eftimation in which I hold his gift, and of the lively

wifh

wifh with which I am impreft, to merit, in
fome way or other, his obliging attentions.

Vienna, March 4, 1771.

## LETTER XXVII.

### TO THE SAME.

YESTERDAY was configned to me, by
Signor *Antonio Baroni*, the new differtation
*De ufu progreffionis geometricæ in Mufica*; and
with the utmoft eagernefs I inftantly began
the perufal; but I foon faw that it was a
kind of reading that I was not qualified to
go through with, haftily. With due attention, I hope, however, to acquire from it
all the pleafure and inftruction of which my
intelligence is capable. In the mean time,
accept my moft grateful thanks for the precious gift : wifhing you, reverend and learned
Sir, a long enjoyment of that life and health,
which you fo laudably employ in increafing
the luftre of our country; believe me to be
with affection, gratitude, and efteem, &c.

It will probably afford fome gratification
to the lovers of Englifh poetry, who are
zealous for the honour of our countrymen,
to be made acquainted with the effect which
a perufal

a perufal of an Italian tranflation of Young's
*Night Thoughts,* had on a man of Metaftafio's
exquifite tafte and found judgment. There
is only one letter in the collection, addreffed
to the perfon to whom the poet confides his
fentiments.

## LETTER XXVIII.

### TO DOCTOR GIUSEPPE BOTTONI.

I HAVE perufed with avidity, and infinite
pleafure, which I never expected to receive
from excefs of melancholy, the firft fix *Night
Thoughts* of the celebrated poet Young, in
your elegant verfion; and am extremely
grateful to you for enabling me to have a
knowledge of the Englifh Mufes, in fpite of
my involuntary ignorance of this excellent
language. Thanks to your affiftance, I
have underftood, and admired, thefe poems to
fuch a degree, that they did not feem at all
to have changed their drefs. I have not
obferved in your tranflation, any of thofe
uncertain and fervile ftrokes of the pencil,
which ufually diftinguifh a copy from an
original; and am perfuaded, that if the fub-

lime

lime author had fung on the banks of the
Arno, he would have expreffed his thoughts
in that flowing, clear, and noble manner;
and with that conftant and varied harmony,
with which you have fo wonderfully tranflated and enriched him.    I can eafily comprehend what infinite pains fuch a difficult
tafk muft have coft you; but it feems well
worthy of your labour,   The extraordinary
merit of this excellent writer appears, even
in his defects; for notwithftanding the want
of order and connexion, his frequent repetitions, determined obftinacy in always
fhewing the dark fide of every object, and
unwillingnefs to conduct us to virtue by any
other way, than that of defpair; in fpite
(I fay) of thefe oppreffive circumftances, he
feizes on the reader, and tranfports him juft
whither he pleafes,

He always thinks for himfelf, profoundly,
and with grandeur.   His colouring is vivid,
vigourous, and fplendid; fo that the abun-
dance of his beauties, makes us overlook his
imperfections; as we are too much dazzled
by the magic of Reubens's colouring, to fee
the defects of his defign.

May the favours of Apollo with which
you have been bleffed, continue during the

progrefs

progrefs of a work fo admirably begun; and
may I be ftill indulged with your partiality.

Vienna, May 23, 1771.

To the following correfpondent of this period (1771) no more than one letter feems to
have been preferved; but as we obtain by it
Metaftafio's opinion, on a fubject as curious in
politics, as that of the preceding letter in poetry, it feems well worthy of infertion here.

## LETTER XXIX.

### TO SIGNOR D. GIACOMO MARTORELLI.

I never doubted, Sir, but that Baron *Van
Swieten*, in his anfwer, would render you all
due juftice; but I am extremely pleafed to
fee my expectations fo fully verified in the
copy tranfmitted to me, and to find in what
high eftimation your opinions and writings are held by fo enlightened a judge: as
you may place entire confidence in the approbation beftowed upon you by a man fo candid, frank, and of a temperament fo entirely
hoftile to flattery.

I am extremely obliged, as you may well
imagine, by the trouble which you have
taken to fend me the epigram lately come

from

from the Ifland of Barataria(r). Your civility to it inclines me to imagine, that you
think it my own; it will not therefore be decent for me to pafs fentence upon it, having
not yet learned to fwim or fifh in the troubled
waters of critical feas. A very learned adept
in the imperial library, to whom I communicated the epigram, believes the author of it
to have been a Greek and not a Roman: founding his opinion upon the error which, according
to him, cannot be that of the ftone-cutter,
and upon fome phrafes which feem to him
tranfpofed. I fhall procure a copy of the literary journal of Florence, and without fear
of being deceived, fhall believe what is there
determined concerning it.

With refpect to this part of the world, literature of every kind is a merchandife for
which there is no vent; and the phyfical reafon for it is, the enormous and ruinous military
fyftem, which obliges the fovereigns, whether they will or no, in order to defend themfelves from each other, to impoverifh both
themfelves and their fubjects. And as there
is no other road by which individuals can
expect advancement, fo princes would be

(r) Alluding to the tranflation of a Greek Epigram, which
afterwards appeared among his pofthumous works.

thought

thought reprehenfible curators of the public fecurity, if the leaft part of that revenue were appropriated to the honour of Minerva, which is hardly fufficient for the expences of Mars. And this too indifputable truth, is the clear folution of innumerable problems, my dear Sig. Martorelli, which appear inexplicable.

Vienna, Auguft 19. 1771. (s)

Of the many prints engraved of Metaftafio, I have never feen one that did juftice, either to his features or expreffion. And the Poet, in the following letter to a Roman painter, who applied to him for a print, or the copy of a picture, which refembled him the moft, feems to have thought himfelf little obliged to the artifts who had made him the fubject of their labours.

(s) The reader will recollect, by attending to this date, the fituation of Germany at the time thefe reflexions were made: the long and ruinous war between Auftria and Pruf-fia, and the mutual jealoufy which thofe powers entertained of each other, feem to have difcouraged and banifhed almoft every art, but that of flaughter. But now, in greater dan-ger from the arms and principles of France, than the fears or ambition of each other, though united among themfelves, their whole attention and refources are neceffarily pointed to the fecurity, not only of the government, religion and laws of the feveral ftates, but the poffeffions, liberty, and lives, of individuals, more important and folid bleffings, than literature or the fine arts!

LET-

# LETTER XXX.

## TO SIGNOR FRANCESCO CARDINALI.

FAME, which blazons the merit of others, however conftant and univerfal, is, howéver, but too frequently the mere effect of chance and good fortune: hence that which procures me the favour of your choice, may very probably be of this kind; but too rigorous an examination into motives, may not be for the advantage of my felf-love; and being indebted to good fortune for the acquifition of your partiality, I fhould not have fufficient courage to take much pains, in analyzing and deftroying it.

Impreffed with a due fenfe of my obligation to you, for the honour you do me, by wifhing to give my portrait a place among the illuftrious men whom you propofe to copy, I cannot, in gratitude, help praying to heaven, that by thus exalting me, you may not difgrace your own tafte and judgment.

It is moft certain, that my picture in the obfervatory of the Arcades at Rome, was fent thither by myfelf, from Vienna, at the requeft of Prince D. *Sigifmondo Ghigi*; and likewife that it was carefully copied from that which

was

was once thought to refemble me the moft; but it feems as if I had no great reafon to be proud of it. In that which I inclofe, you will find the features of my peruke and band per- fectly exprefled; but not thofe of my face.

Yet it did not feem ufelefs to fend it, as ex- ternal, but true circumftances, however tri- vial, frequently contribute to fuggeft the air of an abfent countenance.

Vienna, December 9, 1771.

There are feveral fhort letters of civility in the collection, from the bard to this paint- er; who feems to have merited his efteem, by the modefty and refpect with which he ad- dreffed him.

" The candour and modefty with which you exprefs yourfelf, have not only confirm- ed, but confiderably encreafed my efteem for you: as thefe qualities have their intrinfic and real value, without the affiftance of opinion or chance. I congratulate you on the poffef- fion of fuch qualities, and perhaps more on my own account than yours, as they have ren- dered the poffeffion of your partiality a more valuable acquifition. "

The following letter of this period, will afford the reader an opportunity of knowing

Metaftafio's ideas of a perfect *Canzone*, or detached fong of many ftanzas.

## LETTER XXXI.

TO THE MARQUIS CARLO VALENTI,
*upon a Canzone written by P. Sanbonifacio, the
Jefuit, on the Emprefs Queen's birth-day.*

WHOEVER was the author of the Canzone
which you have been pleafed to fend me, has
great reafon to be grateful to the mufes for
the partial affiftance which they have afforded him, in this pleafing and ingenious production. It is at once poetical, clear, noble,
harmonious, rich in imagery and ideas, and
manifefts, throughout, the effects of that art,
which the writer fo dexteroufly and perfectly
has contrived to conceal. But what has afforded me the moft pleafure, is the author's
exquifite judgment, which difcovers itfelf
both in the choice of his fubject, and in the
fkilful manner of arranging his materials;
which he has diverfified without multiplying
them, and formed into a whole, where nothing is wanting or fuperabundant; I congratulate him on his fuccefs; and while I render

you

you my beft thanks for this new and obliging
teftimony of your remembrance, permit me
to remind you of the conftant and ancient
refpect, with which I have always been, and
ever fhall be, &c.

Vienna, June 10. 1771.

We fhall now return to the Poet's correfpondence with Sig. Saverio Mattei of Naples, with whom he generally difcuffes literary fubjects more amply, than with moft of
his other correfpondents.

## L E T T E R. XXXII.

### TO SIGNOR SAVERIO MATTEI.

THOUGH you always avail yourfelf of a
period equal to the time which I have fuffered to elapfe in anfwering your laft letter, I
fubmit with patience, while I know you are
fulfilling the duties of a parent and a philofopher. And I rejoice extremely, that you
have quitted the tirefome toils of the bar, which
obliged you to exercife your talents at the expence of more luminous and fruitful employ-
ments; I hope thefe are the preludes to a
feries of aufpicious events; and that, for once,

I 2 fortune

fortune will be obliged to unite with juſtice, in favouring merit.

I perceive the partiality of friendſhip in all you ſay of my *Ruggiero;* and the pleaſure which this diſcovery affords me, is a conſolation more flattering, than the conſciouſneſs of ſuperior merit could produce. But whatever my poor drama may be, its worth will certainly receive no encreaſe by the reſpect ſhewn to the Singers of the preſent times; reduced by their own fault to the rank of performers of *Intermezzi,* or buffoon interludes between the ſeveral dances, which are now become more intereſting than the acts of an opera. For the Dancers having uſurped the art of counterfeiting the affections, and of repreſenting human actions, have juſtly acquired the attention of the people, which the others have as juſtly loſt. For contenting themſelves with grating the ears of the audience with a vocal *Sonata,* which is called an Air, often very offenſive, they leave to the Dancers the taſk of occupying the mind and heart of the ſpectators, by which they have reduced our theatre to a ſhameful and intolerable jumble of incongruities.

Vienna, May 30. 1771.

L E T-

# LETTER XXXIII.

## TO THE SAME.

THOUGH I am become callous, by long ufe, to the mangling of my poor dramas, yet your friendly compaffion, in preventing monftrous wens from fpringing out of my *Ezio*, has obliged me extremely. The *Quartetto* which you have written, is decent, convenient, and happy; and if it is well treated by the compofer and performers, I believe it will have a good effect in the reprefentation. Indeed it will render the fecond act fomewhat barren of airs, in which the two principal perfonages will have but one fong a-piece: which would have been thought facrilege, when I wrote the opera; but at prefent, when the heroic Singers have ceded to the Dancers the precedency of reprefentation; and when, by virtue of this ceffion, they are degraded to the performance of a kind of *act tunes* between the feveral Ballets, the more a drama is cut down, the lefs matter remains to exercife the patience of the fpectators. On the other hand, it is a falfe fuppofition, that I ever wrote a *Quartet* for *Ezio*, or that I ever requefted

quefted

quefted one; though it is moft true, that I am,
and ever fhall be, &c. &c.

Vienna, September 18, 1771.


## LETTER XXXIV.

### TO THE SAME.

I HAVE already received advice, that a copy
of the fourth volume of your Pfalms, directed to
me, is on the road; and I feel the utmoft impatience for enriching myfelf with the poffeffion of this new treafure. Not doubting
but this will furpafs in merit its elder brothers:
as the extraordinary vigour of your genius,
is conftantly on the increafe, though its former efforts furpaffed the common ftandard.

I had hoped, that your friendly compla-
cency would have feconded my well-known
repugnance, (whether it proceeded from weaknefs or reafon) to the publication of my
private letters. But I fee, that availing
yourfelf rigoroufly of the rights which your
merit gives you over my will, you have
freely gone to work, and fpared me the diftrefs of doubtful deliberation. The worft of
it is, that by acting in this manner, you have
manifefted an opinion of my productions far
above their value, for which I know not
whether I ought to grieve or rejoice. Yet
I know

know extremely well, that whatever vexation it may have coſt me, my ſufferings are ſuper-abundantly paid by the enviable friendſhip of one like you : wiſhing therefore for its con-tinuance, I am, &c.

Vienna, March 15, 1772.

## L E T T E R  XXXV.

### TO THE SAME.

I HAVE run through the fourth volume of your admirable verſion of the Pſalms, which you have ſo obligingly ſent me, with avi-dity, attention, delight, and profit, from the title-page to the ſage and learned letter, which you have addreſſed to the *Abate Spar-ziani*; and find myſelf amply rewarded for the long impatience with which I was tor-mented, during the expectation of their ar-rival. All ſeem extremely worthy of the preceding volumes; nay, perhaps from the force of novelty, ſome of your reaſoning, as juſt as unexpected, has ſtruck and ſurpriſed me ſtill more effectually. In the 90th pſalm, (our 91ſt) for inſtance, not only the lively and bright colouring of the tranſlation, but the admirable diſſertation on the *Meridian Dæ-*

*mon,*

*mon*, (*t*) from whofe infidious arts, in order
to be able to defend myfelf fufficiently, I
have learned from you even to doubt of my
own exiftence : the happy apology with
which you exonerate David (pf. 109th)
from the odium of the atrocious imprecations
which are ufually attributed to him, fo inju-
rioufly to his benign character (*u*) : the
noble

(*t*) " The ficknefs that deftroyeth in the noon-day." pf.
91. v. 6. Signor Mattei, after giving the different opinions
of the fathers and commentators on the *Meridian Dæmon*,
feems chiefly to adhere to the opinion of Grotius, as the
moft fimple folution of the difficulty; who fuppofed this
*Dæmon* to imply the SUN, *qui itinerantibus in Palæftina
maximè lethalis eft.* This idea was very likely to ftrike an
Italian, who dreads nothing more than *il Colpo del fole :*
" the arrow that flyeth by day." (v. 5 of the fame pf.) or
more vulgarly, *the noontide devil.* The peftilence in-
flicted on the Greeks at the fiege of Troy comes from the
*Sun* :

The infulted fire (his God's peculiar care)
To *Phœbus* pray'd, and *Phœbus* heard the prayer :
A dreadful plague enfues; th' avenging *darts*
Inceffant fly, and pierce the Grecian hearts.

POPE's Il. b. 1. 494.
The *mall' aria della notte*, or " the peftilence that walk-
eth in darknefs," is likewife a figurative expreffion; that is
very intelligible to the inhabitants of hot climates.
(*u*) This is done by affigning to the *Enemy* of David, the
imprecations of this pf. from v. 5. to 18. inftead of fuppofing them to come from the royal Pfalmift himfelf;
who

noble facility and features of the original *Etruscan lamentation*, which you have had the dexterity to transfuse into our language; the fine poetical fervor which reigns in the 82d psalm; the clearness and connection which has been discovered in the 84th, 86th, 105th, and 113th psalms; the variety and spirit of the imagery with which the representations of nature are described in the 102d and 103d psalms; the truly beautiful, as well as moral short cantata, into which you have compressed the 99th psalm; the drama which you have so ingeniously discovered and demonstrated in the 117th psalm, and (not to tire you with an account of the whole volume) in short, every thing has surprised me to such

who says, v. 3. "For the love that I had unto them, lo, they take now my contrary part: but I give myself unto prayer. Thus have they rewarded me evil for good: and hatred for my good will."-Then follow the maledictions of his enemy—after which, v. 19, he retorts the curses of his foes on themselves. "Let it thus happen from the Lord unto mine enemies," &c.—This solution is so easy and satisfactory, that it seems wonderful not to have been at all times the general opinion of divines and commentators; but the first time that I found this opinion supported, was by the late learned and Rev. Mr Keate, in a sermon which he preached at Chelsea College Chapel, before either of us had seen Mattei's Psalms, and when I had only discovered in this letter of Metastasio, that an apology had been made for David, by Saverio Mattei, without knowing in what it consisted.

proofs

a degree, and furnifhed me with fuch new proofs of your enviable vigour, vaft learning, and numerous and wonderful talents, that I fhall very frequently repeat the perufal of this volume, being always certain of acquiring in it, new inftruction, and new pleafure.

I ought to beftow a word or two on the gratuitous praifes with which you fo generoufly honour me, in your printed letters, and in the courfe of this work; but thefe certain proofs of your partiality are not able to appeafe my remorfe at fuch a ufurpation: fo that not to awaken it, I affure you of my ferious gratitude; but as laconically as poffible.

You have been pleafed, at all hazards, to enrol me among *Controvertifts*, by printing my letters concerning ancient mufic, which I had moft privately addreffed to you, in pure obedience. God forgive you! but for my own part, I cannot; nor fhall I ever diffemble my invincible repugnance to a bufinefs fo fuperior to my phyfical powers, as well as abhorrent to my difpofition and inclination. Confole me, Sir, at leaft, by the continuance of your affection, and judge of mine, by the refignation with which I am, &c.

Vienna, April 7th, 1772.

L E T-

# LETTER XXXVI.

## TO THE SAME

I DIRECT my letter to Naples, whither I hope you are at length returned, after four months abfence; a time equally taken up by your books in travelling, which you fent to me before your departure, but which only arrived here laft week. Indulging my impatience, I began with your theatrical differtation, to which I gave the preference for a thoufand reafons. It is a fublime work, and worthy of you; nor is it admirable merely from the profound learning of the writer, but much more fo from the marvellous knowledge of the moft recondite myfteries of the ftage, unknown to the majority even of thofe who profefs the art. But what flatters me the moft, is the accidental coincidence of our notions concerning the ancient and modern drama. The fpontaneous opinion of one like you, gives me courage, and renders me proud of my own: and I now regard thofe learned, but moft inexpert critics, who differ from us, as entirely confuted. If I were to undertake the pointing out all the paffages of your differtation that

are

are worthy of praife, this letter would not
only equal it, but furpafs it, in fize. The
folid demonftrations with which you have
removed all the infuperable difficulties in
underftanding the poetics of Ariftotle and
Horace, fufficiently to render them ufeful in
practice : the art with which you have expofed the abfurdity of reducing the unity of
place, to the narrow limits of a chamber or
clofet : the torrent of paffages from Greek
dramas, with which you juftify and compare
our dramatic *Airs, Duets,* and *Trios* : the happy as well as difficult verfion of the beautiful fcene in the *Hecuba* of Euripides : the
generous modefty of giving the preference
to my cantatas over your own : the mafterly
analyfis of the firft fcene of *Artaxerxes,* and
that of *Sextus* and *Titus* : and every one of
your fage philofophical confiderations, would
require a prolix and diftinct chapter. But,
begging your pardon, I cannot, however, ap-
prove that manifeft excefs of partiality, in
my favour, which reigns in every period.
You, by this means, expofe yourfelf to the
contradictions of thofe who have their reafons for not being of your opinion : and at
the fame time, expofe your friend, by the
moft violent temptations of vanity, to quit
that

that modeſt courſe which it is his duty to
ſteer, temptations from which he is the
leſs likely to defend himſelf, when aſſailed
by a perſon armed with ſuch learning and
ſeducing eloquence.

I ſhould ſay much more, if I did not fear
that my moſt ſincere praiſes would run the
riſk of being conſtrued into a mercantile re-
ſtitution of thoſe with which you have
voluntarily honoured me ; ſo that, embracing
you with my uſual affection, I commit to
your perſpicacity, the care of inveſtigating,
and of figuring to yourſelf, my eſteem and
gratitude.

After the above was written, your letter,
dated from Naples, arrived. Beſides the
uſual faculty which all your letters poſſeſs,
of conſoling, exhilerating, and of meriting
my gratitude ; this laſt, which informs me
of your happy return to Naples, in perfect
health, after a long and inconvenient pere-
grination, has every title to my thanks ; as it
aſſures me, that no inauſpicious circumſtances
have thus long deprived me of the ſatisfaction
of hearing from you : as your family cares and
affections, have had a conſiderable ſhare of
your time, of which you kindly gave me an
account, and as the exceſſive impetus of

3                               ſome

some expressions of friendship in this letter
enables me to judge of that regard which
occasioned it. I am extremely grateful, as
indeed I ought to be, not only on these accounts, but for the assurance with which you
have gratified me, of the favourable remembrance of the admirable princess of *Belmonte*; yet concerning the instances which
you give, I must in all modesty and decorum
be silent.

O how many sweet and exhilerating ideas
has your account, my dear Signor *Saverio*, of
Magna Græcia, awakened in my mind!
Renovating all the happiness of childhood and
adolescence, which I enjoyed in that country,
no less useful than pleasing! It has brought
again to my view all those objects with which
I was then so much delighted. I have again
inhabited the little chamber where the extreme proximity of marine murmurs lulled
me for many months, so delightfully to
sleep. I have, in fancy, crossed the neighbouring sea in a bark to *Scalea*: all the
names and aspects of *Cirella, Belvidere, Ce-
traro*, and *Paola*, have been brought back to
my mind : I have again heard the venerated
voice of the celebrated philosopher *Caroprese*,
who adapting himself, in order to instruct
me

me, to my weak ſtate, conducted me, as it
were by the hand, through the vortices of
the ingenious *Deſcartes*, at that time in high
favour with philoſophers, and of which he
was a furious aſſerter; and indulging my
childiſh curioſity, now demonſtrating with
wax, in a kind of ſport, how globes were
formed by the fortuitous concourſe of atoms:
now exciting my admiration by the enchanting experiments of Dioptrics. I ſeem ſtill
to ſee him labour to convince me, that his
little dog was only a machine: and that the
trine dimenſion was a ſufficient definition of
ſolid bodies. And I ſtill ſee him laugh, after
plunging me for a long time in dark meditation, and making me doubt of every thing,
in proving that I breathed, by his *Ego cogito,
ergo ſum:* an invincible argument of cer-
tainty, which I deſpaired of ever again demonſtrating.

But you have rouſed a hornet's neſt, ſo
that I find myſelf as much ſurrounded by
remembrances and a wiſh to communicate
them, as you by the literary and law caſes
with which you were aſſaulted at your return: ſo that not to rob you of the time neceſſary for theſe more uſeful and neceſſary
conſi-

confiderations, I embrace you affectionately, and leave you in peace.

Vienna, September 1, 1772.

## LETTER XXXVII.

### TO THE SAME.

In your obliging letter of the 12th of laft October, you courteoufly thank me, dear Sir, for the pleafure and profit which I had received from the attentive perufal of the fourth volume of your illuftrious and learned work. Now who would not purchafe the right of a creditor upon fuch eafy terms? You, however, continue to give me fimilar opportunities; but affure yourfelf, that you will always encreafe the load on your own fhoulders by fuch debts. For my part, I fhall repeat all I have formerly faid, adding, that, among other things, I have particularly admired the mafterly, inftructive, and very elegant fonnet, which I have met with at the end of the obfervations upon the 110th Pfalm; and have there obferved the natural analogy, which is ufual between plants and their fruits. I beg of you to congratulate

gratulate the refpectable author of it, in my name, when you have an opportunity ; as I now felicitate you yourfelf on the tender, grateful, and exemplary difpofition of your own good heart, towards fo worthy a father.

I am forry that your engagements at the bar, have confined you to the city, and deprived you, this year, of the refrefhment of your ufual autumnal holidays in the country. But this convincing proof of the juft reputation which your abilities have acquired, a little foftens the idea of many prefent inconveniences, by thinking of thofe fplendid and tranquil advantages, which I fo ardently wifhed and prefage. When, very long ago, under the direction of the celebrated advocate and, afterwards, councellor, *Caftagnola (x)*, I kept thefe courts myfelf, I learned the following axiom, which I have never fince found reafon to doubt: that the fields of *Themis*, (goddefs of juftice, law,) produce in the beginning to the cultivators there (in Naples) nothing but knavery and mere fatigue ; but, afterwards, in the middle of their career, when indeed they have other labours,

(x) This is the Neapolitan civilian, whom moft of Metaftafio's biographers called *Paglietti.*

but which produce fruits proportioned to their toils, they luxuriate in a spontaneous and constant fecundity, exempt from labour. From their last desirable stage I believe you, my dear Sir, at present, not very remote. I beg you to respect and fulfil my vaticination; and to persevere in believing me to be, &c.

Vienna, Nov. 9, 1772.

END OF THE SECOND SECTION.

## SECTION III.

IT was in the Summer of this year, 1772, that I gratified both my curiosity and my heart, by frequently visiting and conversing with the great lyric bard at Vienna; and though an account of these, to me, most agreeable visits and conversations, has been already given to the public in my *German Tour* (vol. 1.) yet I shall here try to recollect what has been omitted in that relation.

During my residence in that city, I discovered that the poet was not more admired for his extraordinary public talents, than beloved and respected for his private virtues and character. The few innocent singularities which have been ascribed to him, for which he frequently accounts in his letters, were so amply compensated, by his constant probity, politeness, friendship, and philanthrophy, that I heard nothing but his praises from persons of every rank, whenever his name was occasionally mentioned. He seems to have supported dignity without pride; and to have acquired universal admiration without vanity or indirect means. His private,

tranquil-

tranquil, and unvaried habits of life, allowed
him no opportunities for the practice of thofe
fublime, fplendid, and heroic virtues of
courage, patriotifm, magnanimity, fortitude, clemency, and beneficence, which he
has fo admirably defcribed and illuftrated in
his dramatic works; but there can be no
doubt of their exiftence in his heart, whence
his fentiments fo manifeftly appear to have
flowed. The private, domeftic, and focial
virtues of filial and fraternal affection, friendfhip, philanthrophy, urbanity, probity, honour, and general benevolence, feem never
to have been practifed with more conftancy
and devotion, than by our bard; who has
been as juftly, as emphatically, called, by one
of his countrymen, not only *the poet*, but *the
philofopher of the heart* (y).

The monotonous manner in which he
fpent his life during his long refidence at
Vienna, has been ridiculed, and thought infipid, by perturbed fpirits; but to the admirers of his writings and virtues, it will
not be indifferent to know how he paffed
his time, which was in a way fo regular and conftant, that there were few perfons at Vienna unacquainted with it.

(y) *Elogj Italiani*, Tom. I.

He

He ſtudied daily from eight o'clock in the morning, till noon. Then viſited his friends, and thoſe families and individuals from whom he had received civilities. Dined at two; and at five received his moſt familiar and intimate friends. At nine, in Summer, he went out in his carriage, viſited, and ſometimes played at *Ombre*, a game which he liked better than thoſe of mere chance, as it afforded him ſome exerciſe of mind in calculation. Men accuſtomed to think, make their amuſements contribute to mental improvement.

He returned home at ten o'clock; ſupped, and went to bed before eleven. In his con-verſation he was conſtantly chearful; fanci-ful, playful, and ſometimes poetical, in his diſcourſe, as well as in his letters; never ſar-caſtic or diſputatious; totally devoid of curioſity concerning the public or private ſcandal in circulation, the morality of his ſentiments reſembled that of his life. His anſwers were elegant, acute, and ingenious; occaſionally learned without pedantry; and full of intereſting and applicable anecdotes of paſt and preſent times. In confidence with few, but polite to all. His affection for his countrymen was great, and extended

to

to ecclefiaftics, painters, muficians, poets, and minifters of Italian ftates, who were all fure of his kindnefs and good offices. His liberality was exactly proportioned to his means: he feemed to wifh for wealth for no other purpofe than to fupply his own wants, without fuperfluity, and thofe of neceffitous friends. He prefented the *Improvifatore* Talaffi, with twelve Sequins, and recommended him to the attention of the great, for higher patronage. His character was never ftained with any vice, or illiberal propenfities. His fenfibility inclined him to the paffion of love ; but as it was fincere, it became a bridle to itfelf, and a ftimulus to virtue ; as his whole life and writings have manifefted.

*Un amour vrai fans feinte et fans caprice*
*Eſt en effet le plus grand frein du vice ;*
*Dans fes liens qui fçait fe retenir,*
*Eſt honnête homme, ou va le devinir.*
                                        VOLTAIRE.

The fureft check to pravity of mind
Is love fincere, to no caprice confign'd ;
Whoever in his heart admits the gueft
Or has no vice, or foon will vice deteft.

                                        " From

"From a natural love of order and regularity (fays the Abate Taruffi) (z) even to fcrupulofity, he ufed invariably to perform the fame offices each day at almoft the fame inftant; and in his own defence, he would tell thofe who contemned fuch exactitude as contracted and frivolous, that he had always found the regular diftribution of time, not only contributed to bodily health, but to ferenity of mind."

Among his moft agreeable evening occupations, the literary converfations with his two ancient and confidential friends, *Count Canale*, and *Baron Hagen*, feem to have held the firft place; thefe grave and learned perfonages, eminent for erudition and probity, were attached to him by all the ties of good tafte and fimilar affections. Greek, Latin, Italian, and French writers of the firft clafs, continued during many years to exercife the critical acumen of this illuftrious triumvirate.

Among the lively farcafms againft our inoxious bard, it has been faid, that the fmallpox, old age, ficknefs, and death, were never

---

(z) *Elogio dell' Ab. Metaftafio.* The author of this Eulogium lived in the greateft intimacy with the poet at Vienna, during many years.

to

to be mentioned in his prefence; but we find them all frequently mentioned in his letters, by himfelf.

Even his not learning the German language during the many years he refided at Vienna, admits of fome apology. His favour at the Imperial court, and fame throughout Europe, depended on his Italian poetry; and it is moft probable, that he was fearful of corrupting his native language by ufing another, too frequently, in converfation. Every Englifhman muft know, that all foreigners who refide a confiderable time in our country, if they learn our language fufficiently to converfe in it, foon loofe the purity of their own, by a mixture of the two tongues, and by frequently thinking in the one, and fpeaking in the other. I have never known a French governefs, or teacher at a boarding-fchool, who, in fix or feven years refidence here, has not loft as much of her own language, as fhe has gained of ours. It is the fame with profeffed language mafters; of whom, if I wifhed to learn a living language with correctnefs and purity, I would, *cæteris paribus*, prefer him who had come laft from his own country. At Vienna, Italian is more generally fpoken

than

than French, particularly among ſtrangers, and the *Corps diplomatique*. Indeed on account of the Auſtrian poſſeſſions in Italy, there are generally more Italians in the capital of the empire, than French; ſo that Metaſtaſio had no occaſion to learn German for the ſake of converſation, though he had acquired according to his own account (*a*), the names of neceſſaries in that language, *per ſalvar la vita*. And I am inclined to believe, that it was neither the harſhneſs of the Teutonic dialect, nor the difficulty of learning it, that ſo much prevented or impeded his acquiring it, as the fear of corrupting his own.

But as his friend and correſpondent, Sig. *Saverio Mattei*, ſays (*b*), "whoever would have an exact account of his cuſtoms, manners, way of thinking of himſelf and others; of the fulfiling his duties, the viciſſitudes of his fortune, his application, and the degree of ſucceſs with which his works were at firſt received, with their influence on the public taſte of Italy, and on every lyric ſtage in Europe, can only find them in his

(*a*) *Muſical Tour through Germany*, &c. Vol. I. Art. Vienna.

(*b*) *Memorie per ſervire alla vita del* Metastasio, 1785.

Letters;"

LETTERS;" we fhall proceed to felect, extract, and tranflate, fuch of them as ftill
remain unnoticed, concerning the fubfequent
part of his life.

## LETTER I.

### TO SIG. SAVERIO MATTEI.

HAVING no experienced and trufty correfpondent in *Triefte*, I have not been able to
avail myfelf of your fage counfel in fixing on
a commiffioner there, who would undertake
to receive and forward to Vienna, the box
which you have fent by that road ; but I am
acquainted with perfons here, who are on
very friendly terms with the conful in that
city, Sig. D. *Giovan Battifta Orlandi*, and I
have already obtained a promife of his affiftance with refpect to the box in queftion ; fo
that we have reafon to hope for better fortune from the prefent expedient than the
paft. The advice which you give me of the
precious contents of this box, makes me
very impatient for its arrival ; after which
you fhall have tranfmitted to you, an exact
relation of the pleafure and profit which
this acquifition fhall have produced. In the
mean

mean time, I beg of you to deliver, in my
name, all due acknowledgments to the
moſt worthy counſellor *Patrizij*, for the
generous alacrity with which he has ſeconded your beneficent intention of enriching me
with his excellent writings ; and aſſure him
of my ſincere reſpeĉts. I have read with
equal delight and admiration, your new,
eloquent, ſage, and learned diſſertation,
upon the Dramatico-Lyrica poetry of the
Pſalms ; and I do not ſee how it is poſſible,
that oppreſſed as you are with the enormous
weight of ſo many legal, profeſſional, literary,
and domeſtic cares, you are able to preſerve
entire and equal to yourſelf, that wonderful
vigour of mind, which is neceſſary to the
continual produĉtion of new works, as valuable for their correĉtneſs, as genius and
variety of knowledge. Then I know not
how to expreſs to you my ſatisfaĉtion, in finding ſuch an exaĉt coincidence in our way of
thinking, concerning the affinity between
the ancient and modern theatre, and that,
without the leaſt communication with each
other on the ſubjeĉt. In an extraĉt from the
poetics of Ariſtotle, which I have lately
augmented, and in which I have endeavoured to combine the dramatic precepts of this

great

great philofopher with my own but too long experience; and likewife in the notes which I am going to amufe myfelf with writing to my old tranflation of Horace's Epiftle to the Pifos, I fee, that your reafoning and mine fet off from the fame fource, though they meet in concurrence by mere accident; and the fpontaneous opinion of fuch a one as you, puts me in humour with my own.

I am forry that your well-known partiality in my favour, fhould expofe you to a participation of the vigour of the learned author of the Roman daily *literary journal* againft me, whofe impatient fincerity has manifeftly *me* for object, and not *you:* but the opportunity which it has afforded you of becoming by this laft production more wonderful, and more celebrated, and me of being able to boaft of fuch an inftance of your affection, certainly demands our gratitude more than refentment. To fay the truth, I fhould rather have expected from my country, a defence than an attack; but it is juft that all private regard fhould give way to the advantages of public correction. As for myfelf, my dear Sig. Saverio, who am rendered callous and impenetrable by old habits (good

or

or bad) contracted by an uninterrupted ufe of
more than half a century, and in which I
have been indulged not with an accidental,
but conftant favour of the public, it would
be manifeft injuftice in me to pretend to fee
or feel the neceffity of the propofed corrections; and upon the inutility of admitting
them, you have written with fo much learning and folidity, that I fhould be utterly unable to add any thing to your reafons, which
would not be repetition and fuperfluous.
Affure yourfelf, therefore, that my affection
for you encreafes, in proportion to the new
and illuftrious proofs which I receive, from
day to day, of your friendfhip.

Vienna, March 11, 1773.

## L E T T E R  II.

### TO THE SAME.

In fhort, we muft never defpair. For
when I had relinquifhed all expectation, that
the box of books, which you had kindly directed to me fo many months ago, would
ever arrive, the inclofed letter of advice
from a courier of *Triefte*, moft unexpectedly
informed

informed me, that all its contents had long
been in the poffeffion of *Ratrop*, the druggift
at Vienna, I fought, and found him. He
has configned to my meffenger, the book
of counfellor *Patrizj*; and the mufic of the
Pfalm, fet by Sig. *Cafaro*, with fix volumes,
that is to fay, two copies of the three firft
volumes of the new edition, in octavo, of
of the poetical books of the bible; and all
this, not only without a box, but without
any kind of envelope, or direction, to inform the druggift how to difcover to whom
thefe goods appertained. It will now be of
no confequence to inveftigate the caufe
of this diforder: I fhall therefore indulge
my impatience, and immediately proceed to
give you an account of the effect which your
precious gift has produced in me, though
hardly *fummis labiis deguftatum.*

———— I began by reading the firft con-
fultations of the very worthy counfellor
*Patrizj*, nor did I defift till I had entirely
admired them all. I am extremely obliged
to you, for having enriched me with fuch a
treafure; and I entreat you to inform the
illuftrious writer, of my true refpect and gratitude, for the honour he has done the re-
public of letters, and his country.

z                                                    Of

Of the masterly Psalm, by the celebrated *Cafaro*(*c*), it does not become me to speak. It is an acquisition for Signora Martinetz to appreciate, not me. She seized, played, and sung it, the instant it was received in my presence; and it appeared too short. We returned to it, and tried it again the next day, more deliberately; when she discovered in it new beauties, and determined to study it constantly for her improvement in harmony. She has commissioned me to render you a million of thanks, for your kind attention; and I join to them my own acknowledgments, for the pleasure which I have received myself in hearing this admirable music performed.

I have still to speak of my new obligations to you, for enriching me with duplicates of the second edition of the three first volumes, of your most learned book. I have already examined them, though *festinanti oculo*, and find that this edition is more elegant, more convenient, more ornamented, and more rich than the first.—The beautiful octave stanza, the learned dissertation on the *traditions* that have been preserved, &c. and

(*c*) Sig: CAFARO, an excellent Neapolitan composer, in a correct, solid, and masterly stile.

what

what you have added, are all worthy of you,
and extremely applicable to the subject. But
what has interested me most, is an unexpected portrait, elegantly drawn, of my dear
Signor Saverio, and that which he has so well
delineated, in words, of his most worthy
father. I have been pleased to find in the
features of the first, particularly in the eyes,
a perspicacious vivacity beaming from the
mind ; and that exemplary filial tenderness
in the exposition of the second, which renders visible the excellent heart of the
painter.

But amidst so many motives of satisfac-
tion, I cannot conceal my chagrin, in perceiving what a number of my letters you
have published, in spite of my continual
prayers and remonstrances to the contrary.
If, Sir, you had believed them sincere, loving
me as you always seemed to do, you would
not have manifested your affection by continuing so constantly to afflict me ; so that I
am convinced you must regard my antipathy
in the same light as Virgil did the shyness
of Galatea : *Quæ fugit ad salices, & se cupit
ante videri.* But if such is your opinion,
you are mistaken, Sir, and wrong me very
much. My timidity, I know as well as you,
                                                             may

may be carried to excefs, but not to hypo-
crify ; and, at prefent, you ought to have a
better opinion of my heart. Pardon, or
rather receive kindly, this tranfport of fcru-
pulous friendfhip, in which all diffimulation
is culpable ; but ftill continue to love your,
&c.

Vienna, May 22th, 1773.


## LETTER III.

### TO THE SAME.

THE violent tenfion of my nerves, particularly in the head, and hypochondriac
affections, which at this time of the year
plague me infufferably, and deprive me of
all activity, and power of application however flight, have not abated my eagernefs to
read your philofophical and very learned
differtation on mufic ; and I have determined
to give it a fecond perufal, for which I fhall
be well rewarded, as foon as I am able to
undertake it with lefs heroifm. In the mean
time, let me confefs, that the partiality in my
favour, which runs through all your writings,
if it does not convince me of my merit,
affures me of your love ; and I am ex-

tremely grateful for fo dear and valuable a
poffeffion.

The truths which you affert concerning
modern theatres, with fo much eloquence
and learning, are fo evident and inconteffi-
ble, and have been but too long remarked
with indignation by myfelf, that in a fit of
difguft, I determined upwards of fifteen years
ago, never to enter any theatre again, except that of the court, which for my comfort, is now wholly fhut up. When abufes
are arrived at their higheft excefs, nature,
and the inftability itfelf of human affairs,
alone can cure them. You may flatter yourfelf with the hopes of feeing this change, but
not I; fo that it is more your bufinefs than
mine to endeavour to haften it.

The ingenious and lively *fcherzo poetico*
(poetical flight) for the enfuing feftival, which
you have been fo obliging to fend me, is
worthy of the occafion. I have perufed it
more than once, with that pleafure which I
always receive from whatever comes from
your pen; and I conftantly find new caufe
of admiration and envy, at the fecundity
with which you treat every fubject, however
barren and common in itfelf. I pray heaven
to preferve you, and forgive the abufe of that
vigour

vigour which it has granted you, by allowing
yourfelf no kind of relaxation amidft fuch
numerous and different applications. Wifhing for the continuance of your affection,
I remain, &c.

Vienna, December 3, 1773.

As no more than two letters from our
Bard to this fpirited and voluminous writer,
remain to tranflate and infert, though their
dates are pofterior to thofe which are ftill
behind, addreffed to other perfons, we fhall
finifh this correfpondence; as the letters being chiefly on learned and critical fubjects,
are too much connected by reference to each
other, to be feparated without fatiguing the
recollection of the reader.

## LETTER IV.

### TO SIG. SAVERIO MATTEI.

THERE is no occafion, my dear D. Saverio,
to reform any of the verfions of the Pfalms
which you have obligingly fent me, they being
already fo advantageoufly adapted for the reception of mufic. I am truly fenfible of the
labour which you muft have had in felecting
L 2      paffages

paſſages favourable to Airs, Duets, and Trios, and in faithfully compreſſing into them the ſenſe of the text, without loſing that noble, clear, and elegant ſmoothneſs, ſo neceſſary to muſic, ſo eaſy in appearance, and ſo difficult to attain. But do not repent of your fatigue. It is concealed in a maſterly manner ; and you have fully accompliſhed what you propoſed; ſo that, at preſent, every compoſer will employ in theſe Pſalms, both the ſpecies into which Ariſtotle divides muſic ; that is, the *plain* and *florid* (as the ancients in the *diverbia*) uſing in the Recitatives the firſt, which is ſo ſimple and unadorned, that it is ſufficiently formed by the mere cadence of the verſe ; and in the ſecond, the more ornate, which acquires the name of Melody in our Airs, as the ancient did in the *cantica, monodia, ſtrophes, antriſtrophes,* and *epods.* This melody is formed (as you very well know) principally from *rhythm* or *numbers,* of which the metres are a part ; but theſe metres do not conſtitute rhythm, if not arbitrarily varied and compounded by a combination of periodical meaſures, which are invented, with more or leſs felicity, by muſical compoſers in proportion to their genius and abilities ; hence ariſes that alluring and infinite variety in the Airs of different maſters

to

to the fame words, in the Subject, Movement, Style, Paſſages, or whatever you are pleaſed to call them. But the convenience which compoſers will find in ſetting your Pſalms to muſic, is manifeſt and endleſs; being now furniſhed with rhythmic poetry, inſtead of the mere accents of proſe, which they were obliged to ſeek and expand or contract into meaſure, for the ſake of their melody. I congratulate you on your ſucceſs in this enterprize, and myſelf, in finding that without previous diſcuſſion, our opinions conſtantly coincide.

I cannot forgive you for unjuſtly calling your eloquent and learned letter, to the journaliſt of Modena, mere *babble*. Such injuſtice merits reparation, and of the ſame kind as that of Longinus, who having called the events of the Odyſſey of Homer mere dreams, immediately repents, and adds: but *they are the dreams of Jove.* If, however, I was diſpoſed to cenſure you, I ſhould perhaps ſay, that the occaſion did not merit ſuch pains. But every thing merits pains, when there is any one, who like you, can turn every ſubject to general inſtruction, as well as to the increaſe of his own fame. All your letters which I have found in the ſheets

which

which you have fent me, are extremely worthy of the writer; but particularly, the elegant, reverential, and decorous Latin epiſtle,
addreſſed to the *Servus fervorum*. In ſhort,
there is no literary province in which you
are not a citizen.

But do not, my dear D. Saverio, imagine
the fame of me; for if I had not a ſmall place
in Parnaſſus, I ſhould perhaps find a habitation no where elfe. What can I therefore
ſay to you about the various eſſays on legiſla-
tion, by yourſelf and others, with which you
have ſo obligingly furniſhed me? It is true,
that I difcover facts in them, that have been
mentioned in your works, and try to underſtand them; but I ſhall never have the
courage to difcover my opinion of them *.
If a poet may be allowed to judge of the
eloquence and hiſtorical part of a work, I
ſhall ſay fincerely, that I have read with infinite pleaſure, the life of the Marquis *Fragianni*, written with elegance, and judgment,
and reduced in the moſt difficult form of a

---

* The late Dr. Johnſon, having been ſhewn a proof-
ſheet of the *Differtation on the Mufic of the Ancients*, by
the Editor of Metaſtaſio's Life and Letters, faid to him,—
" Sir! the words are well arranged: but I do not under-
' ſtand one of them."

 continued

continued dedication to the learned and fage
reports and cafes in jurifprudence, of counfellor *Patrizj*. I fhould wifh to this great
and moft worthy friend, the fame and fortune
of his celebrated mafter Fragianni, if I did
not already difcover that the firft is prepared, and that he is not far from the other:
I fhall therefore rather form wifhes, as you
are inferior to none in merit, and in the
univerfal efteem which that merit has acquired you, that vanquifhing every obftacle
which envy may throw in your way, you
may compel fortune to join in rewarding
your virtue. Continue, in the mean time, to
honour me with your regard, and to affure
yourfelf, of the high eftimation in which I
hold your extenfive knowledge, and wonderful talents; and that I fhall be always, &c.

Vienna, January 15, 1774.

## LETTER V.

### TO THE SAME.

I AM extremely obliged to you, my dear
D. Saverio, for not fuffering me to remain
in ignorance, of your elegant and excellent
poem on the birth of our Saviour. In its con-

tracted

tracted form, the rich mine from which it
has been drawn is difcoverable. Such mafterly miniatures fometimes coft the more
trouble, in proportion to the neceffity of con-
cealing it, in thefe poetic labours, more
than in any other. I have communicated it
to feveral perfons. All applauded it, and I
am flattered by the confirmation of my own
opinion. I am told, that an edition of your
Pfalms, is already printing at Padua; fee
that this moft happy Canzonetta is inferted
in one of the volumes : as thefe fhort compofitions are foon loft, when printed fepa-
rately. I am impatient to fee this Pata-
vinian edition, of which I am told, and
much more, the many corrections which you
fay you have made in thofe places, which
did not fatisfy your extreme faftidious tafte,
though fo univerfally approved by others.
The learned men of that feminary, make
me hope that the edition will be extremely
correct; and I wifh it as much fuccefs as I
do the magnificent edition of my own works,
which is now preparing at Paris.

The cold, horrid, and obftinate winter,
with which we are ftill ftruggling, is not at
all favourable to my hypochondriac affections: the poor nerves fuffer more than
ufual,

ufual, and require a greater expence of patience than my capital can afford. However, there are people who bear petrifaction heroically; but the trade of a hero is a curfed trade.

I am extremely grateful for the valuable acquifition, which your golden writings have procured me, of fo valiant, learned and celebrated a champion, as the Abate *Cefarotti*; whofe vaft knowledge, fublime genius, and wonderful activity, I have long admired, in every fpecies of pleafing and profound literature. I am only forry, that he has armed himfelf with my trifling works againft our foreign foes; but the fmalleft twig in fuch hands, becomes as formidable a weapon as the club of Hercules. Adieu my dear friend. Take care of yourfelf, and believe me ever, &c.

Vienna, February 15, 1779.

Among Metaftafio's literary correfpondents, whom he never faw, or had heard of, till made acquainted with their exiftence by a prefent of their works, was the Abate MAZZA; who, in 1766, fent him two poetical effays, accompanied with a letter, which
the

the imperial laureat acknowledged with his accuſtomed urbanity. Indeed though neither the writings, nor the name of this author ſeem to have penetrated into our country, the elegant and warm encomiums beſtowed on them, by ſo exquiſite a judge, deducting for mere civility and fear of offence, excite curioſity and an eager wiſh to be acquainted with them. "I have read the whole of your preſent," ſays he, in his firſt letter to this Abate, " and almoſt re-read, with the plea-
" ſure and admiration which productions ſo
" rich and elaborate deſerve. You have no
" occaſion for my vote, to be ſure of a diſ-
" inguiſhed place in Parnaſſus. Your own
" talents, learning, indefatigable application,
" and ſmiling time of life, render your elec-
" tion certain. What may we not expect from
" a ſoil, which produces ſuch exquiſite fruit,
" at a period when flowers can hardly be
" expected ? I can ſee no obſtacle which can
" check your flight, but want of volition,
" Natural diſpoſition armed with ſuch vari-
" ous knowledge, wants only ſelf-confidence,
" to enable you to quit the tracts which have
" been ſo long beaten by others, and finally
" to ſeek in your own judgment the true
" paths to utility and delight.——You muſt
" not

" not expect that I fhould fpeak of your elo-
" quent and flattering letter, nor of the
" magnificent fonnet which accompanies it.
" In fpeaking of either, vanity would appear
" through the tranfparent mafk of humility."

In 1771, after praifing in very ftrong
terms, fome other poems which this author
had fent him, Metaftafio adds : " I congra-
" tulate you fincerely on your fuccefs in
" thefe productions ; and from the fmall por-
" tion of prophefy which I may claim as an
" old prieft of Apollo, I venture to predict,
" that you will appear to pofterity, one of the
" brighteft ornaments of the Italian Par-
" naffus."

Again, the fame year, he fays to this
young poet : " from the fuperabundant re-
" turn of praife with which you honour me,
" in your laft letter, I begin to fear that my
" approbation of your lyrical compofitions
" has been regarded by you, more in the light
" of gratitude than juftice : therefore to
" avoid every expreffion that may be con-
" ftrued into panegyric, I muft tell you with
" hiftoric fimplicity, that you have wonder-
" fully united the lively flafhes of genuine
" poetry, with the minute philofophical
" analyfis of the effence and activity of that
" harmony

" harmony which is fought in all the opera-
" tions of nature."

And finally, in 1773, he tells his poetical
correfpondent, that he had repeatedly read
" the three odes on the effects of mufic, the
" hymn to the Creator, and the two fonnets
" to his fovereign on the commencement of
" the new year, and always with new plea-
" fure and admiration : and inftantly dif-
" covered in the richnefs of the metal, the
" mine that had produced it. To fuch
" poetic eloquence, always big with ideas,
" always fonorous, fparkling, and equal to
" yourfelf, it is not permitted for every inha-
" bitant of Parnaffus to afpire"—but the bard
" entreats him not to rifk the difgrace of his
" judgment, by excefs of partiality to him-
" felf, or provoke his readers to examine
" his merit too minutely."

If a fpecimen of Metaftafio's elegant and
polite acknowledgment of unfolicited favours
from new correfpondents was neceffary, perhaps his firft letter to the Marquis *Andreafi*
might be felected, as a model of its kind.

# LETTER VI.

### TO THE MARCHESE LODOVICO ANDREASI, OF MANTUA.

RETURNING home the other day, I found on my table an elegant cafket, big with moſt valuable merchandife, and delivered without direction or letter. Upon enquiry, my fervant told me, that as far as he could gather from the bearer, it was a prefent from the Marquis Andreaſi : but he was unable to difcover the name of the benevolent commiffary, who had undertaken to have it delivered to me : and he therefore ſtill remains incognito. This circumſtance difcovers the author. And who elfe would have thought of giving me fuch a fweet, and flattering teſtimony of his remembrance, which alone, without embellifhment, is always fufficient to fulfil the meafure of my ambition? For if this contrivance had no other merit in my eyes, than the having employed your thoughts on me, for a few minutes extraordinary, 1 fhould think myfelf in a particular manner indebted to it.

Now

Now you have so well sweetened my existence by your gifts, forget not to honour me with your commands, and give activity to the respect and gratitude with which I have the honour to be, &c.

Vienna, June 24, 1773.

---

We shall now return to his old confidential friend, Sig. Filipponi, secretary of the university of Turin.

## LETTER VII.

### TO SIG. FILIPPONI.

THE prolix enumeration of the amiable and respectable qualities of this Count *Scarnafigi* which you have detailed, my dear Filipponi, with such seeming pleasure in your last letter, is but a repetition of what I had long since learned from our friend Count *Montagnine,* who was perfectly acquainted with his merit, and flattered me with the hopes, of some time or other procuring me the honour of so valuable an acquaintance.

My

My felf-love does not rife to fuch a height, my dear friend, as to believe my private letters fit to fee the light, having been written in hafte, and fent away without ever being read by myfelf. The rapacity of printers, who make not the leaft fcruple of enriching themfelves at the expence of an author's reputation, have attempted, without my permifion, in Naples, Florence, and Bologna, to publifh a collection of them ; but thank heaven, I was apprifed of their intention time enough to prevent their putting fuch a defign in execution, and fhall continue to prevent them in future, to the utmoft of my power.

The manifeft inattention with which your royal prefs (at Turin) has publifhed the tenth volume of my poems, does not make me wifh to fee an eleventh volume printed with equal negligence ; you will therefore believe that I fhall not be very diligent in collecting materials for it.

Vienna, May 2, 1774.

L E T-

# LETTER VIII.

### TO THE SAME.

As you had prepared me, my dear friend, for the arrival of the moſt worthy Count *Scarnafigi*, at this court, it is my duty to give you an account of his reception. This miniſter, in the few days which he has reſided at Vienna, has already had the power of acquiring the approbation and eſteem of the whole court, the miniſtry, and the nobles. I was early in paying my reſpects to him ; he has repeatedly honoured me with viſits, and we have already paſſed ſome evenings together, under my roof, in a ſmall ſociety to which I am accuſtomed. So that I have had the advantage of long converſations with him, and found him cultivated, obliging, full of various and uncommon information, and of a gay and graceful commerce, in which he has the faculty of pleaſing, without the leaſt tincture of diplomatic myſtery or dignity hence, I venture, by virtue of my poetical privilege, to predict, that he will fulfil his commiſſion with applauſe.

Hitherto

2

Hitherto he has lodged at a villa in the environs of Vienna; but he has taken a magnificent houfe in the city, where I fhall make my court, when age and infirmities will allow me. He has frequently fpoken of you with regard; and I can perceive, clearly, that he remembers you with affection. But let this fuffice for the prefent, as it is all that my tumultuous hypochondriacs will allow me to write.

Vienna, Auguft 18, 1774.

## LETTER IX.

### TO THE SAME.

You may trace and afcertain, my dear Sig. Filipponi, an almoft immemorable and uninterrupted poffeffion of my tender friendfhip, and are enabled to figure to yourfelf what confolation I muft receive from the affurances of your affection, and the emotions which your laft moft cordial letter muft have occafioned in my mind; I fhall therefore not attempt to defcribe them, nor folicit the continuance of your kindnefs, as neither of us has it in his power now to change his fyftem.

　　　　You

You are now in the midſt of the feſtivity
of royal nuptials; and we have no reaſon to
envy you, as we are likewiſe enjoying the
preſence of his moſt ſerene highneſs the
Archduke Ferdinand, and the charming
Archducheſs his conſort, the Princeſs d'Eſte,
who has endeared herſelf to all the inhabitants of this country, from the court to the
cabin. The magnificent and numerous de-
monſtrations of joy, with which our court
honours and adorns the preſence of theſe
great and beloved gueſts, are truly imperial;
but you will, however, far ſurpaſs us in the
ſtrife of felicitation, as You will preſerve
your acquiſitions, and We are not far off the
painful moment of being bereaved of ours.

Adieu, my dear friend. Preſerve your
health, and continue to believe me invariably yours.

Vienna, October 12, 1775.

This is the laſt letter that ſeems to have
been preſerved, between theſe two old friends;
though Sig. Filipponi lived, and ſeems to
have continued the correſpondence, till the
year 1779. The following letter of con-
dolence to his ſon, is a melancholy record
of

of Metaſtaſio's affliction, on the deceaſe of a
perſon for whom he ſeems to have had ſo
cordial an attachment.

## LETTER X.

TO SIG. LUIGI FILIPPONI,
*Auditor of the Royal Chamber of Accounts to
the King of Sardinia.*

THE melancholy news of the deceaſe of
your worthy father, my old and moſt cordial
friend, Signor Tommaſo Filipponi, did not
arrive without an ill-boding precurſor. The
unuſual long parentheſes which he begun to
make in our correſpondence, had already,
for ſome time, occaſioned black ſuſpicions,
concerning which I was afraid to enquire,
left they ſhould be verified. From my own
great and juſt affliction, I can comprehend
what yours muſt be, wounded at once, in
the two moſt ſenſible parts of the heart.
But if I am not entitled to the ſame degree of
pity as is due to you, diſdain not, at leaſt, to allow me to be no unworthy companion in your
ſorrow, and in that affection which we have
both had in common. Forgive involuntary

brevity,

brevity, and believe me to be with the moſt ſincere and reſpectful eſteem, &c.

Vienna, March 17, 1779.

---

The following letters of this period, will ſhew how dexterouſly Metaſtaſio eluded gratifying the vanity of authors, who ſent him their works, in hopes of obtaining from his candour and politeneſs, ſome token of approbation, as a *certiorari*, in paſſing them through the world.

## LETTER XI.

### TO COUNT DANIEL FLORIO.

*With whom Metaſtaſio, (ſays the editor of his Letters) was in cloſe friendſhip and correſpondence.*

IT is unneceſſary for me to inform you, Sir, of my internal and candid opinion concerning the admirable Pindaric ode, which, with affectionate partiality, you have been pleaſed to communicate to me. It neither is, nor can be, different from that which the productions of your cultivated and admirable genius have always exacted from me ;

me; and which, to do honour to my own judgment, I am never tired of repeating at all times and in all places. To fecond, by my obedience, your exceffive modefty, in a moft attentive re-perufal of this moft neat and finifhed compofition, I have fought, with almoft malignant folicitude, for fome little imperfection, which I might, with the leaft appearance of reafon, point out; but have not fucceeded in finding one; on the contrary, in thefe refearches, I am more and more convinced, that your poetic vigour is encreafed, inftead of diminifhed, by years; and am confirmed in my former opinion, that whoever would be acquainted with the true enchanting language fpoken in Helicon by Apollo and the Mufes, fhould read your verfes. Thefe indifputable truths I am proud to know, and anxious to publifh: hence you may eafily imagine what pleafure it would afford me to feize the opportunity which you would give me of prefacing your incomparable poem, when printed, with a letter; but, for my great misfortune, I am totally unable to avail myfelf of this permif-fion. And here I fhall relate to you the infu-perable obftacle. Many years ago, it was

M 3                           the

the cuftom of a fwarm of very obfcure in-
fects of our Italian Parnaffus, imitating each
other, to fend me their works in manufcript;
and afterwards print them, prefixing, without my permiffion, the letter, which in mere
civility, I had written, in returning the MS.
I did not fail to refent this; but my letter
only produced a formal requeft, that my
opinion (or rather eloge) might be printed
with their works. I reflected, that if I had
only obliged thofe who deferved it, the reft
would have been in a fury; and if I had in-
difcriminately complied with every requeft,
I muft have appeared either like the am-
bling nag of Silenus, or a moft impudent
and barefaced flatterer. Hence, I found it
the fafeft way, to excufe myfelf, modeftly,
to all. This law, which I neceffarily impofed on myfelf, is now become inviolable,
from the juft fear of offending thofe to whom
I owe refpect, and with whofe requefts, for
the reafons juft affigned, I was unable to
comply. Pity me therefore, my dear Count,
for my not being able to avail myfelf of fo
favourable an opportunity of doing honour
to my judgment; and be not offended, if the
*genus irritabile vatum* which impofed filence

on

on Horace, fhould terrify me. I thank you however, for the partiality which fuggefted the idea.

Vienna, April 15, 1775.

## LETTER XII.

TO THE SAME.

AFTER a prolix reply to your laft favour, comes another, with a magnificent Sonnet to my honour and glory. And what excefs of poetic furor could have ftimulated my dear Count, after more than forty years of affectionate friendfhip, to fet about leading into the temptations of vanity, a poor follower of Apollo, who has already laid down the laurel and worn out lyre, and offer to him that precious incenfe which alone belongs to the luminous fons of fortune? God forgive you! If I had not, for the reafon affigned in my preceding letter, been deprived of the power of calling the mufes to my affiftance, and was not bufily occupied in executing the orders of my fovereigns, I fhould perhaps have tried to revenge myfelf, by another Sonnet; but I am very glad of this legitimate excufe, which fkreens me

M 4 from

from the difadvantage of a parallel, particularly with thefe fhort arms, which I am un-
ufed to wield, &c.

## LETTER XIII.

### TO THE SAME.

My poor *Nugæ canoræ* are unworthy of a
place among the choice and learned volumes
which you are collecting. However, if your
fond partiality fhould obftinately determine
on elevating them to fo high a rank, wait at
leaft till they are adorned with their nuptial
drefs, which our intrepid editor is at prefent
preparing for them at Paris; and who, if
he fulfils his promife, will embellifh them
with eleven copperplates, exquifitely engraved, of which he has already fent me fome
proofs. This will be the neateft edition
which has hitherto appeared, and will, in
fome degree, be an excufe for its admif-
fion into your library, as the excellence
of the frame may make fome amends for
the mediocrity of the picture.

Vienna, April 30, 1777.

The following lettter to a young author
of fome rank, in fociety at leaft, if not
among

among poets, feems worth infertion, not
only for the elegance and politenefs of our
author's compliments, but for the judgment
and good tafte with which he gives him his
advice.

## LETTER XIV.

### TO HIS EXCELLENCY DON CLEMENTE FILOMARINO.

A YOUNG gentleman in the firft flower of
adolefcence, to have mounted already fo high
in Parnaffus, is a phenomenon, no lefs rare,
than important. The valuable fpecimens
which you have fent me, are fufficient to
manifeft the uncommon fertility of your
genius, the wonderful perfeverance of your
application, the vigour with which you invent and think, and, above all, your natural
propenfity to a noble clearnefs and perfpi-
cuity, which has not yet been feduced and
contaminated by that obfcure ftyle which has
ftrangely reigned, for fome years, in many
parts of Italy; where, defpifing the favour of
the people, that is, of the moft certain
guarantees of immortality, and affecting pro-
fundity of wifdom and fcience, writers are loft
in the dark clouds of the confufed oracles of

4                                          Delphos;

Delphos: their ftyle has not efcaped the mafterly whip of our great Venofinian bard, in his *Ars Poetica.*

*Et tulit eloquium infolitum facundia præceps :*
*Utiliumque fagax rerum, & divina futuri*
*Sortilegis non difcrepuit fententia Delphis.*

Thus poetry precipitately flow'd,
And with unwonted elocution glow'd;
Pour'd forth prophetic truths in awful ftrain,
Dark as the language of the Delphic fane.

FRANCIS.

Confide, therefore, in your natural good fenfe; remember always, that the firft duty of a writer, is to make himfelf intelligible; that the moft difficult art of being clear, without finking into meannefs, is much more generally tafted, than the begging dignity from darknefs; and I'll engage all my little credit, as an old Deacon of Apollo, to fecure to you a moft diftinguifhed place among the celebrated names of the elect Italian poetical band.

The partial expreffions with which you honour me, are extremely flattering; and I fhall not enter upon demonftrating their exceís, left I fhould bring on myfelf new temptations of vanity from the fame quarter.

Vienna April 6, 1775.
The

The fubfequent letter to the ingenious and
eloquent Ex-Jefuit, EximENO, will probably
gratify the lovers of mufical hiftory. This
bold writer on Mufic, publifhed at Rome,
in 1774, a treatife in quarto, *On the Origin
and Rules of Mufic, with the Hiftory of its
progrefs, declenfion, and renovation*\**. In the
preface to this treatife, the author modeftly
confeffes, that by a combination of circumftances too long to relate, he *chanced* "*four
years ago*, to give a glance at mufic." And
during that fhort period, he not only made
himfelf mafter of the art, but difcovered
great defects, both in its practice and theory.
He propofes in his differtation, nothing lefs
than a total *diforganization* of the prefent
fyftem of counterpoint, which if adopted,
would probably contribute about as much to
the melioration of mufic, as the revolution
in the government of France has contributed
to the happinefs of its inhabitants. He
fhews no mercy to the ancient mafters of
harmony, and as little to the moderns, who
adhere to the old *regime*. This author, a
fcholar, mathematician, and man of tafte

---

\* *Dell' origine e delle regole della mufica, colla ftoria del
fuo progreffo, decadenza, e rinnovazione.* Opera di D.
Antonio Eximeno.

and

and learning in general literature, writes with fire and eloquence, on fubjects within his competence ; but after trying to *pull down* all the ancient temples to Apollo, the buildings he propofes to erect in their ftead, were fo defective in defign and execution, that, they crumbled to pieces before they were finifhed; nor do his plans feem to have been adopted by any man of genius or fcience, in order to propagate his doctrines.

In 1775, this mufical Reformer attacked *Padre Martini*, the moft learned Contrapuntift of the prefent century, in a work entitled, *Doubts concerning his Effay on the fundamental Practice of Counterpoint* *. And if he had confined his cenfures to the too great partiality and attachment of this good father, to the ancient method of building all ecclefiaftical harmony upon *Canto fermo*, he would probably have formed a powerful fect; but, extending his hoftilities to the works of all the fathers of harmony, and to the ancient fundamental principles of the art, his opinions feem to have been no more

---

* *Dubbio di D.* Antonio Eximeno *fopra il faggio fondamentale pratico di contrappunto del reverendiffimo Padre Maeftro* Giambattista Martini. In Roma, l'anno del Giubileo, mdcclxxv. 4to.

refpected

refpected at Rome, or in any part of Italy, on the fubject of mufic, than thofe of Luther or Calvin, concerning religion.

It not only appears from the following letter, but from other letters of Metaftafio, that Signor *Eximeno* had projected a fcheme for printing this poet's operas, with the original mufic in fcore, which had been fet to them by the great mafters of Italy, when they were firft performed. To have affifted him in the execution of this plan, and others which he had in meditation, would have occupied too much of the Imperial Laureat's leifure at his late time of life; nor does it feem likely, that at an earlier period, he would have involved himfelf in labours of fuch a kind, with a man fo decifive, and of fuch difficult commerce, as D. *Eximeno.*

## LETTER XV.

### TO SIGNOR D. ANTONIO EXIMENO.

INDOLENCE (which at my time of life, is but too legitimate an excufe) has not been the only caufe of my tardinefs in anfwering your judicious, learned, and affectionate letter of laft June: a letter which alone is fuf-

ficient

ficient to convince me of the vaft extent of
your talents, the value of the ample treafure
with which your amazing indefatigable application has enriched your mind, the
*fapience* of Horace, that is, the correct
judgment which reigns in all you think and
write, a faculty which has at all times been
uncommon, even among the greateft writers,
and above all, the debt of gratitude for the
exact correfpondence of ideas which loads
me with fuch vifibly exceffive, or rather
affectionate partiality, as that with which
you honour me and my writings: But a
wifh (not a command) of my auguft Patronefs, that I would write fome verfes upon her
delightful Imperial refidence at *Schonbrunn*,
has obliged me to run unexpectedly to Parnaffus, and bring thence in hafte, a tribute of
the few flowers that I have been able to gather
in the humble bourns, beyond which I am
forbidden to afcend. It certainly was not the
merit of my homage, but my prompt obedience which procured in writing, in fpeech,
and in Imperial munificence, fuch marks of
favour from my generous fovereign, and fo
fuperior to my hopes, that I cannot yet re-
cover from my confufion: and thefe, with
the addition of attending the prefs in print-

ing

ing this late fruit of my exhaufted foil, have, till now, entirely abforbed all my activity, which has ever been circumfcribed, but at prefent becomes more and more limited than ever.

After this juftification, let me, in the firft place, thank you for the favour which you have done me in defcribing the darknefs in which you were involved, in feeking for the true and folid principles of mufic : fince the example of fuch enquirers as you, dimi-nifhes my own mortification in fimilar at-tempts, which I foon abandoned, in def-pair.

The immenfe, and extremely expenfive, enterprize, which you have in meditation, of publifhing a new edition of my dramas, with their moft favourite mufic, and with fuch inevitably copious obfervations as you will be obliged to give in defence of your opinions, opprefs my imagination, which reprefents to me the enormous fatigue, the exceffive expence, the little hope of your indemnification by the number of purchafers, and ftill more, with the painful reflection, that I fhall be utterly incapable of affifting you, as an able amanuenfis in this laborious undertaking, the diminution of my phyfical
force

force not permitting me to pay with punctu
ality, or even with fhort anfwers, my debts
to all thofe who honour me with their
letters.

My works, however, would be in want of
but too much correction ; but how could I
plunge into fuch a fea of trouble? I have
already tired the public with too many of
my gingling trifles; and, befides the vigour
and patience which would be wanting to go
over them again, I fhould have to combat
my vicious temperament, which inclines me
always to doubt of myfelf, and not merely
from excefs of modefty, but from infatiable
felf love, which frequently makes me reject
what is good, to run after what is perfect;
by which means I run the rifk of choofing
at laft fomething ftill worfe than the firft.

Add to all this, that the appearing in print
has always impreffed and ftill impreffes me
with fuch refpect, that without abfolute neceffity, I fhould never have had the courage
to rifk its effects. I fhall here give you a
proof of this diffidence. Many years ago, I
undertook and compleated an extract from
the Poetics of Ariftotle, in which, chapter by
chapter, I confeffed what I was able to underftand, and what remained ftill obfcure to
me,

me, in spite of the diligence and sagacity of
the most illustrious commentators ; I tried to
acquire a more clear idea of the nature of
*Poetry, Imitation,* and *Probability.* By examining the Greek and Roman dramas, I have
demonstrated the false foundation of some of
the rules laid down by modern critics; and
have pointed out the authority which the
text gave me, of laying down certain axioms,
which the practice of more than fifty years
has shewn to be erroneous. Even before I
had made this extract, I had translated into
blank verse an exact version of Horace's
Art of Poetry, with the most scrupulous fidelity, illustrated with notes, that were neither
common nor pedantic, but necessary; and yet
these two labours, terminated long since, notwithstanding the solicitations of my friends,
sleep quietly in my port-folio; and there
they will remain undisturbed: as I cannot
possibly muster courage sufficient to publish
them. With this disposition of mind, you
may easily imagine, Sir, what agitation your
affectionate and partial proposition of employing your pen in writing my life must
have occasioned. Drive from your thoughts,
I entreat you, my dear D. Antonio, such
wicked temptations, if you would not ex-

cessively afflict me by your too great desire of doing me honour. It is a perilous generosity to be prodigal of incense so sweet to such as me: it would excite nothing but envy, disputes, and malignity, among partizans; but still if by means of your enchanting eloquence, it were to succeed to your wishes, in obliging the whole world to be of your opinion, and you should lift me up to the skies, I must confess (call it weakness or reason, as you please) I do not feel myself inclined to be a living spectator of my Apotheosis. With the same sincerity as I confess my infirmity, permit me to acknowledge my infinite gratitude and true sense of your partiality towards me, which I regard as a most valuable acquisition. But how would it be possible for Me to inform you of the Best Music that has been set to my operas, having scarcely heard of any but what has been performed in the theatre of the Imperial Court? and of this, the chief part has been set by the celebrated *Caldara*, an eminent contrapuntist, but extremely deficient in expression, and pleasing melody.

The most painful effect of my inability, would be the diminution of your esteem: but you are too just to regard as crimes mere

involuntary

involuntary defects : with this hope I fhall therefore entreat you to believe me to be, with the higheft regard, &c.

P. S. I am impatient to free my confcience from the weight of a great number of correfpondents, who have long been unavoidably neglected, for the reafons fpecified in the former part of my letter, in order to acquire leifure fufficient to enjoy the delight and profit which I expect from the perufal of the books which you have fent me: but in the mean time, let me gratefully thank you for the precious and obliging gifts.

Vienna, Auguft 22, 1776.

In this dexterous manner did Metaftafio extricate himfelf from the wild and unreafonable project propofed to him by *D. Ant. Eximeno,* and it fhould feem, from giving an opinion of his Treatife, and attack of P. Martini ; for we hear no more of either.

The Bard had another Roman correfpondent on his hands about this time, who wifhed to inlift him in a fervice for which he feems at all times to have had an invincible repugnance. His fear of giving offence, and love of tranquillity, made him decline polemics

and

and comparative criticifm, not only with refpect to the works of living authors, but even of thofe who had been dead more than 2000 years. But let him fpeak for himfelf.

## LETTER XVI.

### TO THE ABATE * * *, AT ROME.

THE affectionate partiality with which I am honoured, by a perfon of your uncommon merit, would oblige me, in return for fuch goodnefs, to be more punctual in my anfwers, and more diffufe in my expreffions of gratitude, did not the precarious ftate of my health, and the ravages of time, which confpire day by day to diminifh my vigour and activity, deprive me of the pleafure of correfponding with thofe whom I moft love and efteem, and who have deigned to think me worthy of their regard. From this ingenuous confeffion, you may eafily comprehend whether I can be in a ftate capable of executing your commands, in giving my fentiments on the Works of *Sophocles* and *Euripides:* an enterprife very unfit for me to undertake, who am by nature averfe, even

to

to a vice, to the drawing parallels, which are
generally odious, and subject to the insults
of critics and disputants. I shall therefore
confine myself to the telling you, laconically,
that I regard these two illustrious Greek
poets, as two artists equally excellent: that
*Sophocles* is skilfully majestic; *Euripides* more
simple and tender: that the first is full of luminous ideas, and the second of affections
more true, and natural; and that both
equally astonish, by the conduct of the principal action, by the exact delineation of characters, and by that most difficult power of
modelling, and chiseling from the life, the
passions of the human heart. But I communicate my opinion to you in mere confidence; nor will you think it merits publication, if you have any regard for my credit;
therefore, begging you to spare my blushes,
I remain, &c.

Vienna, June 16, 1775

---

The following letter to the same anony-
mous Abate, who had written a dissertation
on *Modern Music*, a music which Metastasio
seems to have censured with great severity,

will

will difclofe to the reader the poet's ideas on the fame fubject.

## LETTER XVII.

### TO THE ABATE * * *, AT ROME.

If I was not occupied and fatigued with my prefent employment, and rapidly declining and tottering under the weight of years, I fhould not neglect a correfpondence fo valuable as yours, from which I am certain of deriving fuch great advantages ; being well convinced by your obliging letters, with what rich and rare merchandize your ftorehoufe is furnifhed. I congratulate you on the acquifition of fuch ineftimable treafures, and wonder how it has been poffible for you to unite with the noify occupations of the Forum the elegant amufements of Helicon; and that, in fpite of Themis, you are able to enjoy fuch delightful paftime with the mufes.

I have, at length, had the pleafure of reading your differtation on *Modern Mufic,* and affure you that you have greatly furpaffed my expectations. But above all, I have been furprifed at the arrangement of the materials, the

the neatnefs and elegance of the ftyle, the ingenious texture of the arguments, and in fhort, at the artful and mafterly manner in which you have thrown lights on the moft remote and dark antiquity. To thefe incomparable excellencies of profound learning, muft alfo be added, your initiation into the myfteries of harmony, which feems very confiderable, and gives great force, luftre, and weight to your opinions. With refpect to the intrinfic excellence of Modern Mufic, I am of your opinion; and agree with you, that its effects are few and feeble, compared with thofe which Plato afcribes to the ancient. In fact, our mufic * enervates the mind, being fo extremely artificial and refined, that it is impoffible to trace through it, either probability or natural expreffion; and yet, from infuperable habit, it is become the reigning model of almoft all the mufic of every nation : as men judge more by their ears than by reafon †. By divifions and artful modulations of voice, and by the union of fo great a number of different inftruments, the fenfe

* The Italian.

† Mufic is more the object of fenfe than intellect; its ufe is to pleafe the ear, not to improve the underftanding. It has been faid, that mufic can awaken and excite fenfations, but cannot reafon.

is

is flattered and tickled to such a degree, that it remains enfeebled, and almost bewitched, by those long and rapid trills, which, though they resemble so much the warbling of birds, please us much less, because less natural. The pleasure of conversing with you, drags me on insensibly; and pleased with this transport, I flatter myself with the hopes of your affectionate forgiveness.

Vienna, September 8, 1776.

Metastasio, late in life, readily joined in the almost general complaint against rapid and difficult execution in music; and yet, at other periods, he was partial to a Farinelli and a Gabrielli, whose chief excellence was *execution.* The extraordinary talents, perhaps, of these singers greatly encreased the celebrity of his dramas; but when that was firmly established, it was natural for him to wish to simplify music, and render its powers inferior to those of poetry. Indeed there never was perhaps a lyric poet who did not *listen* with an *evil ear* to the rapturous applause given to a singer in performing an air, of which, according to the late Mr. Stilling-

fleet,

fleet, nobody would think of reading the
words, but the author *.

We fhall now return to Farinelli, in the
correfpondence with whom there is a *hiatus
valde deflendus*, from 1769 to 1776, which has
not been accounted for by the editor of his
letters. In 1770, when I faw Farinelli at
Bologna, and frequently mentioned Metaftafio in our converfations, he fpoke of him
as his beloved *Gemello*, fhewed me his picture,
and, in 1772, Metaftafio fpoke of Farinelli
with reciprocal kindnefs : fo that there feems
to have been no breach of friendfhip, cool-
nefs, or diminution of affection, on either
fide, during the chafm in Metaftafio's printed
correfpondence ; and the accident which
occafioned it remains yet to be difcovered,


## LETTER XVIII.

### TO THE CAVALIER FARINELLI.

My poor abortion of an ode to *Schonbrunn*, is really born under the favourable

* Principles and power of mufic.

influence

influence of all the planets *. The approbation which it meets with, to the wonder
and confusion of the author himself, is certainly not merited by its intrinsic worth.
That it should appear marvellous to my dear
Gemello, long blinded and seduced by his old
tender affection, now transformed into nature, is a phænomenon not difficult to explain; but I am at a loss to discover how he
has been able to communicate his partialities
to their severe and enlightened eminencies,
to such a degree as to incline them to honour
me with their benevolence and approbation.
It now becomes your task to endeavour to
preserve the advantages which you have procured me, by representing to them, with
your enchanting voice, my grateful, humble,
and respectful sentiments to the Cardinals
*Borromeo* and *Buoncompagni* : assuring the
first, that I have always present in my mind
his venerated person, with all the train of
great qualities by which it is distinguished ;
and affirm to the second, that notwithstanding the vicissitudes which occasioned my

* This ode, of which the author speaks in several letters to different persons, did not appear in any of the printed
copies of his works which I have seen, during his life. It
consists of twenty-six stanzas, six lines in each.

quitting

quitting my country before he had become a
citizen of the world, I am not ignorant how
much he has honoured it, and how much
his laudable actions, and amiable manners
have encreafed the luftre and fplendour to
which he was born.

It is fome confolation to me, that your
familiar complaints have had the difcretion
to fubfide, for a little while ; mine are conftant ; but I dare not complain : at my age,
I have no right to complain : murmuring
would but irritate my infirmities, and render
exiftence more painful. We have here, as
well as you at Bologna, all the amufements
of the Carnival : operas, plays, Italian and
German, public and private balls, feftivity,
banquets, and vigils, without end ; but all
thefe cannot produce, in this tranquil nation,
that epidemic hilarity, which in our gay climate is transfufed into all characters, not
only thofe that feek it not, but forcing itfelf
even upon thofe who wifh to avoid it. And
at prefent, fuch as I are well off if they can
defend themfelves from the horrible third
winter, which, like the liver of Prometheus,
re-produces itfelf : and it is certain, that
without the valid patronage of our beneficent
ftoves, we fhould at prefent be in the ftate

of

of thofe prefervations which you have certainly heard of, in the mountains of *La
Mancha*, or the *Sierra Morena*, I forget which,
that, without falting, become incorruptible
when buried under a deep fnow. But you
have fet me a fcribbling, though the nerves
of my head proteft againft it. Adieu, dear
Gemello. I do not put you in mind of loving me, as, after fo many proofs, it would
be a fpecies of ingratitude to imagine there
was any occafion for it : but by taking care
of your health, you will give the beft proof
of it, to your moft conftant friend.

Vienna, February 9, 1776

## LETTER XIX.

### TO THE SAME.

It is not to prefent you with the infipid
fruit of my exhaufted foil ; but to fulfil the
inviolable right of our twinfhip, that I fend
you a copy of my ode to *Schonbrunn*, which
is juft come from the prefs, in order that you
may have the diftinction of being firft punifhed, in fome way or other, for the want of
merit, which but too eafily will be found in
my production. I did not accompany my

poor

poor prefent with a letter, becaufe I muft have done the fame to other perfons to whom I owe refpect and gratitude; and the time it would have required, would have robbed me of the merit of folicitude. The more than exceffive clemency, which my moft auguft fovereign has publicly expreffed, in fpeaking, writing, and acts of generous munificence, has filled me with fuch joy and confufion, that I was a long time incapable of thinking of it with any degree of compofure. Be not offended therefore, my dear Gemello, with my innocent filence ; you ought, indeed, the more readily to forgive me, as the fame thing would have happened to your own heart, in fimilar circumftances.

I honeftly difburfed to our friend *Poggi*, the affectionate compliments which you remitted, and he is to reimburfe you, on account, when he fhall again fee the afs's tower *. In the mean time, do you pay on my account two hundred kind remembrances, accompanied with innumerable proteftations of efteem and affection, to my

* *La Torre degli Afinelli.* A celebrated tower at Bologna, three hundred and fixty feet high. This city, at a diftance, has been compared to a fhip, of which the tower *degli Afinelli* feems the maft.

dear

dear and worthy Abate *Taruffi*, who is ever prefent to my thoughts; wifhing him the indemnifications of fortune, who, at prefent, makes a fhamelefs parade of her hoftilities to merit. My health is not what I wifh it; but it is better than I have a right to expect: fo that I dare not complain. Preferve your own carefully, and fail through the alternate good and bad viciffitudes of life, guided by that found philofophy with which nature has liberally furnifhed you, and continue to be always as much mine as I am yours.

Vienna, September 30, 1776.

## L E T T E R   XX.

### TO THE SAME.

HERE comes another moft cordial letter from my beloved Gemello, who, through excefs of affection, repeats the approbation which he had profufely given in a former letter, to my few verfes on the delights of *Schonbrunn*; verfes which have no other merit than what is reflected on them, from the general favour and veneration which the public beftows on every thing that concerns my admirable Sovereign; and this repetition

affords

affords me infinite comfort, not merited by the found of my difcordant lyre, but as an indifputable teftimony of your affection, of which, though I am already convinced by a thoufand proofs, new confirmations are always received with delight. The thought of honouring my dear Gemello with a vifit, is worthy of the generous heart of her Royal Highnefs the Dutchefs of Parma, the illuftrious protectrefs of the fine arts; who is not only an exquifite judge of the abilities of artifts, but appreciates their probity, candour, and fpotlefs morals; rare merchandize, and not always fufficiently valued. I can never forget her performing the part of Apollo, by which, with her enchanting voice and angelic figure, fhe rendered one of my feeble dramatic compofitions, written by order of my moft auguft Patronefs, admirable and fublime, and lifted me up to a degree of happinefs, of which I fhall ever be proud.

The benign gracioufnefs with which I have been remembered by her Royal Highnefs, at once comforts and confounds me, in the generous manner with which fhe has deigned to fignify it repeatedly, to the Venetian Ambaffador, Count *Durazzo*, and to my dear Gemello : and from the fituation of your own

own heart on fimilar unexpected occafions, you may perfectly imagine what muft be the emotions of mine.

Adieu, my dear Gemello, I fhould write a longer letter, if my conftant hypochondriac affections, rendered more troublefome and perverfe by the cold, would let me; but in fpite of all my defects and infirmities, continue to love me.

Vienna, November 13, 1776.

The next letter to Farinelli, dated March 13, 1777, contains little more than thanks for a prefent of various things fent in a cheft, which was not yet arrived; and elegant compliments and grateful effufions to Cardinal *Buoncompagni*, for his partiality towards him, and expreffions of gratitude to a Bolognefe phyfician, who had enriched his difpenfary with a prefcription in pure love of poetry. He finifhes this letter in the following manner: "I fhall not fpeak to you of my incorruptible complaints, which I pretend not to deftroy, and fhall forgive all the plague they occafion, provided they do not furpafs my patience."

The

The *flottiglia*, as he calls the cheſt, being arrived, he writes as follows :

# L E T T E R   XXI.

## TO FARINELLI.

THE day before yeſterday, the 20th inſt. I was informed of the arrival at the cuſtom houſe, of the cheſt, which you had ſent me ; and yeſterday morning, I received, and had it opened in my preſence, and found it full of moſt powerful temptations of every kind. The firſt thing I thought of, was to ſeek and taſte the ſimnel*, choſen by you as a treat for my favourite gueſts. I believe this is the moſt delicate ſimnel that ever came out of the exquiſite ſhop of Parthenope. Oh my poor temperance ! thou art in the moſt imminent danger. And how can ſuch aſſaults be reſiſted ? Theſe famous myrtles too ! Theſe little boxes compoſed and ornamented

---

* *Moſtacciuolo*, is a cake made at Naples, of flour, ſugar, eggs, and ſweet wine, very different from a Shrewſbury ſimnel, which is a rich plum-cake incloſed in an impenetrable caſe, or cruſt made of flour and water, and coloured with ſaffron, which preſerves it from injury and decay in the longeſt voyages to the moſt remote parts of the globe.

for the table of Jove ! Thofe excellent iced-
quinces, with which the maiden care of the
genteel inhabitants of the monaftery of Saint
Lorenzo, difdains not to flatter the palates
of others ; and that inundation of odours,
piquant and exquifite *liqueurs*, with which
you fcruple not to raife a tumult in the too
fenfible nerves of your poor Gemello's head!
But the moft violent feduction of all, and
that which occafions the greateft agitation in
my mind, is reflecting upon the kind manner in which you muft have been for fome
time employed in the fervice of your Gemello, while chufing, ordering, and collecting together, fuch a combination of various, exquifite, and precious merchandife. Accept my
moft hearty and affectionate thanks: but that
I may not abufe your kindnefs to the injury of
my health, and that thefe teftimonies of
your love, may be of long duration, they
fhall be enjoyed with the moft prudent par-
fimony.

I received fome weeks ago, an obliging
letter from Signora *Giacinta Betti Onofrio:*
a lady who voluntarily, a few years ago,
began to honour me with her letters, by
which alone fhe is known to me. I anfwered them ; and as fhe faluted me in your
name,

name, I charged her with my kindeſt compliments to you in return ; pray tell me, at your convenience, whether ſhe executed my commiſſion. Adieu, my deareſt Charles. My head rebels, and has been for ſome weeks more troubleſome than uſual : but in ſpite of it, I have been, am at preſent, and ever ſhall be, while I exiſt, yours.

Vienna, March 22d, 1777.

## LETTER XXII.

### TO THE SAME.

Your moſt kind anſwer of the 8th inſt. permits me not, my dear Gemello, to remain in that ſilence which my renewed hypochondriac complaints but too juſtly authorize ; as, contrary to expeȼtation, the return of winter has driven us back again to the proteȼtion of our ſtoves, which we had abandoned. The peruſal of your letter has been more efficacious in calming my gloomy humours, than all the antidotes of philoſophy, which promiſe ſo much, and perform ſo little. I have diſcovered how precious to me, are the choice and exquiſite dainties with which you have enriched me, by that ava-

O 2

ricious

ricious repugnance which I felt in diftribu-
ting any part of them, even to perfons to
whom I owe the moft fincere gratitude : but
the pain which the facrifice occafioned, has
been recompenfed by the great pleafure which
the approbation of my friends has occafioned,
and by the renewal of the juft praifes beftowed on the qualities of my dear Gemello,
of which, to my great delight, I find the
whole world well informed.

I am confufed, and proud of the partial
benignity with which the moft venerated
Cardinal *Buoncompagni* regards me. And as
you are juridically authorifed to procure me
its continuance, with the opportune and repeated proteftations of my grateful, dutiful,
and profound refpect, I here folemnly declare you, in this moft important negotia-
tion, my procurator, or rather, my ALTER
EGO. Adieu, deareft Gemello, preferve
yourfelf carefully, if you would contribute to
the prefervation of your, &c.

Vienna, April 21, 1777.

L E T-

## LETTER XXIII.

### TO THE SAME.

If you, my dear Gemello, find yourself involved in the difficulties of the *Plagal tones*, I am not among the *Authentic* *. The laft winter affailed me with rheumatifm, tenfion of nerves, implacable hypochondria, and other gentilities : from which the prefent benign feafon promifes to deliver me, though with lefs promptitude than I fhould wifh. But according to the ancient pro- verb, we fhould fuffer under the aufpices of conftant refignation ; *hoping for good, and tolerating evil.——*

I thank you for the important perfonage which you made me reprefent in the con- fiftory held by the three worthy Cardinals in your houfe : and when, and where, either in fpeech or writing, it is in your power, I beg you will not negledt prefenting to them my grateful and profound refpedts.

An intrepid editor at Paris, has undertaken a magnificent and expenfive edition of all my

* Alluding to the ecclefiaftical tones of Canto fermo, an for account of which, fee Hiftory of Mufic, vol. ii. p, 13.

works ;

works ; and in informing me of his defign, has tranfmitted to me proofs of eleven of the plates, already excellently engraved : and if the reft correfpond with thefe, the cornice will be much more rich and elegant than the building. I fhall in due time inform you of the further progrefs of this enterprize.

Notwithftanding my having called for affiftance in devouring the dainties with which your feducing *Flottiglia* has enriched my ftore-room, I have not yet come to the bottom of my ftores : fo that I ftill continue, and fhall, the Lord knows how much longer, to mafticate your favours, and mentally to embrace the amiable donor. Adieu, incomparable Gemello.

Vienna, June 21, 1777.

## LETTER XXIV.

### TO THE SAME.

HAVING read with the higheft fatisfaction, fome weeks ago, in letters from Rome, that his Eminence Cardinal *Buoncompagni* was preparing to return to Bologna, I rejoiced extremely at the thoughts of your happinefs, and wifhed inftantly to congratulate you upon

upon it; but my abominable hypochondriac,
or rather hyfterical affections, were in fuch
a tumult, that I durft not touch the pen.
At prefent, as you have confirmed this pleafing news in your letter of the 25th of July,
which is but juft received, I fly with my
whole mind to Bologna, to embrace and
felicitate you, and to participate of your unexpected happinefs, in fpite of the obftinate
perfecutions of my various maladies. Do
you be my eloquent delegate with this moft
worthy Cardinal, and contrive to convince
him of my veneration, gratitude, and refpect.

What can I fay to the unfolicited generous
partiality of that moft worthy Marchionefs
*Pepoli Spada*, in favour of my poor filly
rhymes? The picture which you have
drawn of her, with the enumeration of her
rare qualities and accomplifhments, render
me proud of the acquifition of fuch a protectrefs, and I fhould be much more fo if I
did not believe her deluded by your *twinly*
feduction. I envy extremely the fate of that
volume of my writings, which the *Abate
Pignatelli* has exalted to the dignity of his
companion : and am only forry that he will
not be better rewarded for the trouble of
taking it with him. Exprefs to both my
gratitude ; you, who are not incommoded

with

with my confusion, may do it much better than me.

I expect soon to receive the Paris editor's proposals: and shall inform you, the instant they arrive, of the plan and conditions of this vast enterprize. He wrote me word some time ago, that he should associate partners, and take in subscriptions; not for advancing money, but to ascertain the number of copies which he may venture to work off. Nothing is to be disbursed till the work comes out, which will be delivered by a volume or two at a time.

Speak not to me, my dear Gemello, of another *flottiglia:* I cannot get to the end of the first; think therefore whether I can allow you to send a second. Besides, more virtue than I possess, is necessary to prevent intemperance in the use of your kindness: and you, my dear Gemello, should be more solicitous for my health, than sensual pleasure.

Adieu, dear Gemello: preserve in yourself a rare model of amiable, honest, generous, and prudent men, in the midst of such scarcity; be assured that I perfectly know you, and therefore can never cease to be truly yours.

Vienna, August 12, 1777.

LET-

# LETTER XXV.

## TO THE SAME.

THE fteady and neat writing of your laft dear letter of the 15th inftant, the chearful humour which reigns in it, and the gay fympofiacs which you defcribe, if they do not entirely make me amends, my dear Gemello, for my afflicion at the news of the cruel and violent hurricane which your health has lately fuffered; I at leaft hope that this unexpected attack which you fo valiantly repelled, was inferior to your remaining vigour: and that it has made no impreffions on your machine, which can difturb its equilibrium. I congratulate you on this circumftance, though I do not wifh you, however, to have frequent occafions for fuch congratulation.

You fhall be obeyed in due time, with refpect to the copies which you wifh of the new Paris edition; but the propofals not being yet arrived, I am unable to anfwer your queries.

I am truly fenfible of the zeal which his Eminence Cardinal Buoncompagni expreffes

for

for corrections in the Paris edition; but
it is difficult to promife them all, as the
editions whence this will be printed, are fo
numerous. I certainly fhall not fail to recommend the meafures he wifhes to have
purfued : and in the mean time, plume myfelf in having my poor labours honoured
with the attention of fo great a Patron.
Prefent to him, I entreat you, my gratitude
and veneration. Affure the moft obliging
Marchionefs *Spada*, and the Abate *Pignatelli*, of my gratitude, and that they fhall
be informed of the method of becoming fub-
fcribers to the new edition, as well as of the
time for paying their money, and receiving
their books, as foon as I fhall know it myfelf; but of which, at prefent, I am wholly
ignorant.

Our honoured friend, Signor *Poggi*, has
been very long in paying you the fraternal
embraces which I configned to his care;
but the pleafure which you exprefs in receiving them, will not allow me to complain of
this delay.

Adieu, dear Gemello : take care of yourfelf for your own fake, as well as mine, for
the reafons given warm from my heart in
my laft letter ; and which you, from gratitude and innate goodnefs, repay me with
                                    intereft,

intereſt, I am pleaſed with your panegy-
rical expreſſions, as proceeding from that
affectionate ſhort-ſightedneſs, which makes
you mine, and me yours.

Vienna, September 29, 1777.

## LETTER XXVI.

### TO THE SAME.

THE hilarity of your dear letter, of the
20th of October, which, I know not for
what reaſon, only arrived yeſterday, has
given me more than uſual pleaſure. If this
ſerenity is a phyſical conſequence of the
good ſtate of your health, I congratulate you
on the ſolidity of your little frame ; and if it
is the fruit of your philoſophical meditation,
I admire the vigour of your mind. My
thoughts have not been inactive concerning
you, during my ſilence : I have always been
thinking of my Gemello, even during an
indiſcreet attack of eryſipolas in my left foot,
which has confined me to the houſe four
entire weeks : and yet I owe it no ill-will,
as it has left me in a better ſtate than it
found me. We are here up to the chin in
froſt and ſnow ; but grown callous, by the
frequency

frequency of fuch favours, we pay little regard to them.

Yet the Teutonic winter will certainly be revenged for our prefent contempt, by fome infupportably cold weather; but we flatter ourfelves that it will not be of long duration, and in the mean time, are preparing for our defence. I envy your vicinity to the venerated Cardinal *Buoncompagni*, the worthy Marchionefs *Spada*, and the moft accomplifhed Abate *Pignatelli*: to all whom I beg of you to prefent my grateful and fincere refpects.

The printer, *Reggiano*, pledges himfelf for what I cannot poffibly give; having repeatedly promifed, long fince, all my inedited works to the publifher of the Paris edition. He had better wait for the French prefs, and copy into his edition all that is new in it: but then thofe pieces will not be inedited. It would be great pity if the whole impreffion, as you feem to fear, fhould remain on his hands. The public would be robbed of the numerous inftructions concerning the dramatic art, which, in this edition, would ornament my poor poetical follies. Adieu, dear Gemello, forget not to believe me, &c. &c.

P. S.

P. S. Upon a more accurate perufal of your letter, I find it dated the 10th of December, and not October. Therefore, it is but juft to exculpate the poft.

Vienna, December 30, 1777.

## LETTER XXVII.

### TO THE SAME.

AFTER a moft beautiful Spring, during the firft thirteen days of the prefent month, that had rendered this country warm and fmiling; the treacherous winter is returned, and has mortified the fields and plants which had put on their green and flowery drefs : fo that your dear letter found me again muffled up in the furs and flannels which I had but juft laid afide, and extremely fcandalized at the difcourtefy of this climate. Since yefterday, it has feemed inclined to behave better; but I fhall not truft to it, and fhall adhere to the fage Spanifh proverb : *Hafta el quaranta de Mayo no te quites el fayo* *.

You are all occupied with the reprefentation of Alcefte; and we are equally employed

* Till the fortieth of May
Fling thy cloak not away.

by

by the facred eloquence of father *Francefco Maria* of Bologna; who, in the Italian national church here, has not only collected and edified a noble and moft numerous audience, by the fermons and difcourfes which he has fo ably given, but greatly encreafed the juft reputation and efteem which he had acquired in this city two years ago. His departure hence is fixed for the next month; he is charged with my moft affectionate and fraternal remembrances, with all the vivacity which could be given to them, confiftent with the ferious and refpectable character which he fuftains.

My health being better, as I have heretofore faid, than I have a right to expect, I dare not give way to the temptation, to which I am but too much inclined, of complaining. I muft, however, perpetually recommend to you the care of your own health, if you have any value for mine. Neglect not to keep me in the remembrance of the moft worthy Cardinal *Buoncompagni,* and in that of the no lefs worthy and noble houfe of *Spada*; accept my thanks for the precious lentils which you have fent me, and believe, without ever facrilegioufly doubting of it, that I am yours.

Vienna, April 23, 1778.

L E T-

3

## LETTER XXVIII.

I wish, my dear Gemello, that our twin-ship made you refemble me lefs in the too frequent irregularities of health; but your dear letter of the firft of this month, convinces me, that you are no lefs obliged to be always upon your guard againft infidious attacks of your tranquillity. I know that the moft fpecific drug for our maladies, is patience; but to put it in practice requires heroifm; and it has ever been my opinion, that the trade of a hero is not long fupportable.

The benign remembrance of me by the Arch-dukes at Milan, at once confoles and confounds me : and I entirely participate in the favour which they have manifefted to you. It is but juft, that he who fhares your pains, fhould partake of your honours. Included in this account, are likewife the vifits which you receive from their Eminences, *Buoncampagni*, and *Simoni* : to the firft of whom, I befeech you to renew the ufual atteftations of my veneration, as well as of my refpect and gratitude to all the illuftrious

family

family of *Spada*, and to all others who honour me with their remembrance; but in particular, to the very worthy father *Francesco Maria* of Bologna; who, in a moſt obliging letter, has given me a very exact account of the ſtate of your health, and of my ſituation in your good heart, as well as of the affectionate and obliging reception with which you have honoured him.

I hope you have already ſeen and read, the propoſals of Molini the printer, at Paris, for publiſhing a complete and magnificent edition of all my works: I ſhould inſtantly have tranſmitted his propoſals to you by the poſt, if I had not ſeen the names of Meſſrs. *Taruffi* of Bologna, in the liſt of commiſſioners for receiving ſubſcriptions and delivering the books, when ready; which rendered my original intention uſeleſs.

I ſhould lengthen my letter, but it is late. and I have people all around me; ſo that with a tender and haſty embrace, I, for the preſent, take my leave.

Vienna, June 18, 1778.

———————

The ſubſequent letters of this year to Farinelli, are chiefly on the ſubject of the

Paris

Paris edition of the poet's works, and mutual complaints of infirmities and declining health. In September, he fays—" Here, the feafon, " which had already threatened us with the " return of winter, is again become ferene, " temperate, and in every particular plea- " fant; I hope that your's is likewife " changed for the better, and that the " indifpofitions of which you complain, will " be all removed. Mine, by dint of habit, " have familiarized me to patience; fo that I " do not complain of them, except fome " phyfical fhock of the machine torments " me more than ufual. Employ yourfelf, " my dear Gemello, as much as poffible, to " divert your attention from thofe gloomy " meditations to which I perceive you in- " clined, and which, inftead of relieving, " encreafe our fufferings. Your former " felicity was not fufficient to make you lofe " your equilibrium; a proof, that your " mind does not want the neceffary vigour " for facing inconvenience. Adieu. I find " that I have already moralized too much. " Do not ceafe to love me, or, at leaft, to " think of me, which did not ufe to put you " out of humour; and I will do the fame: " confoling myfelf always with the pleafure

" I feel,

" I feel, in fuppofing that I am poffeffed of
" your affection."

## LETTER XXVIX.

### TO THE CAVALIER FARINELLI.

IT is not from entertaining the leaft doubt
of your affection, on account of the time
that has elapfed fince your laft letter, but
to interrupt the prefcription of fo long a
filence, that I vanquifh my too reafonable
repugnance to writing, which daily encreafes with my age; and likewife to give
you on paper, a thoufand of thofe embraces
that I never ceafe giving with my heart,
which is always the fame for you. In the
news which has arrived here of the earthquake at Bologna, you have been the firft
object of my reflections. But not having
found your name in any account which has
been received here, I have affured myfelf,
that you and your chattels have been unhurt:
and this I am the more inlined to hope, as
a letter from his eminence Cardinal *Buoncompagni*, addreffed to one of his correfpondents in Vienna, confiderably diminifhes the
horrors of the firft account, which were

extremely

extremely exaggerated. The fame will likewife happen to you concerning the account
of our magazine of powder being blown up ;
which by the force of tragic eloquence in
the firft relators, announced the deftruction
of Vienna. Amidft all thefe events, my
health obftinately preferves a good appearance ; but, though it deceives others, it is
not fufficient to deceive myfelf, who really
feel the infidious progrefs internally making
by the enemy : and, like a theatrical hero, I
am never able to impofe on myfelf in the
fame manner as I do on the fpectators.

Vienna, Auguft 19, 1779.


## LETTER XXX.

### TO THE SAME.

YOUR moft cordial letter of the 12th inft.
as ufual, full of thofe affectionate expreffions,
of which, without ingratitude, I cannot
doubt the fincerity; and feafoned with that
gay and ferene eloquence, which alone can
announce the regular equilibrium of our
humour, has confoled, rejoiced, and furnifhed
me with arguments to confirm me in the
hope, that heaven will long be propitious

to

to my prayers, in preferving your life for the
folace of your friends, and as a model
for thofe who are capable of knowing and
imitating you. I, who feel the weight of a
pen at our time of life, gratefully receive
inftances of that affection, which ftimulates
you from time to time, to comfort me with
your letters. *Padre Guardiano* minutely
informed me of the delightful day which he
paffed with you in your garden of the Hefperides; and I confoled myfelf for not being
of the party, by thinking of your own pleafure
on this occafion, and wifhing you a repetition of that happinefs ; flattering myfelf with
the hopes of the Gemello not being wholly
abfent, though far diftant.

I believe myfelf entirely indebted to your
conftant partiality, for being ftill remembered by the *Spada* family, by Cardinal
*Buoncompagni*, the Duke *Riario*, Signor *Pignatelli*, and Signor *Germani Valdivia :* and beg
of you to continue the tafk of helping me to
fecure fuch an invaluable blefling, by repre-
fenting to them the refpect and veneration
with which I am impreft by their condefcenfion. Prefent particular thanks to Duke
*Riario*, for the pains which he takes in embellifhing one of my poor dramatic children

with

with his elegant mufic: and, in gratitude, I
wifh him patience to perform the operation.

Cardinal *Migazzi*, Count *Rofenberg*, and
the Spanifh Ambaffador, will have your
compliments, whenever I am able to tranfport myfelf into their vortex, which is at
prefent too tumultuous for me.

Forget not, I entreat you, to render particular thanks to our good father *Guardiano*,
for the lively account which he has given
me of the extafy into which he was ravifhed,
at hearing what a valiant defence your voice
has made againft the injuries of time. I have
it ftill frefh in my memory, and I might
fay in my ears, what it was when you firft
afcended the throne of the whole vocal band:
fo that I am not furprifed at his furprife.

Vienna, November 23, 1779.

------

At this late period of the poet's life, he
not only preferved his epiftolary intercourfe,
with furviving old friends, but accepted the
voluntary offers of new correfpondents, who
folicited his approbation, advice, or acquaintance. Of the former clafs, was the Abate
*Galfo*, to whom the firft letter in the collection, that feems to have been preferved, is

dated

dated 1778, when the Poet was arrived at his eightieth year.

# LETTER XXXI.

## TO THE ABATE DON ANTONIO GALFO.

Six days ago, your moſt obliging letter, dated at Rome the firſt of June laſt year, was ſent to my houſe by Count *Erneſt D'Harrach*; which letter (I know not by what accident) having been nine months on the road, has at length put me in poſſeſſion of your ſurpriſing mock-heroic poem. I have attentively read, and greatly admired it ; nor do I ſee it poſſible for me, without being guilty of uſurpation, to arrogate to myſelf the title of your Maſter, with which through exceſs of politeneſs, you have qualified me in your letter. How could I poſſibly communicate to You, that ardent, and prodigiouſly fertile vigour of fancy, which I feel but too ſenſibly I do not poſſeſs? How, immerſed as I have always been, even to a fault, in my conſtant endleſs natural doubts, could I inſpire you with that frank and noble ardour, with which you have dared to open and purſue a road hithero unknown,

unknown, through which you have mounted
to the fummit of Parnaffus ? Ah, my good
Abate, affault not, I befeech you, my due
moderation with temptations fo violent : do
juftice to your well-known merit: accept of
the fincere fentiments of gratitude which I
proteft, both for the valuable gift, and the
manifeft gratuitous partiality with which
you honour me, and which I moft amply
return ; and permit me, inftead of arrogating
the title of Mafter, to fubfcribe myfelf your
faithful Servant.

Vienna, February 26, 1778.

## LETTER XXXII.

### TO THE SAME.

WHOEVER fhall read the lively, moral,
and feftive compofition, entitled *Il Tempio
della Follia*, *The Temple of Folly*, will be
obliged to confefs, that the author of it is
truly a poet, both by art and nature. I
have re-perufed it always with new pleafure ;
I have admired its ingenuity, and harmonious facility ; and have difcovered in it many
inconteftable truths, which have always been
before our eyes, without my ever feeing

them.

them. Congratulate yourfelf in my name, if you pleafe, and in that of the worthy Count *Girolamini.*

In order to avoid much writing, (an œconomy at prefent to me but too neceffary) I anfwer at once the letter which accompanied your poem, and that which you fent with the letter of the Abate *Salvini,* full of affectionate and kind expreffions, which I return from the bottom of my heart.

Drive from your thoughts, my dear Sig. *Galfo,* as evil temptations, the defire of croffing the Alps, in order to undeceive yourfelf concerning my merit; and be conftant to bear with me at a diftance. Convinced of the goodnefs of your heart, I fhall freely avail myfelf of your generous offers, whenever any urgent occafion prefents itfelf: or, rather I fhall begin now, by loading you with injunctions to continue to me your affection and regard; to believe me invariably yours; and never to doubt that I am with the trueft efteem and gratitude, &c.

Vienna, July 25, 1778.

———

The Abate Salvini's application to Metaftafio, being mentioned in the preceding letter,

ter, this feems to be the place for its infertion.

## LETTER XXXIII.

### TO THE ABATE LUCA SALVINI.

I AM extremely grateful for your obliging attention in making me acquainted
with the luminous progrefs of our academy ;
which, as you inform me, is rendered more
illuftrious every day, by frequent and
fublime aggregations; and I fhould be
extremely proud, if it were in my power to
procure it the gratification of which my
worthy colleagues are at prefent fo ambitious. But this is not the time for thinking
of it ; for who would propofe a place in a
literary academy, to a prince not only
occupied with his ftate affairs in Vienna, but actually in the camp of Bohemia,
regulating the motions of two hundred thoufand armed men, who depend upon his nod?
and even if he were in his capital, in the
bofom of the moft profound and tranquil
peace, my due refpect would not permit me
to utter with my lips the propofition which
you fuggeft. So much the lefs, as what

lately

lately happened at Paris is sufficient to difcourage fuch a liberty; where, though the
Emperor honoured a meeting of the moft
celebrated of the royal academies with his
prefence, yet he neither defired, nor was it
propofed to him, as I have ever learned, to
become an integral part of it. Perhaps
fome perfon high in office, honoured with
the familiarity of his fovereign, availing
himfelf of the opportunity of chufing fome
favourable moment, might rifk the mentioning fuch a bufinefs; but thefe are not
operations for fuch as me, obliged by prudence to confine myfelf within the narrow
limits to which I am reftricted by the duties
of my office. You will, I hope, excufe
my perhaps too great timidity, which may
be indulged to an excefs; but remember,
that at prefent, my age will not allow me to
attempt the correction of natural defects, or
bad habits. Punifh me not for this involuntary crime, by diminifhing my favour, and
and believe me, with the higheft refpect
and regard, &c.

Vienna, June 25, 1778,

L E T-

# LETTER XXXIV.

TO SIG. MATTHIAS VERAZI,
*Secretary to his Highnefs the Elector Palatine.*

By the opportunity of a courier, I was
fpeedily furnifhed with a copy of *Europa
riconofciuta,* which you have been fo obliging
as to fend me. In this compofition, I find
my friend, Signor Verazi, always equal to
himfelf: flowing, happy, clear, and rich in
that enviable fertility of fancy which conftitutes the principal merit of dramatic
poetry, and which communicates itfelf to
all the inferior arts employed in its fupport.
I rejoice and congratulate you on obtaining
the favours of fo enlightened a city; and
find nothing reprehenfible in the book you
fent me, except the manifeft excefs of partiality, with which you publicly fpeak of
me : an excefs which I can no otherwife
accept, than as a confequence of that dim-
fightednefs which the friendfhip with which
you honour me occafions.

Vienna, September 3, 1778.

Metaftafio

Metaſtaſio, fearful of offending, and ever doubtful of his own favour, both with the public and his Imperial benefactors, could never be prevailed upon to riſk the diſpleaſure of either; as he would not venture to print any of his writings, till they had been approved in their performance or peruſal while in manuſcript, nor to try his influence at a court which he had ſo long delighted, by ſoliciting benefits either for himſelf or friends. And perhaps to this prudent backwardneſs in ſolicitation, he owed the countenance and condeſcenſion with which he was ſo long honoured. However benevolent and willing to confer favours gratuitouſly, princes may be, it is natural for them to keep at a diſtance the importunate; who by being refuſed what it may be inconvenient, improper, or impoſſible to grant, become active and implacable enemies. The following letter in anſwer to a ſolicitor for court patronage, through the influence of the poet, will enable the reader to judge of his reaſons for putting a negative on the requeſt.

L E T-

# LETTER XXXV.

## TO FATHER FILIPPO STANISLAO MELANO.

THE Sonnet which your reverence has been pleafed to fend me, is worthy of its ingenious and learned author, and I feel all the weight of gratitude which is due from me, for fuch a partial remembrance ; and fhould be proud if it were in my power to manifeft my fenfe of your kindnefs, by a prompt execution of your refpected commands. But as my admirable fovereign is perfecuted with an inundation of bad Italian poetry for the moft part, which fince his journey to Rome, is perpetually pouring in upon him, he has clearly expreffed his determination to receive no more. Now how would it be poffible for me to have the courage to demand an audience (as there are no other means of getting into his prefence), and pretend that he fhould lend an ear to my poetical lecture, at a time when he is immerfed in the ferious affairs of a war, which is at prefent in its moft violent fermentation ? By doing this, I fhould run too great a rifk of injuring both the merit of

4                                    the

the author, and my own character, for refpect and difcretion. I entreat you to fuggeft to me fome more favourable opportunity of demonftrating my obedience, and efteem.

Vienna, January 13, 1779.

———————

In the following letter to the Abate Galfo, we have the poet's opinion of controverfy and polemics.

## LETTER XXXVI.

### TO THE ABATE GALFO.

In the parcel from you, which I received through the favour of the Apoftolic Nuncio, I find impreffions of two of my letters written to yourfelf, in which their only merit is the juftice which I render to your talents; and the having fulfilled this indifpenfible duty, fomewhat diminifhes the mortification which I feel when any of my writings are printed, from that innate want of confidence in myfelf, which through the whole courfe of my life, has robbed me in a great meafure, of the limited powers which were allowed me. I am extremely pleafed at the perfect

analogy

analogy which there appears to be, between my opinions and thofe of the learned journalifts which you mention, and congratulate myfelf on the occafion. I wifh I were able to felicitate you on the acquifition of that tranquil philofophy, which the moft excellent authors want, to render them infenfible to the inevitable affaults of detraction. But remember, my much refpected Abate, that no race of men has been plagued with this abominable contentious fpirit, fo much as men of learning. Think of *Scaliger, Erafmus, Schioppus, Muretus,* &c. I pity humanity for nothing fo much as that infirmity, which by its violence, reduces men, venerable for their doctrine, to the level of actors on a public ftage, for the diverfion of idiots. If you would avenge yourfelf and crufh envy, it muft be done by an encreafe of merit. And the fpecific which I prefcribe to you, is the only one which I have ever propofed to myfelf.

It is neceffary to be feized (as for my good fortune feems your cafe) with an exceffive degree of kindnefs and partiality in my favour, to exalt into a model my old Epithalamium, written during the firft effervefcence of a juvenile fancy, when wholly
ignorant

ignorant how much it wanted a bridle. But this kind of folemn approbation, with which you have honoured it, has reconciled me to it fo much, that I am now blind to its defects, and am proud, that it has in any degree given occafion to fo new, delicate, and pleafing a production as yours ; or rather, that it has in any way feemed to entitle me to a fhare of your praife. I congratulate you on the conftant favour of the mufes, and am, &c.

Vienna, March 28, 1779.

## LETTER XXXVII.

### TO THE SAME.

YOUR moft beautiful Epithalamium, neatly printed, has been delivered to me fome days, together with the remarks of the learned journalifts. I have received new pleafure in the perufal of the firft, by the mafterly manner with which you have contrived to rectify the miftakes of my early inexperienced youth; and in the fecond, have applauded the exact juftice rendered to your extraordinary merit, which encreafes every day—Take care of your health for the honour of our

Parnaffus

Parnaffus ; pity my neceffity for brevity, and give me new opportunities of manifefting my obedience to your commands.

Vienna, October 18, 1779.

Though the following letter, which feems the firft that has been inferted in the collection of our bard's correfpondence to Signor Volta, is dated at fo late a period of his life; the affectionate manner in which he expreffes his regard, appears to indicate a long, tried, and intimate acquaintance.

## LETTER XXXVIII.

### TO THE ADVOCATE LEOPOLDO CAMILLA VOLTA, REGIUS SECRETARY AT MANTUA.

THOUGH extremely eager to receive news of your health and welfare, I have never accufed you, my dear and valued friend, of negligence in tranfmitting it; well knowing with what an inevitable croud of affairs, of every kind, you muft be oppreffed at your return to Italy : I am, therefore, extremely grateful to you for the juftice you have done me, in believing me always, in fpite of long

VOL. III.                Q                filence,

filence, the fame affectionate friend, and
exact calculator of your great merit, admirable talents, and literary treafures with
which you are enriched; but above all,
I fhall ever bear in mind your fweet and
innocent manners, which render you always
pleafing to your equals; and fhall ever
remember my own acquaintance with you
among the deareft and moft honourable circumftances of my life.

Speak not to me, I entreat you, of Theatres,
either tragic or comic. The firft, which
(as far as my powers have enabled me) I
have tried to render lefs abfurd, confpire at
prefent to combat common fenfe: and the
fecond, in the midft of fuch innumerable,
not only fupportable, but good and excellent
examples with which the French have furnifhed us, have not yet found a tolerable
imitator in Italy. A very mortifying circumftance for our nation! But this fubject is
too extenfive and abundant for a worn-out
old writer, which, though in appearance it
feems in the fame ftate in which I left it,
is in reality fubject to all the laws of nature.

Signora Martinetz is extremely flattered,
though confufed, by the academic patent
which does her fo much honour. She renders

3

ders thanks to You for it, as she believes herself indebted to your declared partiality ; and
entreats you to represent in more suitable
eloquence than she has been able to do in
the inclosed letter to her generous promoters,
the most humble sentiments of her unfeigned
gratitude.   Counsellor   Martinetz *,   Don
Domenico, and Ercolino, return you their
best acknowledgments for your kind remembrance ; and I embrace you with the most
tender and cordial affection.

Vienna, August 9, 1779.

## LETTER XXXIX.

### TO THE SAME.

Signor *Angelo Talassi†* delivered to me,
a few days ago, your dear and much respected

---

\* Brother of Mademoiselle Martinetz, Aulic Counsellor,
and first keeper of the Imperial library. Metastasio, on
his first arrival in Vienna, took up his abode in the house
of their father, Signor Nicolo Martinetz, Master of the
Ceremonies to the Apostolic Nuncio, with whose family
he lived fifty-three years.

† The celebrated *Improvvisatore*; who, when in London
about eighteen years ago, by his extemporaneous numbers
on a subject given, astonished even Dr. Johnson; who was
very incredulous concerning this faculty, till he heard
*Talassi improvvisare* at Streatham.

letter,

letter, with a magnificent eulogium on the poetical merit of the bearer, to whom I am ready to do all due juſtice, upon the faith of ſo enlightened a judge as my friend Signor Volta, even before I have had an opportunity of making the experiment myſelf. But I fear he has undertaken a very difficult taſk, in trying to render Italian Poetry familiar and grateful to German ears; eſpecially extemporaneous numbers, which allow not a moment's reflection to the aſtoniſhed hearer. I ſhall do every thing in my power to contribute to his favour. But you, who ſo well know the preſent paucity of my phyſical faculties, muſt proportion to that my hopes of ſucceſs.

All thoſe whom you have ſaluted, ſalute you again; and I, with involuntary and inevitable brevity, moſt affectionately embrace you, and am, &c.

Vienna, Auguſt 18, 1779.

---

The following letter is the firſt which appears in the collection, to a new and unknown correſpondent, ambitious of the poet's approbation.

LE T-

## LETTER XL.

TO THE ABATE GIOVAN GABRIELLO MAC-
CAFANI.

THE violent and paffionate enthufiafm excited in you by the perufal of my poetical trifles, is expreffed in fo lively a manner, both in profe and verfe, that I make no doubt, if you chofe it, but that you might afcend to the fummit of Parnaffus. You have exalted me, Sir, fo far above my merit, that in order not to appear a bribed and feduced judge, it is neceffary for me to be more fparing than I wifh, in rendering due juftice to your talents. But I find it impoffible to be parfimonious with refpect to the candid and affectionate partiality in my favour, which is difcoverable in all your expreffions: This requires gratitude and reciprocation, and I affure you of both, with the utmoft fincerity; and wifh for opportunities to give fuch proofs of them, as fhall render it impoffible for you to doubt of my being with due refpect and efteem, &c.

Vienna, December 20, 1779.

L E T-

# LETTER XLI.

## TO THE SAME.

THE fable of my fufferings and recovery from a dangerous accident, afforded me new information, and an indubitable proof of your cordial affection for me, as well as of your admirable poetical talents; fo that I think myfelf extremely obliged to the ingenious inventor of the report, and congratulate you, Sir, on your abilities in compofing Eulogiums, and on the amiable qualities of your head and heart. The reafons affigned in my firft letter, and the imperious authority of age, which, though it malignantly ftill permits me to write, will not allow me to exprefs fo amply as I wifh, the true value of your obliging and beautiful compofitions, nor the affectionate return, which is due for your candid propenfity in my favour: fo that I am conftrained, moft unwillingly, to confine myfelf to the fincere proteftations of gratitude and efteem, with which I am, &c,

Vienna, March 30, 1780.

LET-

# LETTER XLII.

## TO THE SAME.

THOUGH the bufinefs of writing has long fince become difficult and laborious to me, and by the laws of nature is rendered more heavy every day, my gratitude will not permit that your very beautiful and truly poetical fonnet, which you have done me the honour to addrefs to me, fhould remain unnoticed: as it is not only a teftimony of your exceffive partiality for me, but of your own favour with father Apollo, and the tuneful fifters. I congratulate myfelf on both, and in return, wifh you fubjects lefs fteril and more worthy of your abilities; yet I fhall not ceafe to feel how much I am indebted to them, nor to be with all due refpect and efteem, &c.

Vienna, May 1, 1780.

LET-

# LETTER XLIII.

## TO THE ABATE GALFO.

By means of our moſt worthy Apoſtolic Nunzio *, the infallible Socrates came in perſon ſix days ago, to inform me, that my dear Sig. *Galfo* had courageouſly undertaken, and happily ſuſtained, the difficult enterpriſe of always ſurpaſſing himſelf. The tragedy which has been ſent to me, with its vigorous and ſeducing ſtyle, richneſs of thought, vivacity of imagery, ſolidity of doctrine in the numerous moral maxims it contains, together with the poetical fire which ſo happily ſparkles in ſome of the ſimiles, confirms the

---

* Meaning Monſignore Viſconti, the titular biſhop of Epheſus, with whoſe notice I was honoured at Vienna in 1772. His Excellency was a great collector, and not a mean performer, of Italian Catches and Canons, and condeſcended to furniſh me with copies of ſeveral ſcarce and valuable compoſitions of that kind. See *Preſent State of Muſ. in Germany*, Art. Vienna, p. 285. It was this prelate who obſerved, when I excuſed myſelf for arriving late at dinner, by ſaying, I had been ſtopt in the ſtreet by proceſſions : *Quel genti ſon portaitiſſimi alle proceſſione :* "The Auſtrians are extremely addicted to proceſſions."

aſſertions

affertions in this truly philofophical reprefentation. The inevitable infirmities of age
forbid me a longer ufe of the pen; I fhall
therefore merely fubfcribe to the found judgment of the enlightened journalifts, who fay
of you, that your firft attempts bear the ftamp
of a mafter : *pour des coups d'effai vous faites
des coups de maitre.*

Vienna, Auguft 17, 1780.

## LETTER XLIV.

### TO THE ADVOCATE LEOPOLDO CAMILLO VOLTA.

THOUGH writing, my dear Signor Volta,
is extremely inconvenient to me, yet the not
anfwering your cordial expreffions is impoffible. I too clearly difcovered the eftimable
and amiable qualities of your mind and heart,
during your refidence here; and I have too
much pleafure in telling you how much I
love and efteem you, and how conftantly I
fet that value on your worth which you
have convinced me you fo well deferve. I
hope you will frequently remind my much
revered Marquis *Andreafi* of my refpect.
Pray tell him that the Paris edition of all

2

my

my works, has already begun to be publifhed.
We have already received here three extremely elegant volumes, and next month
are promifed three more. I wonder that
you have not yet received them. If you
cannot procure them from any neighbouring
city, it will be beft to write immediately to
'the Abate *Giufeppe Pezzana* at Paris, who is
the diligent editor.

Signora *Martinetz* is much flattered with
your remembrance, and is joined by her
whole family in a grateful return of your
regard. Our Don *Domenico* will do the fame,
as foon as I fhall inform him of your obliging attentions : affure yourfelf of my regard
and affection, and believe me, &c.

Vienna, July 13, 1780

## LETTER XLV

### TO THE SAME.

By the lively manner with which you
have been ftruck at the fight of the elegant
Paris edition of my works, I form an idea of
my dear Sig. *Volta's* fincere and affectionate
friendfhip; and though I was fure of it before, fuch an obliging proof of it cannot fail
of

of sweetly stimulating my vanity. I will not dissemble the] pleasure which I likewise receive myself, in seeing my children so magnificently cloathed and provided for ; but at the same time, I cannot deny my fears, that this will give a furious opportunity to many people to examine too minutely how well they deserve such an expensive partiality. I believe the edition advances happily; the Abate *Pezzana* having informed me in his last letter, that the first sheets of the sixth volume went to press on the fourth of last month. The sonnet of Count Bulgarini, is truly beautiful. I not only do it all due justice myself, but successfully procure it from every body else; nor shall I fail to put it in the road to our Olympus.

I should gladly lengthen my letter ; but my diminished physical faculties hardly permit me to give you a hasty embrace.

Vienna, September 4, 1780.

END OF THE THIRD SECTION.

## SECTION IV.

THE letters of our bard have for fome time been confiderably diminifhing, both in number and length; and the complaints which he fo frequently repeats of his want of force and vigour to reply, in the ample manner which he ought, to the few perfons with whom he ftill wifhes to keep up a correfpondence, feem perfectly real and fincere. He is now (1780) arrived at his eighty-fecond year, a period to which few mortals are allowed to extend their exiftence. However, his friend Farinelli, after fixty years trial, is not neglected. His letters to him, though fhort, compared with thofe of former times, are not lefs frequent or affectionate. Eight of thefe for the prefent year have been printed, of which we fhall give a tranflation.

## LETTER I.

### TO THE CAVALIER FARINELLI, AT BO-LOGNA.

YOUR letter, written during the laft fighs of the old year, has had the power to difpel

the

the hypochondriacal clouds, which, during this fevere feafon, are generally condenfed to fuch a degree, that I fc 'm in danger of lofing the fmall remains of my obftinate patience. Your letter, which breathes nothing but kind-nèfs, tranquillity, and that wife equanimity, which preferves an equilibrium amidft all the furious tempefts incident to humanity, has infpired me with the wifh and faculty of imitating you. Yes, my dear Gemello, in your neat and fteady writing, and in that chearful eloquence with which you inform me of the gay parties which are formed at your country houfe, I exult in the folid arguments which they afford me, of your being ftill in poffeffion of that folid health of body and of mind, which will not only pre-ferve your philofophical gaiety in misfortune, but ftill have the power of communicating it to thofe with whom you converfe. May that Omnipotence by which you have been fo partially endowed, long allow you the enjoy-ment of thefe bleffings, and fecond the prayers of your conftant Gemello!

I have defcribed the character of your Ambaffador to the Countefs *Figuerola* and Monfignor *Perlas*, prefenting to them, as my credentials, your original letter, which they have

have entirely read, and highly commended ;
your gratitude is due to them for the pleafure
which they exprefs in their remembrance of
you, whom indeed it would not be eafy to
forget, among the many who daily propofe
you as an example of wonderful abilities,
united with candour, and innocent manners.

But I entreat you, who have already
gained me the favour of fo many and fuch
illuftrious perfons, to be careful in preferving it for me, by bearing teftimony to my
gratitude and refpect, and reciprocal return of
wifhes for their profperity. You know that
I am now no longer a man to write letters of
great length; but as an ancient inhabitant of
my heart, you ought to know its moft fecret
and recondite receffes : and therefore, I defire you to inform yourfelf, of all that your
moft faithful friend and Gemello would
write, if he were able.

Vienna, January 13, 1780

## LETTER II.

### TO THE SAME.

Your laft chearful and affectionate letter,
by the pleafant humour which runs through
it

it from the beginning to the end, has nearly
diffipated the dark clouds which obfcured my
hemifphere ; and made me blufh at my
inability to affume a fimilar difpofition,
notwithftanding the pompous philofophical
axioms fo oftentatioufly difplayed in my writings. You, in the midft of frequent earthquakes and the indifcreet irregularities of your
health, are not only able to defend yourfelf
from perturbation, but capable of conceiving,
arranging, and writing, mufical compofitions,
which exhibit all the fcience and practice of
an excellent contrapuntift. The Duet which
you have had the kindnefs to fend me, is
marvellous, not only for the difficulty of the
labour which you have contrived to difguife
in fo mafterly a manner, and the lively expreffion of the words, but for the opportunities it affords to a fine and cultivated
voice, to difplay its powers, in fwells,
fhakes, beats, *appogiature, volate,* and all
thofe extemporaneous and unexpected paffages and embellifhments, which are indebted to you for their exiftence\*. I have
already

---

\* We have here a comprehenfive defcription of good
compofition and excellent performance. The poet, however, fpeaks not only with approbation, but eloge, of his
friend's invention and execution of difficult divifions; talents
which

already heard it performed feveral times, by perfons extremely fkilful and intelligent, not only in execution, but in the laws of harmony; who were fo enchanted with the compofition, as to comply with infinite pleafure with my eagernefs to have it repeated again and again.

We are not perfecuted here with the frightful threats of your earthquakes, but for more than two months we have been ftruggling with the moft horrid and obftinate winter which can be imagined, and without the leaft refpite. Figure to yourfelf all that is moft cruel in this dreadful feafon, and you will conceive fome part of the infults and inconveniences with which we are furrounded: impetuous freezing winds, ice harder than marble, deep, inceffant, and permanent fnow, which covers and renders all objects of one colour: fo that to keep open a little intercourfe between the inhabitants, whole regiments of pioneers, with fhovels,

which he condemns fo feverely in others. Farinelli, with his wonderful, natural, as well as acquired powers, was the Archetype of all the rapid and difficult execution, which has been carried to fuch excefs in modern times, as to fatigue and annihilate admiration; which exifts no longer than its objects are rare and extraordinary.

fpades,

ſpades, pickaxes, brooms and carts, are conſtantly employed, and even theſe are not a
match, with all their fatigue and diligence.
for the quantity of ſnow which is falling
without intermiſſion, and renews and en-
creaſes their work. The Danube, with
new and incredible viciſſitudes, ſometimes
fluid, and ſometimes congealed, has at
length broken all the great bridges, by which
the proviſions are brought to this populous
city from Hungary and Moravia, which are
the chief diſpenſers of its nouriſhment;
and every thing is become ſo dear, that the
common people are unable to procure the
neceſſaries of life. But this *nænia* is
too long, and tireſome. Adieu, my dear
Gemello. Let us preſerve ourſelves for better times, and in the mean while do you
continue to love, and believe me, yours moſt
faithfully.

Vienna, February 24, 1780.

## LETTER III.

### TO THE SAME.

I RECEIVED a few days ago, a moſt affectionate letter from you, with a ſplendid pre-

fent of *liqueurs* and fweetmeats, with which your tender and generous friendfhip, by excefs of kindnefs, puts my moderation, fo neceffary to fecond childhood, to too great a trial. With this *flotta*, I have likewife received, the Aria of *Thyrfis*, of your compofition. I waited for leifure to examine the whole, before I gave an account of all the treafures with which you have put me in poffeffion. But during my delay, comes another letter from you, big with a Cantata, produced on the banks of the *Manzanare*, by the prolific vein of Bonechi, and rendered admirable by the enchanting notes of my incomparable Gemello, who on all occafion, manifefts how much art and nature have confpired to diftinguifh him. The fame golden mine is difcoverable, whence the duet *Mille volte mio teforo*, &c. was dug. But through the uniformity of ftyle, that ingenious diverfity appears, of which expert compofers fo well know the ufe; wonderfully combining together the lively expreffion of two effects, totally contrary. Adieu, my head will not permit me to ufe the Afiatic ftyle to-day. Remember my refpects and falutations to thofe perfons who honour me with their remembrance:

and

and continue yourfelf to me, what has been, and ever will be to you, your moft faith-ful.

Vienna, March 29, 1780.

## L E T T E R. IV.

### TO THE SAME.

On Monday, the 17th inftant, I had ad-vice from the cuftom-houfe, of the arrival of the elegant little Petronian cheft*, big with fweetnefs to feduce both the ear and the palate. My firft care was to have it inftantly brought home, the fecond to pro-cure me the delight of being in your com-pany, at leaft mentally, continuing to drink my delicious ardent liquor from the little flaſk which you had already broached, and to finiſh the remains of the Ferrarefe peaches, defective only in the fmall portion which you had tafted : fo that we have eaten and drank together, by means of your kind inven-tion, in fpite of the enormous tract of land which divides us. I ſhall make grateful and frequent ufe myſelf of the incomparable

---

* St. Petronius is the Patron Saint of BOLOGNA, whence the cheft was fent.

R 2

peaches,

peaches, but much more rarely and fparingly (againft my will) of the fpirituous potation, which by its too great activity, puts all the indocile nerves of my head into fuch a tumult, that they are dancing like thofe of a bacchanal, and continue a long time to deprive me of natural repofe. Imagine not, however, that your favours will remain ufe-lefs; I fhall eafily find coadjutors ready to do juftice to the precious merchandife, and who will be moft grateful to me, for the permif-fion. The Palate fatisfied, I fhall not neglect the Ear, which expects my notice with impa-tience; and the Air of *Tirfi*, excellently per-formed, makes me tafte a new and more exquifite pleafure, by the union of its infi-nite merit with my own felf-love: for though in this Air, not only the humanity, the fweetnefs, and fcience of my Gemello tri-umph, but the genius of the words, to which he has fo wonderfully adapted the melody, that I find them infinitely more beautiful in his mufic, than I was ever able to make them with my pen. The fame moft correct per-former*, at length, without interrupting her pleafant vocal employment, let me hear the

* Mademoifelle Martinetz.

two beautiful Sonatas, which are vifibly the legitimate daughters of my dear Gemello's brain; and pleafe me fo much, that I have refolved to hear them frequently repeated; but by the fame hand: as I fhould efteem it a facrilege to defile them with the inexperience of my own, which deprived of the neceffary practice, imperfectly affifts the little theory with which I have been able to furnifh myfelf. The merit of both thefe pieces is equal; but that of the firft in G natural, in my mind, has fome advantage over the minor fifter*.

If my head would allow me, I fhould be very prolix in my thanks; but that not being the cafe, read them in my heart, where you have fo long been an inhabitant: pay my debts with the dear and venerated perfons who remember me: put not my too neceffary moderation fo often to the trial with your feducing prefents, and continue to believe me, &c.

Vienna, April 9, 1780.

* In the year 1770, when I vifited *Farinelli*, at Bologna, his chief mufical ftudy and amufement, was compofing and playing pieces which he made exprefsly for his different harpfichords, of which he had a great number of the beft and moft curious of the time. See *Prefent State of Mufic, in France and Italy.* Art. Bologna.

LET-

# LETTER V.

### TO THE SAME.

WHEN I anſwered your laſt letter but one, I was at war with my maladies and infirmities, and ſo ſtupified by both, that I knew not whether I was male or female; ſo that I neglected to thank you for a beautiful *Canzonetta* of your compoſition, which I found among your ſweet-meats. I confeſs my ſin, and beg your abſolution. Enquire not, my dear Gemello, after my worthleſs health, ſhe is unworthy of your notice : always the ſame impertinent ſtrumpet. However, I hoped that by the return of good weather, ſhe would be a little reformed——but not entirely to relinquiſh hope, I have recourſe to our Spaniſh proverb, which ſtill allows me a day or two more, ere I give way to deſpair : *haſta el quarenta de maio no te quittes el ſaio\**.

If through caprice, you determined to write down, and execute, ſomething in mu-

---

\* This proverb occurred to our bard on another occaſion, ſee above, p. 205.

fic, imperfectly, you would find the undertaking impracticable: the machine organized
by nature, to the moft perfect harmony, and
the heart fenfible to the beft paffions, as well
as long habit, would oppofe and vanquifh
fuch an extravagant enterprife. So thinks,
and always fays, the ftudious performer of
your productions; who juftly admires you,
having been long fince informed by me, not
only of your profeffional merit, but of the
other invaluable qualities which are peculiar
to yourfelf, and by which you will ever be
diftinguifhed. She is, therefore, proud that
you are pleafed with her approbation, which
does herfelf honour, and will do you no
great harm. Accept it, therefore, and enroll
her among the numerous band of perfons,
who, *avec connoiffance de caufe*, admire and
refpect you.

I would go on, but my head commands
me to *halt*, and I muft obey. Pay my debts
for me, to all my dear and refpectable credi-
tors around you: particularly to the moft
noble houfe of *Spada*, not forgetting father
*Guardiano* of the feraphic family, and continue obftinately to believe me your moft
faithful, &c.

Vienna, June 1, 1780.

LET-

# LETTER VI.

## TO THE SAME.

My worthless head may proteft againft it as much as it pleafes, but it fhall not deprive me of the pleafure of anfwering your moft affectionate letter of the 26th of June. But what fhall I talk about? fhall my poetical whimfies be difcuffed? I have written fo many in my life, and talked about them fo much, that it would be a reprehenfible delicacy to blufh at mentioning them to my Gemello, who *ab immemorabili* muft have feen all my defects; but he on the contrary, exalts them, as laudable and exemplary qualities. One of the moft diftinct merits of the indefatigable Signora Martinetz, is the knowing how to do juftice to your ftudious and enchanting notes, and to fee in them that uncommon art, which diftinguifhes the beautiful from the wonderful; in which talent there muft confequently be a union of natural gifts, with long experience, and an intelligent and conftant application, in order to inveftigate the certain fources of that perfect

harmony,

harmony, which has a defpotic power over the emotions of feeling hearts. In fhort, your admirer believes fhe does honour to herfelf, by honouring you ; and numbers your friend-fhip and patronage among her deareft and moft eftimable acquifitions.

I congratulate you (not without fome little fpice of envy) on the vicinity of your gardens of the Hefperides to the moft vene-rated houfe of *Spada*, and confequently grieve at the painful reflection of the im-poffibility of my ever being of the party.

I feel myfelf very much honoured by the obliging mention which has been made of me to you by the worthy Padre Martini, and his learned companion, the Abate Mingarelli ; the firft ought to be already convinced, long ago, of the high and juft eftimation in which, with the whole world, I hold, and ever fhall hold, his merit. And to the fecond, not unknown to me, I am particularly beholden, for giv-ing me an opportunity of declaring my efteem and ambition to procure his patronage. Adieu, dear Gemello; I am tired, and muft ere this have tired you. Therefore, inform yourfelf, of all that you already know I would fay, if I were able.

Vienna, July 13, 1780.

L E T-

# LETTER VII.

## TO THE SAME.

WHENCE, for heaven's fake, could my dear Gemello have taken the new and unexpected idea of making me independent at his expence, by a pious and unmerited ftroke of generofity ? The very worthy Padre Guardiano, to my incredible furprife, informed me of it by a letter which I received by the laft poft, and has made me conceive all the grandeur of your true affection for me. If my faculties were not abforbed by fo many indifpenfible anterior debts, I fhould profit from your admirable example, and imitate your liberality ; but being utterly unable to change the circumftances of my fituation, I beg of you to accept in return, my grateful and fincere acknowledgment of being your debtor *.

My moft tormenting head obliges me to meafure my words : fo that I muft haften to

* It does not appear by any of the printed letters, in what the generous propofition of Farinelli confifted ; it probably was his wifh that the poet would fpend the remainder of his days under his own roof, at Bologna.

entreat

entreat you to load in my ftead, our exemplary and partial feraphic friend, with all
the expreffions of gratitude which are due to
him on my account, and believe me to be
your moft obliged and affectionate Gemello.

Vienna, Auguft 24, 1780.

## LETTER VIII.

### TO THE SAME.

YOUR moft affectionate letter of the 18th
of laft month, is fo full of expreffions and
fentiments worthy of two fond twins, that I
perfectly conceive by it the full extent of
your regard for me, and what mine ought
to be for you. I fhall take no pains to perfuade you what I am, with refpect to you,
as your ideas would not fo exactly correfpond
with mine, if you had not long fince been
convinced of the fincerity of my affection.

Signora Martinetz has learned to know
your worth from her infancy, by my continual and authentic relations; and encreafing in the manner fhe has done fince, in
harmonical knowledge, indeed to a greater
degree than was intended or expected, fhe
has difcovered by her own fcience, the folid
foundation

foundation upon which my reafoning was built, from which fhe derived her early ideas of your extraordinary merit. She is extremely thankful for your moft obliging compliance with her wifhes concerning your felect mufical labours; and proud of the generous offer of your friendfhip, fhe moft eagerly feeks for fome opportunity of manifefting her fenfe of your kindnefs; and I will be anfwerable for the fincerity of her flattering expreffions.

I congratulate you on having, at length, after fo long a parenthefis, again recovered the worthy family of *Spada* for your neighbours; among whom, by mere dint of wifhing it, I have more than once in a dream, found myfelf. Kifs all their hands for me, moft refpectfully, I entreat you, and affure them of my veneration.

I envy the three firft volumes in great and in fmall, of the magnificent and elegant Paris edition of my writings, being in the hands of my dear Gemello : but I hope their contents will be thought more valuable, thus ornamented, than I could ever perfuade myfelf they would be. Pay, I entreat you, all the debts of compliment for which I am

anfwerable

anfwerable to your obliging and benevolent friends.

Vienna, Auguft 31, 1780.

## LETTER IX.

### TO THE SAME.

Your kindeft of all letters, written the 4th inftant, found me in the moft unhappy and afflicting circumftances that I could poffibly apprehend in the courfe of my life. I have loft my auguft and. ever adorable Patronefs, Benefactrefs, and Mother; a lofs for which I have not the leaft hope of ever confoling myfelf! It is unneceffary to de-cribe my fituation to You; your fortitude has been put to the fame trial, and you know what compaffion fellow-fufferers deferve. I I fhould now be your Gemello, in the virtue with which you fupported your lofs; but with which I confefs I do not feel myfelf provided. Incapable at prefent of fpeaking to you upon any other fubject, I muft entreat you to fay for me all that is proper and refpect-ful to thofe where you are, who honour me with their remembrance and commiferation.

Vienna, December 23, 1780.

This

---

This princeſs, (Maria Thereſa of Auſtria, Empreſs of Germany, and Queen of Hungary) who had been educated with the moſt tender care by the emperor her father, was early initiated into the myſteries of the elegant arts, to which ſhe remained a liberal patroneſs, amidſt all the perils and viciſſitudes of her reign, to the end of her life. Her piety has been thought to border on bigotry; but if we may judge of its effect, by the tranquillity, happineſs, and affection of her people, compared with the turbulence, diſcontent, and deteſtation, of the ſubjects of her unprincipled, philoſophical, and diſorganizing ſucceſſor, we may ſuppoſe that too much religion is leſs miſchievous in a ſovereign, than too little. In the two long wars with her formidable foe, the late King of Pruſſia, ſhe ſupported the frequent reverſes of her fortune with abilities, fortitude, and dignity. And after a reign of forty years, in which ſhe deſervedly merited the title of Parent of her people, ſhe died univerſally regretted, and her name and reign are ſtill remembered with the utmoſt reverence and regret, by her ſurviving ſubjects.

A confiderable part of her life, was employed in beftowing benefits on the indigent,
particularly orphans of both fexes : and
among the laft words which fhe was able to
utter, are recorded the following, to her fon
and fucceffor, of which hiftory has not yet dif-
puted the truth : " If I have done any thing
reprehenfible during my reign, it has certainly been without my knowledge; for I
have always had the public good in view.
My heart has never been hardened againft
the unhappy : and this is the greateft comfort of my laft moments." She had been
made acquainted with the bufinefs of the
cabinet, by her father, at fourteen years of
age, and attended his councils. The frequency of her petitions in favour of worthy
objeéts, made the emperor one day cry out,
" You feem to think a fovereign has nothing
to do but to grant favours,"———to which
feeming rebuke, fhe anfwered : " I fee
nothing elfe that can make a crown fupportable:" and thefe were not words lightly
uttered without feeling. Innumerable inftances of her benevolence and pity for the
diftreffed, are recorded. Having perceived
a fick foldier on duty, at one of the gates
of her palace, fhe immediately ordered him

to

to be relieved, and conducted in a carriage to the hofpital. And being informed that this young man's diforder proceeded from indigence, and his feparation from a mother, whom he was no longer able to fupport by the labour of his hands, fhe fent for the poor woman from Brinn in Moravia, which is 120 miles from Vienna, in order that fhe might be with her fon. "I am delighted, fays the emprefs, to her; on her arrival, to reftore to you a child who is fo tenderly attached to you. I will give you a penfion for your fupport, to indemnify you for the lofs of that affiftance which you ufed to receive from his labour; and I recommend to you both, always to continue to love and cherifh each other. *Thefe are my recreations.*"—The good woman, tranfported to hear her fovereign fpeak to her with fuch condefcending good- nefs, cried out—"Though I have no other child than this which you reftore to me, and whom I love more than my life, I would this inftant fee him expire, if his death could be of any fervice to your majefty." The Emprefs Queen, without any other guard than the hearts of her fubjects, was acceffible to all, without diftinction of rank. " I am only a beggarly peafant, (faid a poor Bohemian labourer)

labourer) but I can fpeak to our good queen, whenever I pleafe ; and fhe liftens to me as if I was a Lord."—The emprefs one day returning to her palace, perceived a woman and two children whom fhe could hardly drag along. Hunger had driven them from their miferable dwelling. " How have I offended Providence, (fays fhe) that I fhould be witnefs of fuch a fight ? " And immediately gave orders that her own dinner fhould be carried to them: and had herfelf no other refection than the tears fhe fhed over the mother and her almoft famifhed offspring. " They are my children (fays fhe) and fhall never again be driven to beggary."—" I lament the time I am forced to give to fleep, as it is a robbery from my people." The partiality of her Imperial majefty, to the character as well as genius of Metaftafio, muft have been long fince difcovered by the reader of thefe Memoirs, and will be further manifefted in the fequel.

# LETTER X.

## TO FARINELLI.

WHILE you wrote to me in your bed in the neighbourhood of Bologna, your moſt kind letter of the 20th of laſt month; I, (like a good twin) was in bed at Vienna, where I was confined by a violent fever, and an eryſipelas in my leg. This accidental ſympathy juſtifies our aſſumed twinſhip. The fever obliged me to keep my bed a few days, and departed; but the departure of the eryſipelas does not yet permit me to quit the houſe.

I thank you for informing me of the ſafe arrival of the books, and for the generous and kind thankfulneſs with which you received them. I dare not enter on the ſubject of my loſs: you know by experience, that wounds of this kind do not ſoon digeſt, and that they never cicatriſe till after a long lapſe of time, if at all!

Signora Martinetz renders you her beſt thanks for your courteous remembrance of her; which ſhe returns with ſincere ſenti-

ments

ments of the high efteem that is due to fuch
excellence as yours. I moft earneftly hope
that you will foon fubdue your importunate
complaints, and am with ufual twinly kindnefs, yours moft faithfully.

Vienna, February, 1781.

## LETTER XI.

### TO THE SAME.

I AT length vanquifh my pardonable lazi-
nefs of old age, to tell my dear Gemello,
that I am always his, in fpite of infirmities,
which as ufual, never negleét to exercife my
tired patience : and to inform him, that I
have configned to Signor *Milani*, a friend
and correfpondent of our moft worthy Padre
*Francifco Maria*, the three fubfequent volumes
of the grand Paris edition of my works : that
is, the 4th, 5th, and 6th, which will be
delivered to you with more punétuality than
the former volumes. Thefe have been fome
time in my poffeffion ; but I kept them back
for three plates which were wanting, from
the indolence of the Paris engraver. I hope
that the other two *livraifons*, which are
to complete the edition, will be more

regular.

regular. Adieu, dear Gemello. Neglect
not your health, as you prize mine : Signora
*Martinetz* will not fuffer me to omit her
devout refpects; and with my old age and
obftinate affection, I continue to fubfcribe
myfelf, &c.

Vienna, April 6, 1781.

## LETTER XII.

### TO THE SAME.

I HAVE this moment received, moft incomparable Gemello, your very affectionate
letter ; and though I wrote to you but three or
four days ago, to inform you that I had configned the 4th, 5th, and 6th volumes of the
Paris edition of my works to Signor *Milani*,
I will not leave wholly unanfwered your
cordial wifhes for my health and peace of
mind. Would to heaven the tranquillity,
which you were able to mufter in writing to
me, had required lefs patience to obtain ;
but at our age, it is no fmall inftance of
divine mercy, that we ftill exift. Signora
*Martinetz*, in this letter, repeats her juft
fentiments of gratitude and efteem, which I
inferted in my laft : and with a thoufand,

and

and a thoufand affectionate wifhes for your happinefs, I am, &c.

Vienna, April 12, 1781.

## LETTER XIII.

TO THE SAME.

YESTERDAY, the 28th inftant, I received your very affectionate letter of the 15th, and anfwer it immediately, from mere eagernefs to talk with you, though this letter cannot depart thefe three days. I perceive that though thefe earthquakes and complaints will not fuffer you to remain in peace, yet, in fpite of them, you have the wonderful courage and ftrength of mind to keep up your fpirits, and to amufe yourfelf with running over the keys of the harpfichord, or with a plate of Neapolitan Maccaroni, which there is lefs hope of obtaining here from our moft learned cooks, than a Cardinal's hat. I do not envy you this enjoyment, becaufe I always feem to partake of whatever belongs to you, be it good or bad; yet, I hope you will not fail to deplore my privation. I wifh a good journey and a profperous expedition to our worthy *Padre Guardiano,* who has fo

S 3

fpeedily

ſpeedily put you in poſſeſſion of the laſt publiſhed volumes of my trifles: and when I
receive the reſt, I ſhall not fail to put them
in the ſame road. You know that my brevity is not a matter of choice; therefore,
receive with good humour, though ſhort, my
tender embraces, and believe me, &c.

Vienna, May 29, 1781.

## LETTER XIV.

### TO THE SAME.

Your dear letter of the 11th inſt. though
a mixture of ſour and ſweet, has comforted
me extremely; as after that abominable addition of *ai! ai!** of which you give me
an account, you appeaſe me by ſpeaking
of dinners, harpſichords, maccaroni with
*zucchillo*, and admirable company; convincing me that ſilence has not robbed me of
the ſmalleſt portion of your love; and I
firmly believe, that you will think the ſame
of me. But, my beloved Gemello, the
whole months of July and Auguſt, and

---

* *Ai ai* is a contraction of *aiuto-aiuto*, help! help!
murder!

ſeventeen

feventeen days of the prefent month, we have inhabited here the torrid zone, without being able to breathe, day or night, from a continual burning and fuffocating heat beyond what has ever been remembered in this country. My poor nerves, which hitherto only dreaded cold, are fcandalized to fuch a degree by this ftrange irregularity, that encreafing their painful tenfions and tremors, particularly in my aching and confufed head, they have rendered me unable to read, write, and almoft to think ; leaving me, however, an outward appearance of tolerable health, which does not augment my own patience, though it confiderably diminifhes the compaffion of others, to which I am but too well entitled. The very worthy Count *Gaddi* has frequently feen me in fimilar fituations, and therefore has given you accounts of the florid and happy ftate of my health, to which I can by no means fubfcribe. I love and efteem this Count extremely, and have here many rivals, whence I hope that your acquaintance with each other, produces reciprocal pleafure.

Divide and diffeminate my thanks and refpects in due proportions among the Marchionefs *Spada*, Meffrs. *Pignatelli*, and *Valdivia*,

s 4                    the

the imcomparable *Padre Guardiano*, the Abate *Mingarelli*, and all thofe in your quarter of the world who remember me : and in return, I fhall have the merit of fecuring the Countefs di *Figueruola*, and *Monfignor Perlas*, as I have already comforted the indefatigable Signora *Martinetz* with your obliging remembrance. Do you continue obftinately to love me with all my infirmities and complaints, which will never be able to make me forget you for a fingle moment.

Vienna, September 27, 1781.

## LETTER XV.

### TO THE SAME.

YOUR amiable letters, full of cordiality, grace, and candour, are always dear to me, and efficacious reftoratives, in refrefhing my worn-out patience, at the obftinate tenfion of the nerves of my head, by which I am eternally perfecuted. I am therefore extremely grateful to you for this fuccour which you adminifter to me from time to time. But that I might enjoy it more amply, I wifh moft ardently, that your importunate complaints

complaints would render the exercife of your
charitable affiftance, which is of fuch fingular
ufe to me, lefs painful to yourfelf.   But let
us change the fubject, and not contaminate
the confolation, which, by our cartel, we are
mutually bound to afford each other.

I rejoice in the new and defirable acquifition which you have made, by your acquaintance with the Imperial minifter, and his
moft worthy noble family, and likewife with
the moft learned *Padre Maeftro Gazzaniga*:
of the merit of all whom I judge by their
efteem for you.   To the laft, whom you
will always have the happinefs of retaining
with you, give, I befeech you, a thoufand
affectionate compliments in my name; and
tell him that I fhall never ceafe to love
and efteem him, and to feel grateful for
his conftant demonftrations of benevolence.   Happinefs attend our incomparable wanderer, father *Guardiano!* who,
among his other innumerable faculties, has
the power to infpire my delightful Gemello
with chearfulnefs and good humour, at his
charming dinners, his harpfichord, and the
converfations of his felect parties.

I am arrived at the 7th, 8th, and 9th
volumes of the Paris edition, and fhall tranf-
mit

mit them to you by the ufual road; but I would firft run them through, to difcover the errors that may ftill remain uncorrected; and at prefent, the tremulous nerves of my eyes are not fit for fuch an operation (as you may difcover by my hand-writing.) If this impediment fhould be obftinate, I fhall poftpone the revifion, which I believe is not very neceffary.

Signora *Martinetz*, in compofing an oratorio, which fhe has juft finifhed, has always invoked your harmonical influence. Adieu, dear Gemello. Affure yourfelf of my obftinate perfeverance in loving you, and believe me, with my whole heart, &c.

Vienna, November 14, 1781.

## LETTER XVI.

### TO THE SAME.

YESTERDAY, December 16th, I ordered the 7th, 8th, and 9th volumes of the new Paris edition, in 4to, to be configned to our faithful friend, Signor *Milani*, in order to forward them to you : and as I am informed, that our Padre *Guardiano* is not at Bologna, I fhall lodge my advice to him in your hands, being

being certain, that he will have notice of this new diſtribution of books elſewhere. We have now three-fourths of the impreſ-ſion, and I hope that our patience will not be put to any great trial, ere we receive the remaining three volumes.

The Grand Duke and Dutcheſs of Muſ-covy, who you ſo much admired at Bologna, and whom we at preſent poſſeſs in Vienna, where they are juſtly adored, not only for their elevated rank, but perſonal qualities, by which they are rendered more illuſtrious and dignified, will abandon us the firſt day of the new year, and I begin already to de-plore our loſs.

Pray combat the winter valiantly, as I ſtrive to do, though I have no reaſon to be proud of my bravery. The female compoſer devoutly ſalutes you; and I, with my uſual doſe from the *vaſi pizzechillo,* aſſure you that I am yours moſt faithfully.

Vienna, December 17, 1781.

———————

No more than two or three letters of this year, except thoſe to Farinelli, appear in the printed collection; ſo much were the poet's ſtrength and activity diminiſhed, as well as the number of ſurviving correſpondents!

L E T-

# LETTER XVII.

TO THE ADVOCATE LEOPOLD CAMILLO
VOLTA;

*Secretary and Prefect of the Royal Library at Mantua.*

An eryſipelas in my left leg, to complete my ſufferings, has confined me to my bed for many days, and which does not yet permit me to quit my domeſtic habitation, is the cauſe of this late arrival of my anſwer to your laſt letter. I have peruſed and re-peruſed the ſonnet, which I find worthy of the ſubject, and of the author: and I am gratified with the praiſes which it receives from thoſe hearers to whom I take care to communicate it. I return you my thanks, not only for being ſo obliging as to favour me with a copy of it, but alſo for the public confirmation of the juſt judgment I formed of your talents from the firſt day I had the happineſs of converſing with you in this capital. Continue to honour me in the ſame manner. Aſcribe my ſilence to the irreparable loſs with which we have been afflicted: accept a
reciprocal

reciprocal return of the compliments with which you commiffioned me for the inhabitants and frequenters of this houfe ; and continue to believe me, with my accuftomed efteem and affection. yours, &c.

Vienna, February 1, 1781.

## LETTER XVIII.

### TO THE SAME.

I RECOGNIZE, my dear Signor Volta, all the fenfibility of your zealous friendfhip in the indignation which you manifeft in communicating to me, the *Canzonetta della vita umana*, printed under my name at Florence. The merit of compofing it is not mine, and I fhould be forry to rob the author of his fame : you will therefore oblige me extremely, by acquainting our friends how much I abhor the character of a Plagiarift. I am ignorant how it happens to be my fortune, that fo many generous poets fhould undertake to affift me in the production of children. The imperfections of my legitimate and natural offspring (not all very well known to me) are fufficient to difturb and plague me, without being burthened with

the

the care of others. But experience has informed me, that this is a diforder like the gout, for which we have no other remedy, than to complain and fuffer. Continue that affection for me which you have manifefted, and be affured of an ample return from, &c.

Vienna, Auguft 9, 1781.

The following letter, in anfwer to one written by a literary correfpondent, who, though an acquaintance of no long ftanding, perfevered in tranfmitting to him his poetical productions for approbation, does not feem to have been aufpicious to his views.

## LETTER XIX.

### TO SIGNOR GALFO.

A MOST kind letter of yours dated at Rome, March 21 ft, with a long poetical compofition, which will doubtlefs be worthy of you, but which I have not yet had leifure to read, were delivered to me at the end of May, by our moft worthy Nuncio: by which you will perceive, that it was impoffible to obey your commands in anfwering your letter by the return of poft; and if chronology had put it in my power, my phyfical faculties would

Would have deprived me of that pleasure.
Oh, my dear Abate! the blind partiality
which you have conceived for me, not only
produces in you an excefs of efteem, but
feduces you to imagine (as is ufually the cafe
with thofe in love) that I am poffeffed of
every poffible human perfection, without
excluding the vigour of youth, or thinking
of the inability or infirmities of age, encreafed by the confternation of my recent and
well-known irreparable lofs, which communicating to the body the fatal agitations of
the mind, has confined me to my bed and to
the houfe, near three months, by infirmities
and flow convalefcence; nor am I yet able
to refume my ufual kind of life, or to find
myfelf in equilibrio with my fufferings. To
thefe phyfical obftacles which limit my obedience to your commands, moral impedi-
ments are now to be added; and of thefe
the following is invincible: a perfon of the
moft illuftrious among the great families of
Rome, a man of vaft learning, uncommon
genius, and excellent manners, has defired
to form with me a regular epiftolary correfpondence, fending me copies of his excellent compofitions in the Tufcan and Latin
tongues, entreating my judgment of each.

2                          A com-

A commerce with which I have been fo
honoured and delighted, would have gratified my vanity in the higheft degree; but
my poor exhaufted humanity, has, at length,
much againft my will, obliged me to afk
quarter; and God knows the difficulty which
I had in obtaining it. Now you will be fo
good, my dear Abate, to tell me with what
face I could fend public documents to Rome,
of my being able to comply with the requeft
of others, after having protefted that it was
not in my power to oblige him? You are in
no kind of want of my fuffrages, and thofe
which I have antecedently given, will leave
no doubt of my refpect for your productions.
I fhall, however, read what you have fent
me, when I can do it with a mind lefs
oppreffed, and with eyes more fteady. In the
mean time, I beg you will not confpire with
nature, in diminifhing your regard, as fhe has
done my activity, but continue to love me
as I am, and believe me, with ufual efteem.

Vienna, June 11, 1781.

---

The following is the only letter that
appears addreffed to the fame perfon. It
feems an anfwer to a letter of thanks from
the author of a recent Italian tranflation
of

of Homer, to Metaſtaſio, for his approbation, of that verſion.

## LETTER XX.

### TO THE ABATE GIUSEPPE BOZZOLI.

THE juſtice which I rendered to your happy Homerical verſions, was not ſo much to increaſe the celebrity of your literary talents, become ſo illuſtrious by univerſal applauſe, as to do credit to my own judgment ; which if it had been different, would have proved, that I was ignorant what learning, vigour of mind, good ſenſe, and conſtancy, were neceſſary to conceive, undertake, and conduct, to a happy termination, ſo long and difficult an enterpriſe. You are, therefore, only obliged to me for the advantages which I have procured to myſelf. Cheriſh, I entreat you, your gratuitous, partial propenſity towards me, and extend a ſimilar indulgence to my age and infirmities, which hardly allow me to aſſure you, in this ſhort manner, of the eſteem and affection, with which I ſhall ever remain your, &c.

Vienna, October 24, 1781.

This

This is, chronologically, the laft letter in the collection, to any of Metaftafio's correfpondents, except Farinelli, to whom we now return.

## LETTER XXI.

### TO SIGNOR FARINELLI.

OUR laft letters on the fame fubjeCt, met upon the road; hence, my dear Gemello, I fhould have had nothing to write about, if luckily I had not an account to give you of an unexpeCted vifit from Signor Filippo Cavalier *Gattefchi*, captain in the fervice of Ruffia, with another officer, and a Greek lady, his confort, who furprifed me, and remained a confiderable time in converfation; informing me of the ftate of Italy, and the north, whither they are now returning. During this vifit, I forgot my complaints, more than ufual, while fuffering from the intenfe cold of this climate and feafon: they fung, fpoke of you, and the memory of my dear Gemello is a fpecific againft all my fufferings. The Cavalier, your relation, is extremely courteous and animated, and I wifh him profperity equal to his merit. If writing were not fo painful

to

to me, I fhould fay much more ; but we underftand each other without fpeaking : that is, prefent my refpects, falutations, and thanks, to thofe at Bologna, to whom I am in debt ; preferve yourfelf carefully, during this horrid feafon; accept the compliments of Signora *Martinetz*, and believe me always more than ever yours.

Vienna, January 3, 1782.

## LETTER XXII.

### TO THE SAME.

I HAVE no materials, my dear Gemello, for a letter to-day, and my head protefts againft the ufe of the pen : and yet I cannot refift the defire of giving you a thoufand embraces, at leaft in writing, and returning you a thoufand thanks for the fincere and kind pleafure you manifeft at the great honour which it has pleafed the northern princes to confer on me. The phenomenon, however, will not produce the fame effect on all, and I have reafon to fear, that many, and perhaps the greater part, will be puzzling their brains in finding out what

T 2 proportion

proportion my merit can poſſibly bear, with ſuch an honourable diſtinction *: an enquiry which cannot be of much advantage to me. But let us have no more of it, at preſent. I think of nothing now, but the pleaſure it has afforded you, and the proof it furniſhes me of your true and conſtant affection, of which, however, I had not the leaſt occaſion. Give liberally, and in due proportion, the uſual return of regard and affection to all thoſe around you, who honour me with their remembrance, and accept the reverence of the female compoſer. Adieu. I ſhall write more fully when the wicked nerves of my head will permit; *in tanto vaſt a bizeffe,* and am, &c.

Vienna, January 24, 1782.

* The Grand Duke and Dutcheſs of Muſcovy, in mak-ing the Tour of Europe, when they arrived at Vienna, made early and earneſt enquiries after the Imperial Laureat, with whoſe merit they were perfectly well acquainted, not only from tradition, but his dramatic productions, which had been as frequently and magnificently repreſented, and as admirably ſ t, ſung, and performed at the court of Peterſ-burgh, as in any great city in Europe. Not content with all the information which they could acquire of others, concerning his private life, theſe great perſonages viſited the venerable bard in perſon; and when his character, talents, and age, are conſidered, the honour of the viſit ſeems reciprocal, exalting the good taſte of theſe princes, as much as the reputation of the poet.

L E T-

# LETTER XXIII.

## TO THE SAME.

AH, Ah! I did not expect this from You! After fo many expreffions of affection, pub- lickly to become my rival in poetry! And that no doubt might remain, a faithful and authentic account has been tranfmitted to me, figned by two unexceptionable witneffes, whom I highly love and honour; and how is this rancourous rivalry and *jaloufie du metier* to be reconciled with the tendernefs of twinfhip? The effort would be vain. It is lucky for you, that your letter arrived to inflame and encreafe my bile, at a time when I was unable to write: not only on account of my nervous head-ach, but a whitloe, that is, *pe no mêmardetto punticio,* in the ftitching or thimble finger (in the good language of feamftreffes) the beft finger of my right hand, which obliged me to have recourfe to the Cæfarian furgeon for affiftance, which I have not yet completely obtained. In the firft impetus of my profeffional jea- loufly, God knows what indecorous expref- fions might have efcaped my pen. But let

us

us change the fubject, as I feel, that fpeaking of it, roufes irrafcibility ; and I believe
it is not your wifh, that I fhould revenge
myfelf upon you in mufic—What would
become of your fame, if I did ?—No, no—
Make as many verfes as you pleafe. I fhall
forgive the infult ; and by the power of
twinfhip, I will fuppofe them to be written
by myfelf. I know not of what *flotta* you
fpeak, if you mean to fill it with poetry, it
fhall be welcome ; but I proteft againft all
things elfe. I can write no more. Act
liberally for me, and for Signora Martinetz,
in giving and taking compliments, and let
us feal our reconciliation, by a million of
mental embraces, and, with ufual wifhes, be
to each other " as we were wont to be."

Vienna, February 11, 1782.

## LETTER XXIV.

### TO THE SAME.

WHAT ! then is envy, in mercy to humanity, no more ? Neither here, nor elfewhere, during this dreadful feafon, can I
find a friend or acquaintance who does not
complain

complain of want of health. We are all equally obliged to have recourfe to refignation : one prays for me, another for you, and all are wifhing better health to their tormented neighbours. My whitloe has at length left me, but it was flow in taking leave ; my other complaints obftinately defend their pofts, and I my patience ; but I will not tire yours : let us therefore talk of other matters.

The great *Servus Servorum,* is faid to be within two or three days' journey of us; and our Emperor, who from an obftinate complaint in his eyes, is obliged to keep his room, would otherwife go to meet him. Heaven fend, for the fake of the Chriftian world, that this unexpected vifit may be profperous! The Petronian cheft, which as ufual, illuftrates the generofity of my dear Gemello, will oblige me to practife a difficult and importunate moderation in the ufe of its contents. But Signora Martinetz, who devoutly reverences you, will heartily fupply my inability, and begins already to thank me for the enviable commiffion. She has happily fet to mufic my oratorio entitled *Ifacco Figura del Redentore* (Ifaac type of the Redeemer). It was yefterday performed

T 4                                in

in the theatre, for the second time : And notwithstanding the rigour of the season, and catarrhs of the singers, it was not defrauded of its merited approbation. This sacred function was performed here for the benefit of the poor widows of musicians, raising by the profits a fund, in order to relieve them by pensions, at the decease of their husbands *.

Oh how many things I still want to say! But what is to be done when we can do nothing! I beg you, my dear Gemello, to act my part with due respect and proportion among the many persons in your neighbourhood, who honour me with their remembrance. The admirable *Carlucciello* is embraced with my whole heart, and the fraternal tenderness confirmed of his immutable Gemello.

Vienna, March 20, 1782.

---

This was the last letter written by Metastasio to his beloved friend Farinelli, and

* This plan was established in imitation of the original English *Fund for the support of decayed musicians and their families*, now called the *Royal Society of Musicians*, and still subsists. See *Account of the Commemoration of Handel*.

perhaps

perhaps the laſt uſe which he made of his pen ! For in leſs than a fortnight after, he was ſeized with a fever, which deprived him of life, and the world of one of its beſt inhabitants and brighteſt ornaments ! But the account of his laſt ſickneſs and deceaſe, which the accompliſhed Mademoiſelle Martinetz ſent to Farinelli immediately after the fatal event, deſcribes the circumſtances ſo amply, and with ſo much feeling and elegance, that we ſhall give it to the reader, as much in her own words as a faithful tranſlation will allow.

### TO THE CAVALIER FARINELLI.

THE loſs of a mortal who honoured humanity, is felt by all; but it is particularly calamitous to thoſe who, like yourſelf and our family, were united to him by the ſtricteſt bonds of a long and ſincere friendſhip. Indeed from the time of the immortal Metaſtaſio's firſt arrival in Vienna, April 17th, 1730, he never quitted our houſe, nor ceaſed conferring benefits and acts of kindneſs on its inhabitants: it will therefore be unneceſſary minutely to deſcribe the affliction of my mind to you, Sir, whoſe ſenſibility of heart

heart and affection for your friend, are fo well known. The ftroke, however, came upon us too fuddenly: as the vigour of his conftitution, fuperior to the age of eighty-four, animated by a conftant and equal vivacity and incomparable wit, were fuch as promifed a longer continuance among us, notwithftanding the habitual hypochondriac affections with which he was frequently incommoded, but which did not, however, deprive him of the enjoyment of fociety, fleep, appetite, ftudy, or other vital functions. In the evening of the firft of April, his fatal malady began. Returning home from his conftant vifit to Count *Perlas*, he complained of a chilnefs, eat very little at fupper, went to bed at his ufual time of twelve o'clock. The next morning, at feven, he called for my elder brother, Giufeppe, and confulted· him whether he had beft rife and go to church, as he had intended, it being Eafter Sunday; but was advifed by him to remain in bed, as his pulfe was very quick: an hour after, the fever increafed to fuch a degree, that it deprived him of fpeech, and he remained opprefled by a heavy lethargic fleep, which continued during two days, with fhort intervals, in which he was only

able

able to take the medicines prescribed by Dr.
Molinari, his physician. The fever diminished so much on the morning of the fifth
day, that he became tranquil, spoke freely,
conversed with some of his friends, who
visited him, and was able, after dinner, to
have the sacrament administered to him.
You may imagine, Sir, what great consolation this afforded us; but our hopes were of
short duration, for at night, the fever returned with such violence, that every day he
became more lethargic, and baffled all the
skill of the most able physicians, who met in
consultation; so that on the 12th of April,
between eleven and twelve o'clock at night,
he finally, without much agony, rendered his
sublime spirit into the hands of the eternal
Creator, in the presence of his confessor,
having three hours before received the general absolution of the Apostolic Nuncio. Now,
since every mortal must pay the tribute of
humanity, it was some alleviation to our
sorrows, for so great a loss, to reflect, that
this illustrious man, after having with universal applause, employed his extraordinary
talents in instructing and delighting mankind, and amply fulfilled all the duties of a
true Christian, of an eminent writer, and
acquired

acquired the indifputable title of the firft poet of the age, fhould enjoy, at prefent, the worthy and everlafting mede of his fevere rectitude, probity, integrity, and morals.

For the Bologna prefent, generoufly intended for me, you muft content yourfelf, Sir, as yet with my fincere thanks: when it arrives here, I fhall be more diffufe in my acknowledgments, and with my information of its fafety, give due praife to its kind contents. In the mean time, accept the moft fincere affurances of the reverence, efteem, and refpectful confideration, with which I have the honour to be, &c.

Vienna, May 9, 1782.

---

His friend and adopted twin, CARLO BROSCHI, commonly called FARINELLI, furvived this event but a fhort time: the poet dying April 12th, 1782, and the mufician September 22d, of the fame year, having arrived at the great age of eighty-one.—Let not libertinifm, indelicacy, or inhumanity, ridicule or degrade this moft excellent and worthy perfonage, for the cruelty of avaricious parents during childhood! His talents
had

had effects upon his hearers beyond thofe of any mufical performer in modern times(*d*): and it may be doubted, whether the moft celebrated muficians of antiquity, Orpheus, Linus, or Amphion, however miraculous their powers over the heart of man, ever excited fuch fplendid and folid munificence in their hearers (*e*). His extraordinary voice and almoft fupernatural powers of execution, have been fo often celebrated in every part of Europe, that nothing need be added here to his *public* profeffional character; and in the courfe of this work, the numerous and impreffive eulogies of fo exquifite a moralift and judge of the human heart as Metaftafio, muft have exalted his *private* virtues and conduct through life, to an uncommon pitch of excellence. In my youth, during the keennefs of curiofity, concerning the life of this portentous performer, I had accounts from the higheft authority, of his modefty, humility, and benevolent propenfities, during his fplendid refidence at Madrid, while in the meridian of royal favour, invefted with

(*d*) See *Italian Muf. Tour*, and *Hift. of Muf.* vol. iv.

(*e*) The King of Spain, fettled a penfion on him for life, of 2000l. (many accounts fay 3000l.) fterl. per ann. with honours, privileges, and prefents innumerable.

wealth,

wealth, honours, and influence, fufficient to excite every fpecies of envy, hatred, and malice, in all the orders of fociety. Yet fo found were his intellects, fo fage and judicious his conduct, that he cannot fo properly be faid to have efcaped the fhafts of envy, as to have prevented their being fhot at him. Of almoft all other great fingers, we hear of their intoxication by praife and profperity, and of their caprice, infolence, and abfurdities, at fome time or other; but of *Farinelli*, fuperior to them all in talents, fame, and fortune, the records of folly among the *fpoilt children* of Apollo, furnifh no one difgraceful anecdote. It was not till after this moft aftonifhing performer and worthy man had defcended with dignity from the height of his former eminence, power, and royal favour, that I had the pleafure of contemplating his manners, and enjoying his converfation at Bologna; but I do not remember that I ever was more fatisfied or lefs difappointed in approximating celebrity. Rouffeau fays of Philofophers, that " the only prejudice of which they cured him, on acquaintance, was the having thought them, at a diftance, fuperior to other mortals." But Farinelli, inftead of lofing
ground

ground in my favour by a clofe examination, confiderably augmented my refpect and ad-miration. With all the eafe and grace of a man of the world of high rank, long accuf-tomed to the practice of urbanity, he joined intelligence, information, franknefs and can-dour. Farinelli's mind was *entire*, whatever mutilations its manfion may have fuffered. If vice, rafhnefs, imprudence, or any thing in which his own volition might be accufed, had rendered him different from his fellow creatures, reproach and contempt would have been juftly his due. But when it is confidered, that ever fince he became a free-agent, his whole life was not only inoxious, but exemplary, in the practice of all the focial, friendly, benevolent, and amiable virtues; that with natural powers, and acquired ta-lents for delighting others in the moft inno-cent and exquifite manner, he never loft his equanimity in the midft of the higheft and moft inebriating profperity and applaufe, but remained humble, modeft, and fteady in his duty, gratitude, friendfhips, and attachment to his family and country; it feems as if the involuntary lofs of the moft grofs and com-mon of all animal faculties, had been the

only

only degrading circumftance of his exiftence (f).

METASTASIO's death illuftrated the principles and practice of his life. Pious and firm
in the belief of the religion of his country,
he courageoufly, in his laft moments, relied
on the promifed propitiation of his Saviour;
and on receiving the facrament a very fhort
time before he expired, exclaimed,

> *T'offro il tuo proprio figlio,*
> *Che già d'amore in pegno,*
> *Racchiufo in picciol fegno*
> *Si volle a noi donar.*
>
> *A lui rivolgi il ciglio;*
> *Guarda chi t'offro; e poi*

(f) It is not eafy to account, rationally, for the total
filence of all Metaftafio's biographers, on the fubject of
his long, conftant, and ardent friendfhip for this extraordinary and worthy perfon; though a volume and half of his
letters are addreffed to him, they feem afhamed to mention
his name. Signor Mattei, indeed, has once condefcended
to fpeak of a letter *to the Eunuch* Farrinelli *—Why this
contempt? If the vulgar and jocofe chufe to fhew fupe-
riority by their farcaftic attempts at wit, they muft not b
robbed of fo obvious and tempting an opportunity; but
that men who fancy themfelves philofophers, and elevated
above plebeian prejudices, fhould join in the cruel confpiracy,
is a difgrace to wifdom and learning.

* *Memorie per fervire alla vita di Metaftafio.* p. 41.

*Lafci*

*Lafci, Signor, fe vuoi,*
*Lafcia di perdonar (g).*

O Lord, permit me, now my race is run,
    While hov'ring o'er the gaping grave,
To offer up to Thee, thy only Son
    In facrifice, my foul to fave.

See whom I offer ; oh, behold him, Lord,
    And for his fake my crimes excufe ;
O turn thine eyes, and then refufe t'afford
    Thy mercy, if thou canft refufe.

Dr. Johnfon, equally pious, and impreffed with the deepeft conviction of the myftery of the incarnation, had too little reliance on his own merits, to think himfelf deferving of falvation, through his redeemer. With all his native courage, inftead of boldly meeting his diffolution, he would gladly have fuffered the moft excruciating terreftrial torments, to have poftponed the event. During his laft vifit to his friend Dr. Taylor, in Derbyfhire, about four months before his deceafe, he fays, in a letter to me, " I ftruggle hard for life. I take phyfic, and take

(g) This prayer was not pronounced extempore, as may be feen in the tenth volume of the *Nice* edition of his works, where it conftitutes (with a fmall difference) the laft Stanza of his *Paraphrafe on the Miferere*, or fifty-firft pfalm, a pofthumous work.

air; my friend's chariot is always ready.
We have run this morning, twenty-four
miles, and could run forty-eight more. *But
who can run the race with death ?*"

Metaſtaſio was interred in the pariſh
church of Saint Michael, in Vienna, the
14th of April. The funeral rites were performed with ſplendor, by his grateful heir,
Signor Joſeph Martinetz, in deſpite of the
poet's injunctions, who had forbidden all kind
of pomp. The inheritance of Signor Martinetz conſiſted in a well-furniſhed habitation, a coach, horſes, a great quantity
of princely preſents, a very ample and ſelect
collection of books, with a capital of one
hundred and thirty thouſand florins; from
which, however, were to be deducted, twen-
ty thouſand for each of the executor's ſiſters,
and three thouſand for each of his younger
brothers.

The poet's attachment to the *Martinetz*
family, was of long ſtanding. In the year
1730, on his arrival at Vienna, the firſt
houſe in which he took up his reſidence, was
that of Signor Nicolò *Martinetz*, maſter of
the ceremonies to the Apoſtolic Nuncio in
that city. The eldeſt ſon of this gentleman,
whom he appointed his heir, was aulic coun-

ſellor

fellor and firft keeper of the Imperial library.
Signora Marianna, his eldeft daughter, educated under the poet's eye, and univerfally
admired for her talents and accomplifhments,
particularly in mufic (as has already been
related) not only as an excellent performer
on the harpfichord, and an exquifite finger,
but for her genius and abilities as a compofer.
She was an eléve of the admirable Dr. Haydn,
who refided three years under the fame roof
with Mataftafio, during her mufical ftudies.
She had leffons in finging from the celebrated *Porpora*, who had many years before
been the poet's own mufic-mafter. The
productions of Mademoifelle Martinetz, were
communicated to, and approved by the
greateft mafters of Italy, and her name is
infcribed as a member of the Philharmonic
academy in Bologna and Mantua.

Signor Saverio Mattei, one of the moft
ufeful of Metaftafio's biographers, though
he rather gives advice to others, with loofe
and indigefted materials, than a regular life
of the poet, fays, that " whoever wifhes to
acquire an exact knowledge of his cuftoms,
manners, way of life, opinions of himfelf
and others; of his precifion in fulfilling his
duties, of the changes in his fortune, his

appli

application, and the different degrees of favour with which his feveral productions were at firft received, their chronology, the influence they had on the tafte of Italy, and on that of all Europe, with refpect to the melodrama, or lyric ftage, can only acquire fuch information by the perufal of his LETTERS."

The reader has now been prefented with entire tranflations of the principal letters contained in the five volumes of his correfpondence, publifhed at Nice, in 1786, and extracts from the reft; and it feems as if thefe would eftablifh his character as a benevolent, amiable, and virtuous man, as firmly as his dramatic works and mifcellaneous pieces have enrolled him among great poets.

His letters (fays the moft ample and accurate of all his Italian biographers, the Abate *Criftini*, editor of the Nice edition of his works) " will do honour to all Italy, while they difcover his moft intimate attachments, his moft fecret thoughts, his favourite opinions, and the hiftory of a man who was all heart and all virtue."

Thefe letters, like his dramas, are written without preface or text: he plunges at once directly into the bufinefs, whatever

it

it is ; and in the firft line makes known the fubject. He is as fhort and laconic as the matter will allow, without omitting a fingle circumftance neceffary to be known; and with the moft natural fimplicity, beautifies whatever he defcribes or explains. He rifes above the common ftyle, without affectation or fingularity, and has invented a new fpecies of writing, free from extravagance, that renders the moft trifling circumftance interefting which he has occafion to mention. He has political, theatrical, critical, philofophical, and encomiaftic letters, and all are pleafant and feducing. His genius, fays Signor Arteaga (*h*), "may be compared to the goddefs Chloris of the Greeks, who in flying through the air, fcattered rofes wherever fhe went." The fame grace, facility, and elegance of ftyle, appear in his *profe*, which have rendered his *poetry* fo juftly celebrated. Indeed, till I faw thefe letters, I ufed to think, that there was no Italian profe fo eafy to comprehend and conftrue, by young ftudents in the language, as the dramas of Metaftafio. But I am now con-

(*h*) *Revolutioni del Theatro Muficale Italiano.* To. 11, p. 92.

vinced,

vinced, that, in point of *facility*, the profe
of our author is to his own poetry, what
the profe of others is to their verfe.

What renders thefe letters infinitely more
natural and fatisfactory, is, that, like the
*familiares* of Cicero, they were not written
with the leaft view to publication ; as the
reader muft have obferved by the lively complaints he makes to his correfpondents, who,
for the gratification of their own vanity, had
betrayed his confidence. Indeed, what Metaftafio fays of the unlicenfed publication of
his private letters by bookfellers and others,
might be faid by the ghoft of Dr. Johnfon,
and would come perhaps with equal propriety from the living and the dead. In a
letter to Signor Diodati, July 14, 1769, he
afks, " What right can men have to the
poffeffions of others, without their confent ?
Is all idea of *meum* and *tuum* annihilated ?
Thefe invaders muft know, that every man
fays things in converfation and correfpondence
with friends, that he would not fay to the
whole world ; and that fuch remarks on perfons and things as are inoffenfive in private,
become injuries when publifhed." And it is
moft certain, that there is no man, however
candid and prudent, whofe private opinions
and

and converfations would not give pain to, and draw on him the refentment of perfons whom he would be forry to offend.

Metaftafio was an enemy to that pompous, verbofe, and obfcure ftyle which prevailed in his country a few years ago ; and was perfuaded, that the firft duty of a writer, whether in profe or verfe, was to be underftood.

" The ftyle of Metaftafio (fays an Italian critic) never fails to pleafe thofe who give way to their own feelings, more than perfons of profound meditation ; and I would rather be accufed of partiality to him, whom I venerate and love, than ranked with cold philofophers and deep thinkers, whom I may refpect, but cannot love."

All Metaftafio's biographers feem to agree in his being of obfcure birth ; and almoft all allow of his father having been a common foldier, but with fome education ; as when he quitted the army, before he opened a kind of huckfter's fhop, he became a copyift or writer, probably for the lawyers. Our poet's origin was fo long a myftery, that many wild ftories of his firft profeffion, have been circulated ; fome have bound him apprentice

tice to a *Goldfmith*, others to a *Stone-cutter*. But whatever was his genealogy, it cannot have been' fo high as to be degraded, or fo low as not to have been fufficiently exalted by fuch worth and talents, to rank with illuftrious anceftry. A worthy nobleman of our country, as refpectable for literary abilities as titled dignity, has faid, " I had rather be the firft peer of my race, than the hundredth (*i*)." High birth moft affuredly does not imply or preclude genius. The foul may be elevated by education and example ; but even thefe cannot fertilize a barren foil. The gifts of nature are common to every clafs of human beings. How many great talents have been brought to light by mere accident ! How many have burft out, in fpite of parental difcouragement and oppofition ! The great mufician, Handel, was intended for the law; and our ingenious countryman, Dr. Arne, ferved a clerkfhip to an attorney. We know not very well for what employment Shakefpeare was educated ; probably not for

(*i*) Defcription of the collection of pictures at *Houghton-Hall*, Norfolk, in 1743.

poetry,

poetry, or a learned profeffion. Pafcal's genius difcovered itfelf very early. Without genius, all the education and example of a great father, fuch as Cicero, could not make a great fon. The melancholy and beautiful reflection of Gray,

> " Full many a rofe is born to blufh unfeen,
> And wafte its fweetnefs in the defart air,"

is true, with refpect to natural intellects, in poverty and obfcurity, being thrown away upon the world; yet, perhaps, " whatever is, is right," at laft : there muft be " hewers of wood and drawers of water."——A nation of philofophers, poets, painters, or muficians, without agriculture, ufeful handicraftsmen, and labourers, would be ftarved to death, or extirpated by wild beafts. There is, perhaps at prefent, a fufficient proportion in every ftate of Europe, of fcientific and learned men, as well as of elegant artifts; and *equality* of any one kind in a ftate of fociety, though all were to be Lockes, Newtons, Bacons, or Boyles, feems not only phyfically and morally impracticable, but the very attempt appears pregnant with mifchief, mifery, and ruin to all.

Metaftafio,

Metaſtaſio, notwithſtanding the indigence
of his parents, fortunately received an excellent education from his adopted father,
Gravina; which cheriſhed and expanded the
natural qualities of his good heart, and found
intellects (*k*). He was learned without pedantry, pious without cant or ſect; breath-
ing the true ſpirit of Chriſtianity, without
fanaticiſm or bigotry; and practiſing its benign precepts of morality, ſo favourable to
the tranquillity and happineſs of mankind.

The emperor, Charles VI, found in Metaſtaſio, a man who encouraged and confirmed
his love of virtue, decorum, and propriety;
and Metaſtaſio found in his patron, a prince
ſuſceptible of receiving favourably his recom-
mendations of the moral and ſocial, as well
as heroic virtues. Indeed the poet and patron
ſeem to have been made for each other.

Metaſtaſio delighted in virtue ſo much,
that when he deliniates eſtimable characters,
he refines upon the good qualities which hiſ-
tory or tradition has aſſigned them; and

(*k*) The Abate Criſtini, ſays, " Gravina, not only
had him inſtructed in the civil law, but in the true ſpirit
of religion, the government of the paſſions, diſintereſted-
neſs, love of honeſt fame, humility, modeſty, probity, and
the practice of every ſublime virtue."

by his exquifite and tranfparent colours, gives to his pictures the utmoft degree of per-fection. Indeed his virtuous characters are more divine than human; but they are ren-dered fo amiable and worthy of imitation, that they excite a wifh in the reader or hearer to copy, or at leaft encourage and venerate fuch excellence. A true poet, fays Horace (*l*), unites the fweetnefs of verfe with the utility of his precepts: and no author has penetrated fo far into the refine-ments of the art, as Metaftafio. His heart was a copious and durable fountain of deep morality; the pureft harmony flows from the fame fource; and thefe running together, partake of the quality of each other, emanat-ing by turns both vigour and fweetnefs. Virtue cannot appear in a more pleafing and alluring garb to humanity. His heroes, it has been faid, ftart at the fight of death, becaufe they are human; but they advance, becaufe they are virtuous.

Few writers have been fortunate enough to enjoy the favour of the public fo completely during their lives, as Metaftafio. But this felicity is not to be more afcribed, perhaps, to the excellence of his writings, than to

(*l*) *Omne tulit punctum, qui mifcuit utile dulci.*

his

his modesty, candour, and determination neither to give nor take offence by censuring the productions of others, or resenting the censures of his own. He seems to have seen with due horror, the effects of literary war on the combatants (*m*).

His whole life appears to have been of that even tenour, which nothing but great accidents or public calamities could disturb. His veneration and gratitude for his patroness, the Empress Queen, seem, during the last years of his life, to have been the strongest passions to which he gave admission in his breast. When unfortunate in war, or on account of the sickness or death of any of her family, he was as much agitated, as any of her most faithful and best subjects. But when her own life was endangered by disease, his equanimity and philosophy totally left him. Then yielding to the natural sensibility and tenderness of a heart, neither chilled by apathy, nor petrified by stoicism, he became a common man; not too stubborn for affliction, or too proud and obdurate for the impressions of calamity. The sickness of his brother, and death of the

(*m*) See his letter of March, 1779, to the Abate Galfo.

Countess

Countefs d'Althan, are likewife illuftrations of this occafional fenfibility. And if the well-known precept of his favourite poet is right, a man poffeffed of fuch irrefiftible pathetic powers over others, muft have felt fenfibly and painfully himfelf (*n*).

That celebrity which he enjoyed fo indifputably during life, was not diminifhed by his deceafe; his works are ftill in every hand: the philofopher, the courtier, the bigot, the man of the world, auftere and gallant females, all equally read them, and all find them equally beautiful. His moral maxims are daily cited, and his productions are become the code of lovers. The fetting and finging his verfes, have rendered Pergolefi, Venci, Jomelli, Sacchini, and Farinelli, Caffarelli, Pacchierotti, and Marchefi, as celebrated in all parts of Europe, as Corneille, Racine and Voltaire. Had his dramas been regular tragedies, written for declamation, without mufic, perhaps we fhould never have heard of them in England; but mufic being an univerfal language throughout Europe, they are certainly obliged to

(*n*)    *Si vis me flere, dolendum eft*
    *Primum ipfi tibi.*

the

the compofer and finger for a great part of
their fame, at leaft out of Italy, notwithftanding the complaints of Metaftafio himfelf, and the admirers of tragedy who are
inimical to mufic, that they have been injured
by compofers and performers. Particular operas, and perhaps, at fome time or other, all
his dramas may have fallen into the hands
of compofers without genius, and fingers
without talents ; but upon the whole, excellently written as are Metaftafio's dramas,
and exquifite as is the Italian language, it
muft be owned, that mufic has been the
vehicle in which the operas of Metaftafio
have travelled into foreign countries. Cato,
Regulus, Themiftocles, Artaxerxes, Olimpiade, and Demofoonte, are allowed to
breathe a true tragic fpirit, even through
the effeminate languor of lengthened tones,
and long divifions ; but it is in the perufal,
perhaps, not the vocal performance, that
the force and beauty of Metaftafio's dramatic
fcenes, have been difcovered out of Italy.
When an air has been encored, it has not
been for the beauty of the poetry, but the
compofition or performance of that air. It
muft be allowed, however, without the
leaft deduction, that Metaftafio's genius, good
tafte,

tafte, and found judgment, firft achieved the
difficult tafk of rendering fo wild and incon-
gruous a compound of feemingly heterogeneous ingredients and abfurdities, a rational
entertainment.

Whether the fubjects he chofe for his dramas or fugitive pieces were facred or fecular, hyftorical or mythological, they are
treated with equal purity and delicacy. Dr.
Johnfon's high character of Richardfon, as
a *moral writer in profe*, is not more his
due, than Metaftafio's among *moral poets*.
Though love could not be excluded from his
fecular dramas, it is of that refined and delicate fort which will mend and purify, not
corrupt and deprave the heart. Decorum,
probity, innocence, and good-faith, were
equally inviolate in his actionsand writings.
And his conftant wifh feems to have been
through life, to infpire in mankind, a love
of virtue, and deteftation of vice.

Even the church has defended his morality.
The ci-devant Jefuit, father CORDARO, in
his Eloge of our poet, fays, " I well know,
that Metaftafio has been accufed by fome of
having brought the paffion of love too forward in his dramas, at the rifk of feducing
and

and enervating the heart and virtue of the hearers. How shall we defend him from this charge? He would certainly have done better if he could have confined himself to the love of glory, and of our country, in displaying the virtues of valour, fidelity, and canstancy, without medling with the follies of lovers. But there are certain noble affections, concerning which the vulgar have but little knowledge, and less taste. On the contrary, every one understands love; and without that seasoning, every representation, at present, seems insipid. It is the predominate passion of the times. He was perhaps necessitated to comply with it; but with what precaution and reserve! Has an unchaste word ever escaped him? Or an idea that is not strictly within the limits of the most perfect delicacy? This may be said of his secular dramas taken from profane story; but his sacred dramas are not only exempt from blame with respect to the passion of love, but sufficiently pure in morals and doctrine, to serve as correctives to whatever the most morose critics may object to his productions for the stage."

The four critic, *Boileau*, disputes not the theatrical dominion of love:

*——L'Amour*

*————L'Amour fertile en tendres sentimens*
*S'empare du theatre—————*
*De cette passion le sensible peinture*
*Est pour aller au cœur la route la plus sûre.*

Art. Poet. Chant. III. v. 93.

Lord of the manor, love has seiz'd the stage,
There to display his joy, his grief and rage ;
Though other passions may attention find,
'Tis that alone, which int'rests all mankind.

If the world could go on without love,
the playful character which our poet makes
the urchin give of himself, would fright
timid and sober folks from having any thing
to say to him.

*————D'ogni costume,*
*Bella diva, io son capace :*
*Son medesto, e sono audace,*
*So parlare, e sò tacer.*
*Serbo fede, uso l'inganno :*
*Son pietoso, e son tiranno ;*
*E m'adatto al mio talento*
*Al tormento, ed al piacer (o).*

I've ev'ry virtue, ev'ry vice,
Now hot as fire, now cold as ice ;
Am sometimes modest, sometimes bold,
Loquacious now, now silence hold.

Both truth and falsehood have their turn,
I'm tender swain, or tyrant stern ;
And can, as best my measures suit,
Give rapture sweet, or pain acute.

(o) *La pace fra la virtù, e la Bellezza.*

Metaſtaſio's meaſures, in the ſongs with
which he terminates the ſcenes of his dramas, are ſo ſweet and varied, that they have
often ſuggeſted to muſical compoſers, by the
mere peruſal, melodies of every kind.

It has been doubted by ſome eminent ſcho-
lars of our country (unacquainted, perhaps,
with his adoption and education by Gravina)
whether Metaſtaſio was able to read the
Greek tragic poets in the original. This
ſcepticiſm concerning the extent of the
Poet's learning, ſeems to have ariſen from
the little uſe that he has been found to make
of the ancient fathers of the Drama in his
own works, either by directly copying them,
or by imitations; but this he might eaſily
have done, by the help of Père Brumoy, and
others, from tranſlation. Whoever has read
with attention his *Abſtract of Ariſtotle's Art of
Poetry*, and remarks on the doctrines it contains, will not only find it impoſſible to
doubt of his acquaintance with the Greek
language and theatre, but clearly ſee his
reaſons for not implicitly adopting their
practice, or ſervilely copying their ſentiments. That he has highly taſted and re-
verenced the great Grecian models in every
ſpecies of literature, and frequently tinctured

tured his writings with infufions from their
ineftimable productions, has been locally indicated by fome of his learned countrymen,
who have been moft fevere upon the few
imperfections which they could difcover in
his works.

It has been faid by Arteaga (*p*), that no one
has fo happily adapted the Greek ftrings to
the Italian lyre, as Metaftafio; he having
feized the very foul of the Greek poets more
fuccefsfully than any of his predeceffors in
Italy, not even excepting *Chiabrera*, who
was certainly a great man, but who, in imitating the ancients, wanted the true philofophical fpirit (*q*).

It is not fufficient (continues Arteaga) for
an author to call an irregular ode Pindaric, becaufe it is divided into *Strophe*, *Antiftrophe*, and
*Epode*, if devoid of the true Pindaric genius,
the Greek *coftume* and character, and if conftructed in meafures wholly untuneable, forgetting that mufic and poetry were infepa-
rable in ancient Greece. It is the fame

(*p*) *Ubi fupra*, Vol. II. p. 84.

(*q*) Chiabrera, born at Savona in 1552, is faid by Apoftolo Zeno to approach Pindar in dignity, and Anacreon in
fweetnefs. *Nella dignità fi accofta a Pindaro, nella dol-
cezza ad Anacreonte.* Bibl. dell' Eloquenza Ital. di Fon-
tanini con le Annotazione d'Apoft. Zeno.

with

with moſt of thoſe who fancy they reſemble
Anacreon, when their ideas ſeem to ſpring
from his gay ſyſtem. But how different
from the productions of theſe pretenders is
the golden hymn of Metaſtaſio in the Olympiade: In which, whoever is poſſeſſed of a
ſoul for poetry, and free from pedantry, will
recognize the true Grecian ſpirit.

*Del forte Licida,* &c.

The genius of the famed celebrator of
Bathyllus appears with equal felicity in the
hymn which Achilles ſings in the opera of
that name:

*Se un' Alma annodi,* &c.

In which our Poet's muſe reſembles the
dove of Venus, quenching his thirſt from
the cup of Anacreon.

Some of his dramas, however, were certainly written under reſtraints and diſadvan-
tages at the court of Vienna. He was not
only obliged to ride poſt to Parnaſſus, occaſionally, upon very ſhort notice, but circum-
ſcribed to very narrow limits in other reſpects; particularly in writing for the performance of the Arch-dutcheſſes. At ſuch
times he was obliged to relinquiſh the eſtab-
liſhed rules and prejudices of the theatre;
even the number of perſonages was preſcribed,

fcribed, as well as their habits, figure, age, and manners. A *Stock piece*, fit for general ufe, is a jack boot, that will fit any leg; Metaftafio, however, was obliged to cut out to one meafure, and finifh to a particular laft. But of thefe difficulties, we have his own account in various letters.

The ten firft years of his refidence at Vienna, will determine the point of elevation which his glory attained. He regarded *Attilio Regolo* as his beft OPERA, *Betulia Liberata* as his beft ORATORIO, and ARTASERSE as the moft FORTUNATE of his dramas : for however fet or fung, it was always fuccefsful.

It was an intelligent obfervation of the late accomplifhed mufician *Abel*, that the genius of Emanuel Bach would have been more expanded and of more general ufe, if, inftead of being confined to the Hans town of Hambro' without a rival, he had refided in a great capital, fuch as Paris, Naples, or London, where he would have been ftimulated to diligence and exertion by competitors, and obliged to ftudy and refpect the public tafte. But Metaftafio, confined to the Imperial theatre at Vienna, without an opponent, or fear of either public caprice or private cabal, though the performers were

not

not always of the firſt claſs, or his auditors,
ſuch formidable critics as thoſe he would have
had to encounter in Italy, was ſo ſure of ſuc‑
ceſs in the ſtyle which he had formed early
in life, that he had no occaſion to try experi‑
ments in order to excite curioſity, or awaken
attention in an audience leſs able to judge of
the poetry than the muſic, and not allowed
to be ſevere, if diſpleaſed with their enter‑
tainment.

His monotonous reſidence at Vienna, ſeem‑
ed perfectly to ſuit with his natural love of
order and tranquillity. Though late in life,
when he felt " the cold gradations of decay,"
he was ſometimes a little hurried and op‑
preſſed by the number of Imperial com‑
mands to write, yet he was not among the
celebrated authors *qui ploravere ſuis non
reſpondere favorem Speratum meritis.* Many
inſtances have already been given of the
favour and ſenſe of his worth, manifeſted by
his patrons; but more ſtill remain, which
equally deſerve to be recorded.

When he had finiſhed his opera intitled
*Il Re Paſtore, & l'Eroe Cineſi,* the Empreſs
Queen ſent him a gold candleſtick, with a
green ſhade *to protect his eyes* from too great
a glare of light, which condeſcending care
of

of his *fight*, the poet regarded as infinitely more valuable than the gift itfelf.

His drama of *Athenais* procured him from his Imperial patronefs the following note, which will always be an honourable monument to literature.

"In this opera, and in the extreme alacrity with which it was written, I find the great Metaftafio full of all the fire and force of his extraordinary genius. And it pleafes me the more, as it affures me of the good ftate of the health of a man who has no equal, and of whom I have always regarded the poffeffion as one of the happieft circumftances of my life. This opera has enabled me to pafs an hour in the moft delightful manner, and I am extremely grateful for it."

Upon another occafion (the rapid production of a *Complimento*, or a fhort Ode for Mufic, to be performed by Arch-dutcheffes on a birth-day) the Emprefs Queen wrote him the following flattering note, in French:

"*La promptitude de la furprize m' ft d'autant plus agréable, que je vois mon ancien Maître (r) parfaitement confervé, qui fait la*

(r) The Emprefs Queen had received from Metaftafio her laft inftructions in the Italian language.

*gloire*

*gloire de notre fiecle, & plus encore de ceux
à qui il s'eft voué.* " MARIE THERESE."

All his biographers mention the offer of
the dignity of COUNT, BARON, and *Counfellor of the Court*, from the Emperor
Charles VI, after he had written *Achille in
Sciro* ; and fimilar honours by the Emprefs
Queen, of which he declined the acceptance.

He feems, fyftematically, to have declined all honorary diftinctions which might
excite envy, detraction, and obloquy, in his
peers, and fill his own mind with humiliating thoughts and mortifying reflections.
When the coronation of the *Improvifatrice*,
CORILLA, was in meditation at Rome, the
Emprefs Queen, juftly fuppofing that the
honour of the laurel crown, which Petrarca
had not difdained to accept, could only belong to Metaftafio, fent Baron Hagen to defire the Poet to accept of it ; but he, with
equal firmnefs and humility, declined the
offer.

Before we proceed to fpeak of his numerous productions, it may be neceffary to ob-
ferve, that the French, ever afpiring at
univerfal empire, not only in territorial dominion, but arts, fciences, literature, and
every

every fpecies of ingenuity, deny Metaftafio
all claim to *invention*, and clafs him only
among *imitators* of the tragic poets of
France. He certainly did not invent the
ftories and names of his heroes and heroines, which are generally the moft grand
and illuftrious of ancient hiftory, and fuch
as had not only been previoufly treated by
writers of other countries, but of his own ;
but has he ftolen or imitated the thoughts
and conduct of his predeceffors ? Has he,
like Quinault, confined himfelf to ancient
mythology for his fubjects, or always to the
fame heroes, or chofen the fame virtues and
vices to difplay, as Corneille and Racine ?
Even the names of many of his pieces are
not to be found in the works of thefe tragedians. Why then deny him the merit of
invention, in treating fubjects that have
never been brought on the French ftage ; in
delineating fuch characters, painting fuch
fituations, and colouring paffions with fuch
new, fublime, and touching fentiments, as
are not to be found in the dramas of any
other writer, ancient or modern ? Then let
it be remembered, in writing for modern
mufic, how circumfcribed and limited he
muft have been in the length, meafures, and
diction

diction of his dramas ; in drawing to a kind
of epigrammatic focus the bufinefs and fentiments of a whole fcene, in the AIR by
which it is terminated, and to which it is a
kind of epilogue. Who is able to read the
melodramas of his predeceffors, in Italy, or
elfewhere ? But, though fo truly lyric, and
happily fimplified and polifhed for mufical
expreffion, there are few tragedies written
for declamation in any other language which
pleafe and intereft more in the perufal,
without mufic, than the Operas of Metaftafio. And yet he is denied the merit of
*originality !* His fimplicity, elegance, grace,
propriety, and even morality, are original
*on the ftage.*

Thus far we have only confidered Metaftafio as a dramatic writer ; but he would
have merited a very diftinguifhed place
among the lyric and mifcellaneous poets of
his country, if he had only produced his *Can-*
*tatas*, *Canzonets*, and fugitive pieces, fuch as
*La Liberta*, *La Partenza*, *La Primavera*,
which, perhaps, have never been equalled
in his own or any other modern language.

As the fedentary, and ufually, uniform,
life of a man of letters, feldom affords
a greater variety of incident than that of a

Monk,

Monk, the chronology, plan, and reception of their moſt intereſting productions, are, perhaps, the moſt uſeful materials which their biographers can boaſt. We have theſe reſources ſtill in ſtore; and theſe Memoirs, which, with little deduction, may be ſaid, from the great portion of each volume which is occupied by the poet's own letters, to be written by Himſelf, ſhall be terminated with an ample liſt of his writings, claſſed under different heads, beginning with his *Operas*, the great pillars of his fame.

Metaſtaſio, in one of his letters to a friend, who tried to perſuade him to continue to write, tells his correſpondent, that, " After having treated almoſt all the modifications of the human heart, the intenſe application neceſſary for the invention and texture of a dramatic compoſition, became to him an exceeding hard labour (s)." In the following catalogue of his dramatic works, will be indicated the *moral object* which the poet had chiefly in view, while he was writing each piece; in which he has not only adminiſter- ed cathartics to the irregular paſſions, ac- cording to Ariſtotle, but anodynes to virtue.

(s) See Vol. II. Letter VII, to Saverio Mattei, p. 393.

A CHRO-

A

# CHRONOLOGICAL LIST

OF

## METASTASIO'S SECULAR DRAMAS, OR OPERAS,

SPECIFYING THE TIME, AND PLACE, WHERE THEY
WERE FIRST PERFORMED, BY WHOM SET TO MUSIC,
AND THE MORAL OBJECT OF EACH.

—————————

1. DIDONE ABBANDONATA, was written and firſt repreſented at Naples, 1724. Set to muſic by *Sarro*. The dire effeɛts of the in‑conſiderate paſſion of *love*, and the conſe‑quent rage of *diſappointment* and *deſpair*, are diſplayed in this drama.

11. SIROE. Firſt performed at Venice, 1726. Set by *Leonardo Vinci*. A parent's *blind par‑tiality* for one unworthy ſon, and ill‑treat‑ment of another, whoſe *filial duty* and *af‑feɛtion* are proof againſt diſgrace and ſuffer‑ing, are the vice and virtue chiefly diſplayed in this opera.

111. CATONE IN UTICA. Rome, 1728. Set by *Vinci*. In this piece, no one need be told that its hero's love for his country, and the
freedom

freedom of its inhabitants, are painted under the well-known virtue of *Cato*, called *Patriotifm*.

IV. EZIO, or ÆTIUS. Set by *Porpora* for Rome, 1729. *Valour* and *Fidelity* to the hero's fovereign, in fpite of ill-treatment, are the principal virtues of the Protagoniftes in this drama.

V. SEMIRAMIDE RICONOSCÌUTA, 1729. Set by *Porpora*, for Rome. In this drama *Vice is detected*, but not punifhed ; and no extraordinary efforts of virtue have been exerted by the fuccefsful characters. However, it is allowed by the fevereft critics, that the beauties of the poetry are fufficient to compenfate for the defects of the fable ; and that any one, except Metaftafio, who has ever written for the lyric ftage, would be glad to have been its author.

VI. ALESSANDRO NELL' INDIE, 1730. Set by *Vinci* for the Roman theatre. The *magnanimous Generofity* and *Clemency* of Alexander the Great, are the moft prominent virtues in this drama; which, though it has ever been a favourite of the public, is not allowed by Italian critics to rank with the author's productions of the higheft clafs. The words of the fongs, however, are in fuch favour with Italian compofers, that they have them by heart, and frequently choofe one of them, occafionally, for a detached air, to difplay the

the abilities of a concert finger, without any dramatic connection.

VII. ARTASERSE. Set for Rome by *Vinci*, and for Venice by *Haffe*, 1730. The principal virtues inculcated in this celebrated drama, are the *filial duty* and *affection* of Arbaces.

VIII. ADRIANO IN SIRIA. The *triumph* of the Emperor Adrian, *over the paffion of love*, is the moral leffon of this drama, the firft which the author produced at Vienna, for his Imperial patron, the Emperor Charles VI. 1731. It was fet by *Caldara*, of Venice.

IX. ISSIPILE. Vienna, 1732. Set by *Conti*. The virtue that is chiefly difplayed in this affecting drama, is *filial affection:* the heroine rifking her own life, and that of her lover, to preferve her father.

X. DEMETRIO. Firft performed at the Imperial theatre in Vienna, 1732, to the mufic of *Caldara*. The moral inculcated is *the facrifice of love to duty*.

XI. OLIMPIADE. Set by *Caldara* for the Imperial court, 1733. The fubject of the fable turns upon a moft heroic *facrifice to friendfhip and gratitude*. The fongs, in general, of this admirable drama, are among the moft poetical and happy of Metaftafio's lyric compofitions.

XII. DEMOFOONTE. Firft performed at Vienna, 1733, to the mufic of *Caldara*. In this moft interefting and affecting drama, which, for

the

the fublimity of the thoughts, the energy and force of expreffion, and the grace and elegance of the language, may be regarded as the moft perfect of Metaftafio's productions, *marital affection* is proof againft the moft humiliating difgrace and terrific danger.

XII. LA CLEMENZA DI TITO. *Clemency*, the fubject of this drama, was rooted in the heart of Metaftafio; and the luxuriance with which it fprung up and flourifhed, was never more manifeft, than in the *benignity* with which he has embellifhed the character of Titus, and eftablifhed his right to the title of *deliciæ humani generis*. This admirable leffon for his Imperial patron, was firft performed at the court theatre in Vienna, 1734, to the mufic of *Caldara*.

XIV. ACHILLE IN SCIRO. Written at Vienna in 1736, for the marriage of the Arch-dutchefs Maria Therefa with the Duke of Lorrain, and fet by *Caldara*. *The conqueft of glory over love* is the principal moral bafis of the piece. The character of the young Achilles in this drama is the *Hercules infans* ftrangling the ferpents in the cradle. It has been faid by an Italian critic (*t*), that if Metaftafio had written no other drama than this, it would have placed him in the high rank which he fo defervedly attained.

(*t*) The Abate Colomes.

XV. CIRO

xv. Ciro riconosciuto. Vienna, 1736. Set by *Antonio Caldara*. In this drama, a *fond* and *diſtreſſed mother* is the moſt intereſt-ing agent in almoſt every fcene : where ſhe is by turns anxious, terrified, enraged, and enraptured. The ſubjeƐt of this piece is manifeſtly the fame as the Merope of Maffei, Voltaire, Aaron Hill, and the tragic writers of all ages and countries, from the time of Euripides.

xvi. Themistocles. Written for the court of Vienna, 1736, ſet by *Caldara*. This opera abounds with more noble ſentiments, moral maxims, and patriotic effuſions, than any one of Metáſtaſio's works. There is not, perhaps, in the annals of mankind, a more re-ſpeƐtable and intereſting charaƐter than that of Themistocles. And this drama, of which he is the Protagoniſtes, has been lately pro-nounced in Italy (*u*) worthy of the beſt age of Athens, the happy, but ungrateful mo-ther of this hero.

xvii. Zenobia. Vienna, 1740. Set by *Pre-dieri*. This is ranked among Metaſtaſio's beſt dramatic produƐtions. In Zenobia's charaƐter, to the virtue of *filial obedience*, is added an extraordinary portion of *conju-*

(*n*) *Oſſervazioni di varij letterati ſopra i drammi dell'abáte Metaſtaſio*. Tome II. p. 193. In Nizza, 1785.

*gal*

*gal fidelity* to a hufband whom her father's fituation and entreaties obliged her to marry, though long paffionately attached to a fond and worthy lover of her own and her parent's choice

XVIII. ATTILIO REGULO. Written 1740, for Vienna, but not performed till 1750; when it was firft fet by *Haffe*, for the court of Drefden. It was an enterprize of great difficulty to fupport the character of *patriotifm* in three different dramas, without monotony of fentiments, or deficiency of intereft in the plot or perfonages. But the poet has fo contrived to difference thefe patriots, as to avoid copying himfelf. The character of *Cato* is fevere and inflexible; of *Themiftocles*, grand, tender, and refolute; and of *Regulus*, magnanimous, rigid, juft and almoft divine.

XIX. ANTIGONO. Written for the court of Drefden, and fet by *Haffe*, 1744. The focial virtues of *parental generofity, filial duty, affection*, and *obedience, friendfhip*, and *fidelity*, are all in action, and put to the teft in this drama.

XX. IPERMESTRA. Vienna, 1744. Set by *Haffe*. *Conjugal affection* is here manifefted, at the imminent rifk of life, by the heroine of the drama.

XXI. IL RE PASTORE. Vienna, 1751. Written for ladies of the Imperial Court, by whom

it was firſt performed to the compoſitions of
Signor *Bonno*. *Humility*, *moderation*, and *con-
tentment*, are beautifully illuſtrated, and rendered deſirable, in the ſentiments of the
Shepherd King. When it is remembered
that this drama was written exprefsly for
great perſonages to perform in the preſence of their Imperial Majeſties, inveſted
with abſolute power, the bold and vigorous
ſentiments on the duty of ſovereigns, which
the Poet ventured to put into the mouth of
one of the characters, do equal honour to his
Imperial patrons, who could liſten to them
with pleaſure, and to the Laureat who had
the courage to preach ſuch doctrine in a
court.

XXII. L'EROE CINESE. Repreſented for the
firſt time by perſons of diſtinction in the
Imperial garden at Schonbrunn, 1752, to
the muſic of *Bonno*. The heroic *loyalty* and
*fidelity* of the principal perſonage in the
piece, are ſuch as muſt appear unnatural
and exceſſive to Europeans unacquainted
with the Chineſe veneration for their princes
and fathers of families.

XXIII. NITTETI. Written for the Court of
Madrid, 1756. Set by *Conforti*. The hero-
iſm in this drama is wholly female. The
character of *Beroe* is the triumph of Virtue,
exhibiting an admirable example of gene-
roſity

rofity and fortitude in a female that is at
once young, beautiful, full of fenfibility, and
in love! Though this is not one of Metaſtaſio's beſt compoſitions, yet the delicacy
of fentiment and expreſſion of fome of the
fongs, frequently equal thóſe of his moſt
celebrated productions.

XXIV. IL TRIONFO DI CLELIA. Vienna, 1762.
Set by *Haſſe*. *Patriotic enthuſiaſm* is the prominent feature in the opera of *Clelia:* a
heroine neither coarſe nor maſculine. There
are not, indeed, in this drama, thofe tender
and touching ſtrokes, thofe fentimental and
elegant airs, and happy fimiles, which occur in moſt of his other theatrical pieces;
but, if we recollect the Roman *coſtume* at the
early periods of conqueſt, we ſhall find *la
feroce virtu republicaine* admirably painted.

XXV. ROMOLO ED ERSILIA. Written at Vienna,
1765, for the marriage of the Arch-duke
Leopold, and ſet by *Haſſe*. This drama,
which has never been popular, is, however,
not without infinite merit in its fimplicity
of plot and delicacy of fentiment. The hero
determines to wave the exerciſe of power,
in hopes of obtaining by affection what he
could command as a conqueror; the heroine
is ready to facrifice every inclination and
hope of felicity, rather than rebel againſt

*the will of her father, and the rigid laws of her country.*

XXVI. IL RUGGIERO, OVVERO L'EROICO GRA-
TITUDINE. Written at Vienna, for the nuptials of the Arch-duke Ferdinand with the Princefs of Modena , and firft performed at Milan, 1771, to mufic compofed by *Haffe*. This was the laft production of the great Poet, and excellent Mufician ; who had both exceeded their 70th year. The *heroic gratitude* of *Ruggiero* towards a rival to his fame and love, who had generoufly faved his life and refcued him from prifon, is the characteriftic virtue of this drama. Superficial young critics have pretended to difcover the coldnefs and fterility of old age in the words and mufic of this opera; but however inferior to the more early productions of thefe illuftrious authors, more intelligent and candid judges difcovered fcene and fentiments in the poetry, and elegance and propriety in the mufic, of which, at the time they were produced, none but Metaftafio and Haffe could have been the authors.

THE

THE prefent Work having been undertaken as a kind of fupplement to the *General Hiftory of Mufic*, it is hoped that the mufical reader will not be offended if a few reflections are added here concerning each clafs of Metaftafio's poetical productions for mufic. And firft, of the OPERA, or *Secular Mufical Drama*, in the ftate to which it was brought by our Lyric Poet.

The moft judicious critics of Italy, where the Melodrama is beft underftood, after analyfing the dramas of this author, and witneffing the failure of his fucceffors, are of opinion, that " good tafte in theatrical reprefentations in mufic was born and died with Metaftafio." All the great Tragic Poets of Greece preceded the formation of the rules of the art by Ariftotle. Rules are now drawn from the dramatic works of Metaftafio, which can never be fulfilled but by imitation. And as poetry is derived from foul and fentiment, not from line and rule, and genius is an enemy to reftraint and violence, whoever thinks it neceffary to

imitate

imitate Metaſtaſio, even with equal genius, muſt be in trammels. And yet, if *he* is quite right, what can new candidates for dramatic fame, in writing for muſic, do better than to imitate him? It is impoſſible to diſcover new, eaſy, and pleaſant roads, in a country which he has ſo often interſected, without purſuing, or at leaſt croſſing, ſome of his paths.

Apoſtolo Zeno ſeems to have been the Eſchylus, and Metaſtaſio the Sophocles and Euripides of the modern Melodrama. What preceded and is ſubſequent to them, appears equally to partake of the wildneſs and weakneſs of their predeceſſors and ſucceſſors in Greece and Italy.

When any *ſtyle* of poetry or muſic is brought to perfection, little is left to be done for a long while, but to imitate and vary the thoughts and paſſages of that ſtyle. Milton's epic, Pope's ſatirical and epiſtolary ſtyle, in poetry, and Pergoleſi's in muſic, muſt be worn out and nearly forgotten, perhaps, before new ſtyles can be formed or favoured. Handel left nothing new to be done in *his* ſtyle of compoſition. Imitations are ever timid and feeble. What has been happily accompliſhed without rules or model,

del, cannot be achieved with the fame energy, enthufiafm, and effect, by a *Receipt.* All great originals, fuch as Homer, Pindar, and Shakfpeare, either preceded, or defpifed rules.

Novelty is wanting at prefent, both to Poetry and Mufic ; but the time, or at leaft the daring and inventive genius, is not yet arrived for either. The Oratorios of Handel, fublime as are the choruffes and many of the fongs, from having been fo often heard, have tired the public ear, and yet no other attempts are liftened to with patience. It is fo with opera airs and playhoufe fongs : eternal imitation and repetition of what we have heard a thoufand and a thoufand times, renders our mufical theatres a confufed and ill-bred *converfazione,* more than an interefting performance of poetry and mufic (*x*).

Signor Saverio Mattei, in his differtation *on the Philofophy of Mufic* (*y*), has made

(*x*) This complaint is confined to the generality of *Vocal Mufic.* The new Symphonies of HAYDN preclude all converfation, by their never-failing novelty, and the inexhauftible fertility of his invention. Almoft all other mufic is little more than a *Cento,* which can never grapple with *attention.*

(*y*) SALMI, Tomo V.

many

many juft reflections on the declenfion of
the mufical drama in Italy, which are not
totally inapplicable elfewhere. He fays, that
" every fpecies of voice, from the ambition
of foaring with the lark, and mounting to
fublimity, has loft its true quality and character. The *Bafe* tries to rival the Tenor,
the *Tenor* the Counter-tenor, the *Counter-
tenor* the Soprano, and the *Soprano* the Fla-
geolet, or bird-pipe.

The improvements in mufical inftruments
and inftrumental compofition have been the
ruin of vocal mufic. Inftruments, for want
of vocal expreffion, multiply notes and
long divifions. But it degrades a finger to
run races with hautbois, flutes, and fid-
dles. Let inftrumental performers fhew
their power of hand, and the genius of their
feveral inftruments; but let not the human
voice quit the fentiments and expreffions of
humanity, and the paffions that belong to
its nature : let inftruments imitate birds and
beafts ; but let not the human voice imitate
the tricks and tones of inftruments, to
which it fhould ferve as a model : let its in-
flections be purely *vocal*, and fuch as will
pleafe, not difgrace, humanity.

Another obfervation of Signor Mattei,

3                                    feems

feems naturally to account for the rapid decline of the Opera, as far as concerns Poetry and Mufic. " At prefent," fays this judicious Critic, " the emoluments of the principal perfons employed in a mufical drama are fettled in a direct contrary ratio to what they ought to be. At Naples, the manager of the Opera affigns to the firft Dancer 2000 fequins; to the firft Singer 1000; to the Compofer 200; and to the Poet 50; whereas the whole arrangement fhould be reverfed : the higheft falary fhould be given to the Poet; the fecond to the Compofer; the third to the Singer; and the fourth to the Dancer." And perhaps, if thefe falaries were fettled, like an Englifh county election, by public fuffrage, this would be the general opinion. As it is, fays Signor Mattei, " Opera talents are proportioned to the pay : the dancer is better than the finger, the performance of the finger better than the intrinfic merit of the *fcore* or compofition, and the worft of all is the poetry, ftolen from Metaftafio, and totally fpoiled by the poetafter, who botches it together." From this ftate of things it muft appear in vain to hope for a good Opera, or a reform in the eftablifhed fyftem.

Subjects

Subjects of dignity, heroifm, and great paffions, are ruined in the Italian Opera, by the kind of voice which ever claims the principal part. If, then, the ftyle of finging were a little fimplified, and fele{Et} *Tenor* voices, highly cultivated, were affigned the principal parts, the poetry would have its effect, as well as the mufic ; and *Cato*, *Themiftocles*, and *Regulus*, would appear with dignity and propriety, though they fpoke in fong (z). If the exquifite voices and refinements in finging of the *Evirati* cannot be difpenfed with, let them be employed in female parts, as is conftantly the cafe at Rome, and as, in our Shakfpeare's time, was the cafe with all the female parts on our ftage, which were performed by boys.

Italy, ever fertile in genius, cannot be in want of men of abilities equal to the difficult tafk of finding out a new path in an art thought to be already brought to perfection.

The prefent fyftem of giving the principal man's part to a *Soprano* voice, muft confine the Poet to love, tendernefs, and effemi-

(z) There can be no doubt but that the little fuccefs and infrequency of the performance of thefe heroic dramas, were occafioned by the principal part being written for a *Tenor* voice.

nate

nate characters and paffions. At prefent, the Italians condefcend to imitate the noife, machinery, and *Balets analogues* of France; and thefe often fupply the place of good poetry as well as mufic. A *Spectacle*, however fplendid, muft fatigue the eye, if the mind has nothing to do.

It feems neceffary here to take fome notice of the mutual complaints of Metaftafio himfelf, and his learned friend Mattei, of the neglect of Poetry and abufe of Execution on the Opera Stage.

It is natural and juft that poets fhould wifh to fimplify *Dramatic Mufic*. But perhaps it would not be for the intereft, even of the words, to ftrip it of all ornaments and opportunities of difplaying a fine voice and fuperior vocal abilities. Some latitude may furely be given to the compofer and performer in the airs, when it is confidered that the whole bufinefs of the Drama, in carrying on the plot and developing characters in Metaftafio's Operas, is tranfacted in the *Recitatives*, and that the airs are merely recapitulations of each fcene, and illuftrations of the principal incident or affection on which it is founded. I would willingly facrifice all fuperfluous ornaments and fcience

in

in the compofition of *Mufical Dramas*, out of refpect to the POETRY ; but I cannot join in the contempt which lyric poets put upon inftrumental mufic in general. Good finging is infinitely more uncommon than good playing ; and though the moft pleafing power an inftrument can poffefs, is that of imitating' the voice, yet both ftringed and wind inftruments of the firft clafs have their peculiar qualities both of expreffion and execution. The productions of Corelli, Geminiani, Handel, and Tartini, for violins, long gave lovers of mufic infinite delight, when well executed, without the affiftance of the voice ; and fince their reign, the productions of Stamitz, Bach, Abel, Boccherini, Haydn, Vanhal, Pleyel, &c. have fo much merit of compofition, and effect in performance, that they not only make us forget our cares, but all the enchantments of vocal mufic.

---

## SACRED DRAMAS,

OR,

## *ORATORIOS.*

1. LA PASSIONE DI GIESU CRISTO. Written in 1730, at Rome, by order of the Emperor Charles VI. Set by *Caldara*, and performed in

in the Imperial Chapel at Vienna, in Paſſion-
week.

II. SANT' ELENA AL CALVARIO. Written at
Vienna for Paſſion-week, and ſet by *Caldara*
for the Imperial Chapel, 1731.

III. I A MORTE D'ABEL. For the ſame place
and occaſion, 1732. Set by *Reutter*.

IV. GIUSEPPE RICONOSCIUTO. Set by *Porſile*,
for ditto, 1733.

V. BETULIA LIBERATA. 1734. *Reutter*, for ditto.

VI. G OAS RE DI GIUDA. 1735. Ditto.

VII. ISACCO FIGURA DEL REDENTORE. 1740.
Ditto.

Beſides the above ſeven Oratorios for the
Imperial Chapel, he wrote a Sacred Drama,
PER LA FESTIVATA DEL SANTO NATALE,
at Rome, in 1727, for *Cardinal Ottoboni* (*a*),
which was ſet by *Giovanni Coſtanza*, and
performed in a theatre, with ſcenes, and in
action (*b*).

Calſabigi (in the Preface to the Paris Edition of Metaſtaſio's Works, 1755) in ſpeaking of theſe Oratorios, ſays, that " Metaſta-

(*a*) It is ſaid, by ſome of Metaſtaſio's biographers,
that *Cardinal Ottoboni* was his god-father, and that the
Poet received the name of *Pietro* in honour of this illuſtrious ſponſor.

(*b*) In the *Nice* edition of theſe Oratorios, all the texts
of Scripture are indicated in the notes.

fio, by adapting his beautiful poetry to facred ftory, under the moſt ſevere laws of the Drama, has produced Tragedies as perfect as this kind of compoſition will allow." And Saverio Mattei, who is of the ſame opinion, and ſeems anxiouſly to wiſh for a theatre at Naples wholly appropriated to *Sacred Dramas*, during Lent, ſays, that " the Greeks went to a play as to a *ſpiritual exerciſe*, or as we go to a ſermon." And it is well known from Livy's account, that the Romans, in times of public calamity, flew to the theatre; and that the firſt introduction of Dramas with Muſic was occaſioned by the plague.

Mattei wiſhes the muſic of oratorios to be grave, learned, and ſublime. " Young muſicians (ſays he) are merely taught counterpoint; which is no more than *concordance* in grammar; but they know nothing of the *philoſophical* or *poetical* part of muſic. Their whole knowledge is mechanical, and they are never out of the grammar. As to different ſtyles of compoſition, they are ſeldom allowed to ſtudy any but that of their maſter. The vocal ſtyles of Vinci, Pergoleſi, Haſſe, Jomelli, Cafaro, and Piccini, are all different, yet all good."

In

In eftablifhing a *facred tragic theatre*, Mattei not only wifhes the inimitable oratorios of Metaftafio to be new fet by the greateft mafters, without humouring the caprice of fuch fingers as are only capable of finging in one ftyle, or of executing a particular paffage or trick, which muft neceffarily be introduced in every fong they fing; but, above all, to have the poetry refpected, and the precepts of *Joafh*, *Jofeph*, *Judith*, &c. heard with reverence. His plan extends to the works of the moft folid and fcientific compofers of the laft age; fuch as Leo, Haffe, and Jomelli, which he would have revived, and performed without changing a fyllable or a note (c).

Befides his regular oratorios, in two parts, Metaftafio wrote feveral facred poems, which breathe great fervour of devotion (d).

ODE

(c) It does not appear that Signor Mattei wifhes to have facred dramas performed in *action*; that would be a revival of *Myfteries* and *Moralities*. Oratorios have long been performed in feveral churches at Rome every Sunday evening, in the ftill manner of HANDEL's Oratorios in England, but to a light and feeble mufic, and executed by an inferior band.

(d) Metaftafio was very firm in his religious faith, and difcouraged fceptical and light difcuffions of facred fubjects:

ODE SOPRA IL SANTISSIMO NATALE; or, Ode
for the birth of Chrift.

PARAPHRASE ON THE MISERERE, or Fifty-firft
Pfalm.

HYMN TO SAINT JULIAN.

This laft was written about the year 1751,
for the Italian chapel at Vienna, where it
ftill continues to be fung. In a letter to his
brother Leopold, about this time, he expreffes his own pious rapture at the unexpected commiffion which Pope Benedict XIV
had given him to inform the poet of his
Holinefs's paternal and benevolent remembrance. And, finding that the *fervus fervorum* was much pleafed with his hymn to
St. Julian, he fays, " It is hardly to be imagined what pleafure the people of Roman
catholic ftates in Germany, have in fuch
fpiritual fongs, when allowed to fing them
in their own language ; or the raptures which
pious fentiments, clothed in majeftic harmony, excite. But it is not an enterprife
for every one to attempt. With the affiftance of *Jomelli,* and better health, I fhould

jects : telling his friends, that, " for the peace of his
confcience, he found religious myfteries more eafy to
believe than to inveftigate."

be

be tempted to venture in this fea; but thefe are only *pia defiderata (c).*"

---

## OCCASIONAL DRAMAS

### FOR

### MUSIC AND THEATRIC REPRESENTATION,

#### OF ONE AND TWO ACTS ONLY.

La Galatea, Endimione, Angelica; Sere-natas, written at Naples between the year 1721 and 1723, and fet by *Porpora.* Thefe were never meant for action, but to be per-formed in ftill life, like our oratorios.

Gli Orti Esperedi, written for the Emprefs Elizabeth's birth-day, 1721.

L'Isola disabitata, written in 1752, for the court of Spain, fet by *Bonno.*

---

## FESTE TEATRALE,

### OR

#### FESTAL DRAMAS FOR MUSIC.

La Contesa de'Numi; or, Contention of the Gods, written at Rome, 1729, and fet by

(c) His brother poet, our countryman, Mafon, like-wife writes divine hymns, and encourages metrical pfal-mody in our parifh churches.

*Vinci*, for Cardinal Polignac, in celebration of the birth of the Dauphin, father of Louis XVI.

Il Tempio dell'Eternita, written at Vienna, for the birth-day of the Empress Elizabeth, and set by *Fouchs*, 1731.

L'Asilo d'Amore, written at Vienna, 1732, and set by *Caldara*; afterwards augmented, 1765, and new set by *Gasman*.

Le Grazie vendicate, "Defence of the Graces," written at Vienna, for the performance of the two Arch-dutchesses, Maria Teresa, and Marianna, with a Lady of the Imperial court, on the Empress Elizabeth's birth-day, 1735. Set by *Caldara*.

Il Sogno di Scipione. "Scipio's Dream," written for the birth-day of the Emperor Charles VI, 1735. Set by *Predieri*.

Il Palladio conservato. Set by *Reutter*, 1735. Performed by two Arch-dutchesses and another Lady.

Le Cinesi. Written first for three Ladies only, at the Imperial court, 1735, and set by *Reutter.* But afterwards, with an additional character, it was performed by professed singers, at the Prince of *Saxon-Hilburghausen's*, in the presence of their Imperial majesties, Francis I, and Maria Theresa, 1752.

Il Parnaso accusato, e difeso. Set by *Reutter*. Vienna, 1738.

La Pace fra la Virtù, e la Bellezza. For the

the birth-day of the Arch-dutchefs MARIA
THERESA, 1738. Set by *Predieri*.

In this little drama, VENUS's ELOGE on Beauty,
is admirable.

—————————————*Luce divina,*
*Raggio del Cielo è la Bellezza, e rende*
*Celefti anche gli oggetti in cui rifplende.*
*Quefta l' alma più tarde*
*Solleva al ciel, come folleva il fole*
*Ogni baffo vapor. Quefta a' mortali*
*Della penofa vita*
*Tempra le noje, e ricompenfa i danni.*
*Quefta in mezzo agli affanni*
*Gl'infelici allegra : in mezzo all'ire*
*Quefta placa i tiranni : i lenti fprona,*
*I fugaci incatena,*
*Anima i vili, i temerarj affrena ;*
*E del fuo dolce impero,*
*Che letizia conduce,*
*Che diletto produce ove fi ftende,*
*Sente ognuno il poter, neffun l'intende.*

The light divine of beauty's heav'nly ray
   Gives power celeftial wherefoe'er it fhines ;
The fluggifh foul it renders light and gay,
   As vapours grofs the fun to mount inclines.

The ills of life it tempers, clears its gloom,
   And pays the labour of the hardeft toil ;
Affliction cheers in fate's fevereft doom,
   And fooths the horrors of defeat and fpoil.

The

The fierceft tyrant's rage it foon can quell,
 Can fpur the flow, and chain the fugitive;
Can animate the dull, the rafh repel,
 And joy ineffable to all can give.


Astrea Placata. For the Emprefs's birth-day, 1739. Set by *Predieri*.

Il natal di Giove. For the Emperor's birth-day, 1740. Set by *Bonno*.

L'Amor prigioniero. Vienna, 1741. Set by *Reutter*.

Il vero Omaggio. Set by *Bonno*, 1743.

Augurio di felicita. A cantata. Set by *Reutter*, and performed by three Arch-dutch-éffes, 1749.

La rispettosa tenerezza. For the perform-ance of three Arch-dutcheffes, on the Em-prefs queen's birth-day, 1750. Set by *Reutter*.

Tributo di rispetto e d'amore. Performed by three Arch-dutcheffes, on the Emperor's birth-day. Set to mufic by *Reutter*.

La Gara. Performed by an Arch-dutchefs, and two Ladies of the Imperial court, on the birth of the Arch-dutchefs Maria Antonia, afterwards queen of France, 1755. Set by *Reutter*.

Il Sogno. Performed by the Arch-dutchefs Marianna, and two Ladies, 1756. Set by *Reutter*.

LA

La Ritrosia disarmata, Peevifhnefs dif-
armed.  Written for the court of Spain,
1759.

Alcide al bivio.  Written for the nuptials of
the Arch-duke Jofeph, 1760, and fet to
mufic by *Haffe*.

L'Ape, or the Bee.  Written for the court of
Spain, 1760.

L'Atenaide, ovvero affetti generosi.
Written for the performance of five Arch-
dutcheffes.  Set by *Bonno*, 1762.

Egeria.  Set by *Haffe*, for the coronation of
Jofeph II, king of the Romans, 1764.

Il Parnaso confuso.  Set by *Gluck*, and performed by four Arch-dutcheffes, at the fecond
nuptials of Jofeph II, 1765.

La Corona, a drama of one act, for the performance of four Arch-dutcheffes.  Set by
*Gluck*, 1765.

La pace fra le tre Dee, a feftal entertainment, written for the court of Spain, 1765.

Partenope ditto, written at Vienna, for the
marriage of Ferdinand IV, king of the
two Sicilies, with the Arch-dutchefs Maria
Josephina, 1767.  Set by *Haffe*.

———————

In thefe compofitions, however fhort, we
always find vivacity in the action and dia-

logue,

logue, grandeur and truth of character, a happy delineation of the affections, clearnefs, fpirit, a melodious arrangement of the words and phrafes, force in the recitatives, and elegance in the airs; the moft found philofophy in the fentiments, and fancy and good tafte in the decorations and machinery. So that it is manifeft, that it was the poet's wifh at once to feed the imagination, delight the ear, enlighten the underftanding, and move the heart.

Thefe feftal pieces, though too fhort for operas, or a whole night's entertainment, may be compared to the French *petites piéces*, or our fhort dramas (not farces) of one, two, or three acts.

It has been obferved by an Italian critic (*d*), that, " In thefe fhort pieces the poet has frequently treated of ferious and philofophical matters, too profound and complicated for a mixt audience in a public theatre: fuch as the immortality of the foul, harmony of the fpheres, or of creation; but in all, we find the pureft principles of virtue and morality given to the interlocutors, who

(*d*) Giamb. Aleff. Morefchi.

were

were generally Arch-dukes and Arch-dutcheffes."

Court poems, birth-day odes, &c. ufed to be compofed of fuch childifh mythology, and naufeous flattery, as no man of good tafte and found judgment would even deign to read ; but thefe feftal compofitions of Metaftafio are fuch, as not only the lovers of poetry, but moral philofophers, will read with equal pleafure.

## CANTATAS.

The firft cantatas which our author feems to have written, were twelve, which he produced exprefsly for Porpora, before he left Italy. Saverio Mattei avers that he has found a copy of thefe cantatas at Naples, with the mufic, in the hand writing of Porpora, who calls them twelve *Cantate dell' Abate Metaftafio*. In 1735, while this compofer was in England, he publifhed his mufic to thefe cantatas, in 4to, and dedicated them to his Royal Highnefs FREDERIC PRINCE of WALES. I have a copy of this work now before me ; and though time has robbed the airs of fome of their priftine

novelty

novelty and grace, the recitatives are ftill admirable. Indeed, the Italian recitative, which received its laft forms and polifh chiefly from the elder SCARLATTI (Aleffandro) and PORPORA, feems as fixed and permanent as a dead language ; and, while melody is as fluctuating as the waves of the fea, recitative feems in ftability to refemble *terra firma.*

The poetry of fome of thefe cantatas was improved and polifhed by Metaftafio, and publifhed with others, in editions of his works, which, late in life, he fuperintended. Seventeen cantatas appear in the laft Paris edition, which have been fet by Sarti, Mortellari, and the principal compofers of the prefent times.

Befides thefe, there appear in the *Nice* edition, two cantatas of a comic caft :

LA CIOCCOLATA,
ED
IL TABACCO,

Suppofed to be written in his early youth ; with two others, for two voices, in dialogue :

LA DANZA
ED
IL CICLOPE.

And

And the five following fhort pieces, written
for the Imperial Court, which are likewife
ftiled CANTATAS :

I. LA VIRTUOSA EMULAZIONE. 1751. Set by
Reutter.

II. L'AURORA, & L'ESTATE. Set by Wagenfeil, 1759.

III. L'INVERNO, ovvero LA PROVIDA PASTO-
RELLA. 1760. Set by Wagenfeil.

IV. IL QUADRO ANIMATO. 1760. Wagenfeil,
for two voices.

V. L'ARMONICA. 1769. Set by Haffe (e).

---

## CANZONETTE.

CANZONETTA, for a dance of ruftics, fet
by Bonno, in 1740, for the Arch-dutchefs
of Auftria, Maria Therefa, afterwards
Princefs of Lorain, and other ladies of the
Imperial Court.

I. LA PRIMAVERA, Spring. Written at Rome,
1719.

(e) This cantata was written by fovereign command,
for Mifs CECILIA DAVIES, to *fing* at the Imperial Court
to the accompaniment of her fifter, on the *Harmonica,*
or *Glaffes.*

II. L'ESTATE,

---

## SONNETS.

On the celebrated mufical compofer, Gasparini, at Rome, 1719.

With Twenty-eight more, on various fubjects and occafions.

Metaftafio owns, in one of his letters, that he does not think his genius happily formed for a *Sonnetteer* ; and it *does* feem, as if he had felt the reftraint and difficulty of its conftruction. His fonnets being by no means fo fuperior to thofe of other lyric bards, ancient and modern, as many of his more happy productions.

---

## COMPLIMENTI.

Thefe are fhort poetical felicitations, which were fet to mufic by Haffe, Wagenfeil, and Reutter, and performed at Court on birth-days,

days, by the Arch-dutcheſſes, before their
Imperial Majeſties. They appear in the
*Nice* edition, for the firſt time, among the
poſthumous works of our author, eight in
number, ſome for one, and ſome for two
voices.

---

## STROFE PER MUSICA,

### DA CANTARSI A CANONE;

#### OR SHORT STANZAS TO BE SUNG IN ROUNDS, OR CANONS.

These amount to Thirty-five, many of
them appear in the Italian Collection of
Catches, Rounds, and Canons, brought to
England, by Boroſini, and publiſhed by
Walſh, about the year 1748. Metaſtaſio is
ſaid to have ſet thirty of them himſelf, in
three parts, which are ſuppoſed to be in the
poſſeſſion of his executors, the family of
Martinetz.

---

## INTERMEZZI.

Theſe, two in number, were written by
our author in 1724, to be performed (as was

4                                        then

then the fashion) between the acts of his
DIDONE ABBANDONATA. The dialogue is
carried on with a considerable degree of hu-
mour, between a fantastical and capricious
*Primadonna* (or first woman) and an absurd
*Impresario* (or manager) of an opera.

***

## SIFACE.

This is an old musical drama, of the last
century, which was new written by Metastasio for the use of his friend and music-
master, Porpora, at Venice, where it was
performed, in 1725. We have an ample
account of this labour in one of our author's
letters.

These are his chief works that were written for music.

Of GIUSTINO, a tragedy, produced at
fourteen years of age, on the Greek model,
it has already been said, that it was not
intended for music or recitative in the dialogue, though the chorusses, which terminate
each act, require measured melody. The
resemblance observed (Vol. I. p. 7) between an incident in this tragedy, and
Shakspeare's *Romeo* and *Juliet*, cannot ge-
nerate

nerate a fufpicion of plagiarifm in Metaftafio, if it be remembered, that the plot of
Shakefpeare's tragedy was taken from Ar-
thur Brooke's imitation of the Italian ftory
of *Giulietta*, by *Luigi da Porto* (*f*); and it
was more likely for Metaftafio to copy this
affecting circumftance from his countryman,
than from Shakfpeare, whofe name, at this
early period of his life had probably not arrived at his knowledge; and who had not
availed himfelf of all the advantages of this
afflicting incident, but let Romeo die, before
Juliet revives. And, upon examination, it
appears, from Metaftafio's own declaration,
that the whole plot of his *Giuftino* was taken
from the *Italia liberata* of *Triffino*.

Giuftino, with all its imperfections, is
perhaps the moft grave, regular, and accurate drama, that has ever been produced at
fo early a period of life.

---

## MISCELLANEOUS POEMS

### NOT INTENDED FOR MUSIC.

LA STRADA DELLA GLORIA. *Sogno.* The
Path to Glory; a Dream. Written at Rome,

(*f*) See Malone's Edition of Shakfpeare, 8vo. 1790,
Vol. IX.

in 1718, on the death of his Preceptor and Patron, *Gravina* ; and read by the Author, at a public meeting of the Academy of the Arcadi.

II. La Morte di Catone. The Death of Cato.

III. L'Origine delle Leggi. The Origin of Laws. An Elegy.

Thefe three Poems are written in *Terza Rima*, the verfification of Dante.

---

## EPITALAMI.

I. On the Nuptials of the Prince and Princess di Belmonte. Written at Naples, 1720.

II. On the Marriage of Signor D. Giambatifta Filomarina, 1722.

III. On the Nuptials of Signor D. Francefco Gaetano, and Donna Giovanni Sanseverino. 1723.

---

## IDYLLIUMS.

I. Il Ratto d'Europa.

II. Il convito degli Dei,

III. Teti

III. TETI, E PELÈO.

IV. ODE on the Imperial Refidence at Schon-brunn.

V. I VOTI PUBBLICI, per Maria Terefa, Im-peratrice Regina, 1766.

VI. LA PUBLICA FELICITA. On the Emprefs Queen's Recovery from the Small-pox. 1767.

VII. LA SCOMESSA. The Wager. 1755.

This Quatrain was written, by defire, on the following occafion :——The Emprefs Queen, when pregnant of her youngeft daughter, afterwards Queen of France, laid a wager with Count DIETRIECKSTEIN, that the promifed offspring would be an Arch-dutchefs. As foon as brought to bed, her Imperial Majefty fent word to the Count, that *a Princefs was born, and that two drops of water did not more refemble each other, than the Mother and her Child.* The Count paid his loft-bet with a figure in porcelaine, repre-fenting his own perfon, kneeling on one knee, and holding in his right-hand the following verfes, written on a fmall flip of paper :

*Io perdei : l'Augufta Figlia*
*A pagar mi ha condanata ;*
*Ma s'è ver che a Voi fomiglia,*
*Tutto il mondo ha guadagnata.*

The

The Wager's loft—a Daughter's given!
And I fubmit with joy unfeign'd:
For if like You this gift of Heaven,
'The world entire a prize has gain'd.

VIII. VERSETTI. Lines fent with fome prints
of the Poet's head, to the Marchefa ZAVA-
GLIA.

> Quefte poche immaginette
> Sono, è vero, opre imperfette
>   D'un Artifta dozzinale;
> Ma per me gran pregio avranno
> Se impedirvi almen fapranno
>   D'obbliar l'Originale.

'Tis true thefe little off'rings feem
Unworthy objects of efteem,
  Thus clumfily engrav'd;
Yet bleffings I fhall on them fhower,
If from oblivion, by their power,
  Th' original is fav'd.

IX. Madrigal for Prince HILBERGHAUSEN, to
fend to the QUEEN of ENGLAND, with an
ivory fhuttle, turned by himfelf.

---

## TRANSLATIONS.

III. Tranflation of the Sixth Satire of the Second Book of Horace, in *Terze Rime*.

IV. ———— of the Fifth Epiftle of the Firft Book of Horace, in Stanzas.

V. ———— of the Third Satire of Juvenal.

The *Treatife on the Italian Theatre*, which Metaftafio promifed *Bettinelli*, the Printer, foon after his arrival in Vienna, feems to have ended in his *Eftratto della Poetica d' Ariftotile*; of which, as it is his fole work in Profe, if we except his Letters, and being pofthumous, but little known, we fhall terminate the Catalogue of his Works by fome account.

VI. Estratto dell'Arte Poetica d'Aristotile, *e Confiderazioni fu la Medefima.* An Abftract of Ariftotle's Art of Poetry, with Remarks.

Metaftafio's Introduction, to explain the object of this Abftract, is the following :

" The reputation of Ariftotle, eftablifhed and defended by the univerfal confent and veneration of twenty-two centuries, if not due to the wonderful extent of his fublime talents, and the immenfity of his acquaintance

with every fpecies of fcience, would have
fufficient weight to command the refpect
and gratitude of all fubfequent times, if it
were only remembered, that he was the firft
Philofopher in all antiquity, that we know
of, who was able to form a clear, minute,
and indifputable analyfis of human reafon;
and who, furnifhing it with diftinctions and
divifions, as fo many fecure and neceffary
beacons, has difcovered the road by which
we may moft fafely and courageoufly travel
in the fearch of truth. The having recourfe,
therefore, to fuch an oracle in our doubts
is laudable, efpecially for Poets, whom he
has particularly fupplied with the rules of
their art.

"Perfuaded from my earlieft youth of this
indifpenfible duty, I propofed to acquaint
myfelf, fundamentally, with the poetical doctrines of fuch a mafter : and for this purpofe,
it appeared to me, that the fafeft and moft
certain way to obtain this knowledge pure
and uncorrupted, would be from the original
fountain itfelf, whatever labour it might coft
me: but, perplexed every moment in the
courfe of my labour, fometimes with doubts
concerning a rule which admitted of two
fenfes, fometimes by the obfcurity of an ex-

3                                          preffion

preffion which to me appeared myfterious; now by one precept being apparently contradictory to another, now by a new definition of the fame fubject, totally different from that which had preceded it, and by a hundred difficulties at every ftep, wholly infuperable to my limited faculties; I perceived, at length, with infinite mortification, that, with the inconfiderate temerity of a young man, I had unadvifedly plunged into difficulties, and purfued an intricate road, without companion or guide.

" I had recourfe, therefore, to the moft learned and eminent critics and commentators of Ariftotle's Poetics; and I fhould be ungrateful if I did not confefs myfelf indebted to them for the literal fenfe of many obfcure paffages in the text: but I fhould likewife be very infincere, if I did not declare, at the fame time, that, after all my laborious refearches, I found myfelf, to my great mortification, much lefs enlightened, nay, rather infinitely more perplexed, indetermined, and confufed, than I was before. And, indeed, who could avoid being confounded by the conftant difagreement of men fo refpectable for their learning? Who could help being tired with feeking inftruc-

tion

tion in fo many ufelefs and prolix metaphy-
fical and fcholaftic treatifes, in which the
art they promife to illuftrate is fuffocated?
Who could refrain from indignation, when
fearching in the Greek dramatifts, and in
Ariftotle himfelf, for the paffages cited by
the moft renowned critics as the foundation
of their fovereign decifions, he finds them
(as has frequently been my cafe) *diametri-
cally oppofite*, for the moft part, to their opinions? And, befides this, who could fafely
rely on men, however fkilful in languages,
that were totally without experience in
theatrical matters, and yet convinced of
their own infallibility?

" To extricate myfelf in the beft way
I was able, from fo many doubts, and not
entirely to lofe the fruits of my ftudy and
application, I determined rigoroufly to examine myfelf, and to re-perufe, from the
beginning, Ariftotle's whole Poetics, extract-
ing, chapter by chapter, whatever I could
clearly underftand; and confeffing my ignorance and uncertainty as to the reft; pointing out fuch precepts as, though ufeful perhaps when given, the enormous change of
manners, in fuch a long period of time, has
rendered impracticable; and difcovering what

rules

rules have erroneoufly been affigned by modern legiflators of the drama to the Greek tragedians, and even to Ariftotle himfelf; and by this means form for my own ufe, from the text, a clearer and more diftinct idea of the nature of *Poetry*, *Imitation*, and *Probability*, than is commonly received.

" The indifpenfible duties of that employment to which I had for fo many years been fortunately deftined, had not, till now, allowed me fufficient leifure to execute this tafk as completely as I wifhed : but fince, I have not neglected, at fhort intervals, to meditate on the fubject as much as my neceffary occupations would allow, and to collect together all the materials I was able towards the intended edifice. The day is at length come, when an unufual repofe has finally been granted me by my moft gracious Sovereign ; and I have now, as far as my powers would enable me, fully and exactly terminated my defign.

"But Heaven forbid that I fhould have the prefumption to think of forming by this extract a new Art of Poetry ! The feducing rank of inventor has already produced more Arts of Poetry than will ever be read, or at leaft ftudied and put in practice : indeed,

they

they are more than fufficiently numerous to confound, difcourage, and wholly render dry and arid, the moft happy, courageous, bold, and fertile genius, which the wifdom of beneficent nature can produce.

" The fole object of my labour, was, as much as poffible, to juftify my own conduct to myfelf, who am naturally (for my mif-fortune) the leaft circumfpect of all my judges; and to procure the felf-confolation of being convinced, that all thofe defects from which an uninterrupted experience of more than fifty years, and the inceffant en-deavour to inftruct myfelf, have not been fufficient to exempt me, fhould be numbered among the painful and inevitable confe-quences of human weaknefs."

The title of our author's firft chapter, is the following :

CHAP. I. " That Poetry is one of the arts of *Imitation.* In what it differs from other arts. Explanation of the terms *Me-tre, Rhythm, Harmony, Melody,* and *Modes.* Refutation of the opinion, that compofitions written in profe, can be called Poems. That it is not fufficient for a poetical production to be harmonious, and in meafure ; it ought, likewife, to be noble and elegant."

His

His definitions of the technica of ancient mufic, particularly attracted my attention; and I was flattered to find that they generally agree with thofe that have been given in the *Differtation on the Mufic of the Ancients*. He likewife is of opinion, that the Greeks meant by *Armonia*, what we mean by *Melody*, founding his opinion upon a paffage in Plato: *The regulation of the movement is called* RHYTHM; *but the regulation of the* voice (with refpect to high and low) *is called* Harmony (*g*).

And this is Padre Martini's opinion: *Harmony*, with the ancients, meant the regulation of a fingle voice, with refpect to the intervals of a given fcale or key.

*Melody*, indeed, is not defined as in the Differtation above-mentioned: Metaftafio makes it only a more airy and elegant *kind* of melos; but Ariftotle, in a paffage which he has quoted from him (*h*), does not oppofe *artificial* and *florid* melody to *fimple* and *plain*, but *mufic fung* to *inftrumental mufic:* for ψιλη μυσικη, or ψιλον μελω, *naked* mufic, feems always to imply *inftrumental* mufic, or

(*g*) *De Legib*. Lib. ii.

(*h*) Τὴν δὲ μυσικὴν πάντες εἶναι φαμὲν τῶν ἡδίστων καὶ ψιλὴν ὅσαν καὶ μετὰ μελωδίας. Arift. Polit. Lib. viii. Cap. 5.

*mufic*

*muſic without words. Melodia,* is *melody ſung;*
that is, poetry ſung.

Metaſtaſio thinks *modo* ſometimes confined
to key, and ſometimes to meaſure. Our
old writers on muſic, down to Morley and
Ravenſcroft, applied the word *mood* only to
time or meaſure; but the word *modo,* in Italian, always means key. To the terms *modus,*
*tonos, tropos,* Metaſtaſio gives great latitude,
and refers to Padre Martini for more minute
information. He ſeems of opinion, that,
in antiquity, there was no poetry without
*numbers,* or without *ſinging* (*i*). The *diver-*
*bii* of the ancient Romans, he calls *recita-*
*tive*; and ſuppoſes that in the *cantici,* ſtrophes, antiſtrophes, and epodes, as well as in
the chorus when ſung by all, or by a ſingle
actor, melody (or as we call it *air)* was
uſed.

CHAP. II. Here our author treats
" Of the different objects of imitation.
Difficulty of determining what Ariſtotle
meant by dividing imitable characters into
*beſt, worſt,* and *middle* claſs of good and
bad."

(*i*) In modern times, however, in the church, and in
many of our oratorios, proſe is ſung to meaſured muſic.

CHAP.

Chap. III. " Of the various ways in
which Poets may avail themfelves of the
means and fubjects of Imitation. In what
refpects Homer and Ariftophanes refemble
each other. Reafons affigned by different
people of Greece, for arrogating to themfelves the invention of the drama."

Chap. IV. Poetry is deduced " from the
natural inclination which men have to imitation and fong. Proofs of this opinion produced by Ariftotle: other proofs not given
by him, with regard to mufic, which, perhaps, he did not think neceffary. Differ-
ences between an *imitation* and a *copy;* the
ignorance of which diftinction, produces the
greateft abfurdities. Indifpenfible neceffity
of fong (mufical tones) in fpeaking to the
public. Proofs that all dramas, comedies,
as well as tragedies, were fung throughout
by the Greeks and Romans, are given by
Metaftafio from ten different ancient authors.
Examination of the opinion of Ariftotle,
that Sophocles perfected tragedy, by the
introduction of a third perfonage on the
ftage."

Our author has manifefted much learning
and ingenuity in the courfe of this chapter.
He is, in general, clear and intelligible on

2                                the

the fubject of Imitation : allowing a natural tendency in human creatures, above all other animals, to imitation. " On the ftage, we imitate all kinds of characters, good and bad. We can even imitate the noifes of inferior animals."

His Eloge of Mufic, after faying that the love of it is a natural inftinct of humanity, entirely coincides with my own.

" Who can doubt (fays he) of the efficacy of Mufic on our minds ? Who is it, that has not felt its effects on himfelf, and obferved them in others ? Who fees not that our paffion for this art has introduced it into all human actions? In the fervice of religion, in feftive affemblies, in funeral pomp, and even in military fury, mufic has a confiderable fhare. The moft barbarous and favage nations are pleafed with it : infants liften to it even in the cradle, before the fenfes are perfect, and it calms their complaints. The criminal in a dungeon, the flave in chains, feeking alleviation from their affliction and labour, find it in fong (*k*)."

(*k*) See Preface to *Prefent State of Mufic in France and Italy*, publifhed twelve years before thefe extracts appeared, and anterior to the author's interview with Metaftafio.

*Crura*

*Crura fonant ferro, fed canit inter opus.*

Tibull. L. ii. Elig. 7

—— The fetter'd flave, the drudge of fate,
*Sings,* fhakes his irons, and forgets his ftate.

GRANGER.

Metaftafio gives further reflections from " the ingenious and acute Caftelvetro," on the neceffity of addreffing perfons at a diftance, in mufical tones (*l*). His proofs from Ariftotle, Cicero, Livy, Virgil, Horace, Ovid, Suetonius, Donato, &c. have almoft all been previoufly cited in the *Differtation on the Mufic of the Ancients,* from the fame places, in favour of the opinion, that all the ancient dramas, tragic and comic, were entirely fung, and accompanied, by inftruments.

Dramatic poetry is not only the *imitating* the characters and manners of men, but the imitation of another art: that of mufic. As, according to Metaftafio, " there is no poetry without mufic : the arrangement of words, and different metres, is mufic." In painting, indeed, an artift has natural objects to copy; in poetry, he has them to

(*l*) See *Differtation on the Mufic of the Ancients.*—Chap. on Dramatic Mufic,

defcribe;

defcribe; but what, it may be afked, has a muſician, in *nature*, to *imitate?* Does muſic, in its nature, imitate poetry? I never could clearly underſtand Ariſtotle's meaning, as to muſic being an *imitative art.* Is it an imitation of poetry, in its meaſures and rhythm; and in the tones of ſpeech, lengthened, poliſhed, and impaſſioned?

But my learned and excellent friend, the Rev. T. Twining, in the Second Diſſertation prefixed to his Tranſlation and Notes on ARISTOTLE's TREATISE ON POETRY, has cleared this matter up more to my ſatisfaction than Metaſtaſio, or any of Ariſtotle's commentators that I have ſeen.

The title of my friend's Diſſertation is this: " On the different Senſes of the Word *Imitative*, as applied to Muſic by the Ancients and Moderns." In which he confines muſical *imitations*, to the raiſing *emotions* and *ideas*. And I think the former will include the *paſſions.* There are mere inſtrumental movements, which awaken ideas of *joy*, *ſorrow, tenderneſs, melancholy, ſolemnity, contrition, military ardor*, &c. Thus far it may be allowed the title of an *imitative art.* As to muſic *imitating* human ſpeech, which Dr. Beatie denies, but which Mr. Twining ſeems

to

to have eftablifhed, as much as a matter
that depends on fancy, feeling, and prefent
humour, *can* be eftablifhed ; it is an opinion
to which I fubfcribe (*m*).

Indeed,

(*m*) Mr. Twining, in his Second Differtation, p. 51,
fpeaking of the *imitative* powers of mufic, with admirable
ingenuity, has affigned a ufe for the ancient *enharmonic
genus*, which feems more probable than any thing which
has hitherto been fuggefted on that dark fubjeçt. " *Dramatic* mufic (fays he) is often *ftrictly imitative*. It imitates, not only the *effect* of the words, by exciting correfpondent *emotions*, but alfo the *words* themfelves *immediately*, by tones, accents, inflexions, intervals, and rhythmical movements, *fimilar* to thofe of fpeech. That this
was peculiarly the charaçter of the *dramatic* mufic of the
ancients, feems highly probable, not only from what is faid
of it by ancient authors : but from what we know of
their mufic *in general*; of their fcales, their *genera*, their
fondnefs for *chromatic* and *enharmonic* intervals, which approach fo nearly to thofe fliding and unaffignable inflexions
(if I may fo fpeak) that charaçterize the melody of
fpeech."

It may be thought too fanciful, perhaps, but it feems to
me, as if dancing, mufic, and poetry, were reciprocally
imitations of each other ; it is certain, at leaft, that they
are nearly conneçted, and refemble each other : mufic
imitates the fteps of a dance, and the numbers of verfe.
Hence poetical proportions are, perhaps, called *feet*, and
mufical, *rhythm*. Mufical meafures, times, accents, and
bars, are equally wanted by all the three arts ; and all three
mutually affift each other in the Italian *ballata* (whence our
word

Indeed, I have long experienced and allowed, that by flow, quick, gay, and forrowful movements, mufic, without words, can excite fenfations of various kinds, and remind us of former events and feelings. Farther than this, mufic does not feem an *imitative art.* If it imitates any thing human, important, and impreffive, it is perhaps, the cry of paffion, whether of joy or forrow. It can laugh and be gay; it can grieve and lament, with a little help of imagination. When it has words to exprefs, it fhould be the compofer's and performer's ambition to lengthen and tune the tones of fpeech and paffion ; to imagine what tones of voice, in a certain fituation, would beft, in the language of mufic, excite and enforce the ideas to be expreffed.

The movements in mufic, and meafures in poetry, have fo great an affinity, that their rhythmical effects arife from the fame caufe. An heroic verfe, in grave and folemn fubjects, refembles mufical movements in *adagio, grave,* and *largo,* in common time. This may be purfued to a much greater

word *ballad)* which originally implied an air that was fung to words, and danced at the fame time.

extent than we have room for here (*n*).
But as far as concerns Ariſtotle's doɛtrine,
Mr. Twining's extenſive learning and reading, joined to his knowledge, praɛtice, and
experience in muſic, have enabled him to
explain this hitherto dark and unintelligible
ſubjeɛt, better than a mere ſcholar, or muſician, however deep in his particular faculty,
could poſſibly have done.

Chap. V. of Metaſtaſio's *Eſtratto*, treats
" Of comedy and its authors. Of *comédie
larmoiante*, or ſentimental comedy. In what
particulars epic poems and tragedies agree,
and in what they differ. Of the *unity* of
*time*, of *fable*, and of *place*." In this chapter, the *unities* are admirably explained, and
their doɛtrine, to my comprehenſion, well
confuted, and relinquiſhed, by Metaſtaſio ;
who has proved, that the Greek tragic writers themſelves had no ſuch narrow limits.
He gives the *time* and *place* of the chief dramas of antiquity, Greek and Latin, in all
which theſe unities are violated. The unity
of aɛtion or fable, ſeems more particularly

(*n*) M. Marpurg, of Berlin, has written a Treatiſe in
German, on the comparative length and accents of muſical
notes, and lingual ſyllables. *Anleitung zur Singcompoſition.*
4to. 1758.

recom-

recommended by Ariſtotle, and more conſtantly obſerved than either of the other
two, by the ancients. This precept, Metaſtaſio tells us, he has himſelf obeyed, as much
as poſſible : " as the fixing the attention of
the ſpectator upon one illuſtrious and intereſting character, muſt produce a more ſenſible and perfect effect, than when divided."
But even this rule, he ſays, muſt be conſtrued with diſcretion and exceptions, or elſe
what would become of the beautiful epiſodes
of Homer and Virgil, and the ſecondary
characters in the ancient dramas ? Metaſtaſio, in his more than fifty years ſtudy and
experience, has by his works, diſcovered
what *can* be practiſed with effect, and what
ought to be avoided, better than all the poetics
of mere theoriſts, can ever teach to dramatic writers (*o*).

CHAP.

(*o*) Mr. Twining, in a liberal and comprehenſive note
on that part of Ariſtotle's poetics which treats of the UNI-
TIES, after proving that Dacier, and other commentators,
have erroneouſly aſſerted that the Stagirite literally and
rigorouſly meant by the *unity of time* to confine the action
of a tragedy to the limits of a *ſingle day*, or nearly ſo ;
and that the Greek tragic writers *have always adhered to
this rule*, ſays : " For this, and other inſtances of the
ſame kind, I muſt content myſelf with referring the reader
to

CHAP. VI. " Definition, divifion, and explanation, of the feveral parts of tragedy. Purgation of the paffions confidered—and whether it is produced only by means of terror and compaffion ?"

CHAP. VII. " Of the component parts and length of tragedy."

CHAP. VIII. " The unity of hero (the principal character) does not imply unity of action."

CHAP. IX. " Difference between a poet and an hiftorian. A piece in verfe, though the fubject is neither epic nor dramatic, is neverthelefs a poem. Of epifodic fables. Of furprize, and its different degrees."

CHAP. X. " Divifion, and explication of fables. Defence of Corneille."

to the fenfible and well written *Eftratto della Poetica d'Ari-ftotile*, publifhed among the pofthumous works of Metafta-fio, and which did not fall into my hands, till all my notes were written. It contains many ingenious and fagacious obfervations. The fubject of the dramatic unities, in particular, is difcuffed at large; and, I think, in a very mafterly and fatisfactory way. And, with refpect to the ftrict unities of *time* and *place*, he feems perfectly to have fucceeded in fhewing, that no fuch rules were impofed on the Greek poets by the critics, or by themfelves—nor *are* impofed on *any* poet, either by the *nature* or the *end* of the dramatic imitation itfelf."

Chap. XI. " Of difcoveries and revolutions, and their different kinds and effects. Of paffion. Doubts concerning the modern French rule, of not fhedding blood on the ftage."

Chap. XII. " Of the length and proportion of the feveral parts of tragedy. Of the chorus. Of the number of acts and perfonages. Of the airs in modern operas."

The chorus, for the lofs of which the enthufiafts for antiquity make fuch heavy complaint, was originally a religious hymn to Bacchus, at the time of vintage. The acts of the drama were long called *epifodes*, after they became of more confequence than the chorus itfelf; but the public, long ufed to them, would not fuffer a drama to be performed without a chorus, even when it had no connexion with the fable. At length, it became fo vulgar and uninterefting, that, like a company of modern pfalmodifts in a country church, the choral fingers were left in the midft of their performance by the audience, at the end of the piece, who would not ftay to hear them longer than they could help. But though Metaftafio cenfures the abfurdity of this permanent chorus to every drama, he does not think it neceffary to

banifh

banifh every fpecies of chorus from the
ftage. " The theatre would lofe the privilege of availing itfelf with dignity, delight,
and probability, of a chorus in facrifices,
triumphs, feafts, and on many fimilar occafions, in which it is extremely natural to
fuppofe, that many perfons may concur in
the fame fentiments, and exprefs themfelves
in the fame words." He gives many other
inftances, where a chorus may be introduced
with propriety.

He then proceeds to confider the number
of acts, into which a dramatic fable fhould
be divided; and difputes the rule which
feems to be laid down by Horace for five
acts; fhewing, from a paffage in one of
Cicero's letters, that the ufual number of
acts in that orator's time, was three. And
this was fo long eftablifhed into a law for
operas in Italy, that feveral attempts at five
acts, were there much difcountenanced. The
late philofopher, Diderot, was of opinion,
that three acts would be the beft divifion of
every drama : as they furnifhed a *beginning*,
a *middle*, and an *end* (*p*). However, to fave
the expence and trouble of a third DANCE

(*p*) This divifion includes the perfect *whole*, required
by Ariftotle.

B B 2                                    (at

(at prefent the moft attractive part of an opera) the whole bufinefs of mufical dramas, whatever it may be, muft conftantly be huddled into *two acts*. Metaftafio candidly and liberally fays, that " the number of acts in every drama fhould more depend on the bufinefs to be tranfacted, than on rule and cuftom." But that operas, originally written in three acts, like all thofe of this poet himfelf, fhould be cut, mangled, and *crufhed*, rather than compreffed, into *two acts*, for no better reafon, is treating the remains of the venerable bard with the utmoft indignity, not to fay ftupid barbarity.

After an ample difcuffion of the chorus and number of acts and characters, in the ancient tragedy, Metaftafio fays: " Before we quit thefe fubjects, it may be neceffary to enquire into the *Revolutions* of the chorus, and to what end its different motions were eftablifhed; fometimes moving to the left, like the *primum mobile*; fometimes revolving, like the planets, to the right; and fometimes remaining ftationary, like the earth. But of the ufe and beauty of thefe aftronomical reprefentations, invented by the ancients, or afcribed to them by the ingenuity of modern critics, let every one judge

for

for himfelf. All that feems neceffary for us to fay on this fubject, is, that (in performing the odes) the fongs or ftanzas which the chorus fung in thefe revolutions, took the names of *ftrophe*, that is, *revolution; anti- ftrophe, counter-revolution*; and *epode, addi- tion to the fong.* That the poet, in writing thefe ftrophes, antiftrophes, and epodes, compofed them in a different meafure from the reft of the tragedy; fometimes quitting the Iambic, availing himfelf of the more quick and lively anapæftic and trochaic feet: connecting together a certain determinate number of verfes, adapted to a particular periodical melody, which might be often repeated to other words in the fame meafure and cadence: that this more artificial mufic, which took its name from the revolutions above-mentioned, was not only fung by the chorus alone, but fometimes by turns with the actors, and fometimes by the actors without the chorus. And finally, it is ob- fervable, that thefe determinate melodies, which may be repeated to different words, are exactly of the fame kind as the odes, fongs, and canzonets, in Italy, which have been faithfully preferved in their form and name, being ftill univerfally called *ftrofe* and *ftro-*

*fette.*

*fette.* Now what elfe are the AIRS of our mufical dramas, but the ancient *ſtrophes* (*q*)? And why fuch an out-cry againſt thefe viſible and manifeſt relics of the Greek theatre; and from thofe very learned folks, who are always recommending to us the imitation of it?

CHAP. XIII. " Of the Protagoniftes, or principal character, and of the unhappy cataftrophe, recommended by Ariftotle."

CHAP. XIV. " Of terror, compaffion, and the wonderful. Of the different kinds of tragical actions."

Ariftotle allows of but four events, that are proper fubjects for tragedy. The *firſt* is when the principal perfonage knows the evil which he or fhe is perpetrating : as Medea, when fhe murders her children.

The *ſecond*, when the hero or heroine is ignorant of the atrocious deed, till after it is committed : as Oedipus, Alcmœon, and Telegonus.

(*q*) This defcription feems almoſt to fit our old opera fongs, in times of *da capo*, if the ftrophe and antiftrophe be imagined the firft and fecond ftrain of the air, and the epode, *the addition to the ſong*. And a number of verfes to the fame periodical melody, refembles our ballads, or fongs of many ftanzas, to each of which the fame air is repeated.

The

The *third*, when the perfonage, through ignorance, is on the point of committing fome horrid action, but is prevented by a fudden difcovery, as Merope and Iphigenia.

The *fourth* (which Ariftotle regards as the worft and moft contemptible) when a character is about to commit a crime, but ftops fhort at the inftant he is going to execute his defign : as Hæmon, in the Antigone of Sophocles, who was determined to kill his father.

" Now this fourth tragic circumftance (fays Metaftafio) which is fo much difapproved by Ariftotle, appears to me (with all due deference to fo great a mafter) capable of being excellently treated. If Hæmon, for example, when in the laft agonies near his dying Antigone, fhould have fuddenly feen his father Creon appear, who had fo unjuftly and barbaroufly been the caufe of her death, and in a blind impetus of paffion had determined to kill him, but in the very act of giving the blow, overcome by the paternal looks and voice, which he had been accuftomed to reverence, had found himfelf unable to fummon courage fufficient to overcome the compunctions of nature and long habits ; and, therefore, being unable to fave

B B 4

his

his wife, or to avenge her death, in the
violence of his rage and defpair, if he had
killed *himfelf*, the cataftrophe would have
been one of the moft fpirited and affecting,
that can be imagined : fince it would exprefs
at once the higheft degree of intereft, which
love, nature, rage, and defpair, united, could
produce. Nor would there be wanting the
indifpenfible Ariftotelian *pathos*, that is, the
emotion which arifes from the view of the
dying and the wounded."

With refpect to confining all the fenfations
excited by tragedy, to terror and pity, Metaftafio fays : " All the juft refpect which I
feel for this great philofopher, is not fufficient to convince me, that tragedy, in its
operations, can avail itfelf of no other inftruments than Terror and Compaffion. It
appears to me, that the admiration of virtue, under a thoufand different afpects; as
friendfhip, gratitude, patriotifm, fortitude,
generofity to foes, and innumerable other
modifications ; as well as the abhorrence of
the vices of the human heart, which often
impede and oppofe thefe virtues ; all thefe,
I fay, appear to me efficacious, and fair
means of affording delight and inftruction,
without eternally condemning the fpectator
to

to tremble with horror, or weep with affliction."

From this paffage, and from the whole tenour of his life and writings, it is manifeft, that Metaftafio was no *terrorift*. And though Ariftotle, in the thirteenth chapter of his Art of Poetry, has pronounced, " *that* to be the beft conftructed tragedy which ends *unhappily*;" yet Mr. Twining, in his notes on this chapter, after allowing that " nothing feems more juft, or more accurately expreffed, than Ariftotle's idea of the end of tragedy; that it is *to give that pleafure, which arifes from pity and terror, through* imitation" — την απο ελεας και φοβε δια μιμησεως ηδονην παρασκευαζειν—Cap. xiv, (Tranfl. P. II. fect. 13.) very much to my fatisfaction, adds, " but the Greek tragedians will be thought, I believe, by moft modern readers, to have fometimes pufhed this principle rather too far, and to have excited a degree of horror, which even the charms of imitation cannot well be conceived to have foftened into pleafurable emotion ; and it appears to to me, that Ariftotle himfelf inclined to this opinion, and that he intended this chapter as a leffon of caution to the poets againft this excefs. He feems plainly to have confidered

4 the

the *actual* murder of a mother, a fon, a
brother, and the like, as incidents rather
too horrible to be exhibited in *any* way.  If
the deed *muft* be done, let it, he fays, if
poffible—if the ftory will permit it—be done
ignorantly.  But it will be ftill better, if you
can avoid doing it entirely ; if you can contrive to make the *expectation*, combined with
the *atrocioufnefs* of the event expected, anfwer your purpofe, by raifing as much anxiety, commifferation and terror in the fpectator, as may confift with the *pleafure* which
is the end of tragedy, and then relieving
him at laft, by prevention, at the very moment of execution."  And this has been
almoft invariably the practice of Metaftafio.

The excellent interpreter and commenta-
tor of Ariftotle, juft quoted, has cited a paffage from Roufleau, againft the excefs of
*tragical terrorifm*, which feems perfectly in
unifon with Metaftafio's opinion on the fubject.  In concluding his *Nouvelle Eloife*, the
citizen of Geneva fays : " I am unable to
conceive what pleafure the authors of many
of our tragedies can take, in imagining characters fo full of wickednefs and horror, and
*putting themfelves in the place of thofe they*
*reprefent,*

*reprefent*, making them act and fpeak fuch things, as it is impoffible to fee or hear without fhuddering."

With refpect to the ufual practice of terminating operas *happily*, it may afford fome gratification to the curiofity of thofe who intereft themfelves in fuch exhibitions, to trace it from the firft dramas of modern times, that were recited in mufic.

*Rinuccini*, author of *Eurydice*, the firft regular opera, treated the well-known ftory of Orpheus differently from Virgil, in order to terminate his piece *happily*. In this drama, Orpheus obtains Eurydice from the fhades, by the power of fong, *unconditionally :* indeed, the author apologizes to his patronefs, Mary of Medicis, in celebration of whofe nuptials with Henry IV of France, in 1600, it was written, for having dared to alter the termination of the fable of Orpheus ; juftifying himfelf by its being a time of jubilation ; and adding, that it was the practice of the Greek poets in other fables : Sophocles, in his Ajax, had deviated from Homer in a fimilar manner. Rinuccini, eight years after, wrote a fecond opera, ARIANNA, which he calls a tragedy, though this likewife terminates *happily*, by comforting the unfortunate

unfortunate princefs, who had been abandoned by Thefeus, with a celeftial fpoufe,
in the character of " Bacchus, ever fair and
young."

Thefe two firft mufical dramas, perhaps,
ferved as models for fubfequent exhibitions
of the fame kind: for in examining a complete collection of all the operas that have
ever been performed at Venice, from 1637
to the prefent time, " Medea's murdering
knife" feems never to have been ufed; and
the Protagoniftes, contrary to the precept of
Ariftotle, generally proceeds from *bad* to
*good*, and not from bad to worfe, or from
happinefs to mifery (*r*).

Not one of Apoftolo Zeno's numerous
operas, has an unhappy cataftrophe; and
out of twenty-fix dramas of Metaftafio,
only three, *Dido*, *Cato*, and *Atilius Regulus*,
terminate in a difaftrous manner. When
Cato was firft performed at Rome, in 1728,
and killed himfelf in the third act, the piece

(*r*) Indeed the modern *Pyramus* and *Thifbe*, died like
two fwans, in an opera of that name, in 1774; they were
half an hour in the tuneful agonies of death: and the performers *Rauzini* and the *Schindlerin*, being refufcitated
by an *encore*, delighted the audience with their own *death-
fong*, a fecond time.

was

was ill-received; and the next day, an advertifement was found on the ftatue of Pafquin, " inviting the company of death to the funeral of Cato, who lies *extinct* in the Theatre *delle Dame*."

It has been faid that the emperor Charles VI, having an utter averfion to terrific terminations of the dramas that were performed at his court, and wifhing to fend the audience home in good humour from the theatre, Stampiglia, the imperial laureat, and his fucceffors, Apoftolo Zeno, and Metaftafio, to gratify the tafte of their patron, reverfed the Ariftotelian canon, and changed the fortune of their heroes from *bad* to *good*. But this feems to have been the general practice of much more ancient lyric poets than thefe. In all Metaftafio's beft dramas, which terminate with the happinefs of the principal characters, there are previous fcenes of infinite diftrefs and pathos, arifing from events and fituations of fuffering virtue. To fee a magnanimous and virtuous character, after great trials and fufferings, by which he has gained our affection, pafs from mifery to a ftate of happinefs, is more inftructive, as well as more grateful, to the human heart, than the death of villains, or of thofe who,

who, like Oedipus, fuffer every fpecies of woe for inevitable crimes, committed through ignorance. It is rather *danger* than *terror,* which awakens our pity in the tragedies of Metaftafio.

The cavalier Planelli (s), one of the beft Italian writers on the melodrama, or opera, fays : that " the diminifhing the horrors of tragedy, whatever *Mifanthropes* may fay, is a certain proof of the progrefs which urbanity, clemency, and benevolence, have made in modern times. The ancient Greeks, defcended from the barbarous and ferocious nations which firft inhabited that country, retained, in their moft civilized cities, a tafte for terrific and fanguinary exhibitions. The tragedies which remain of the three great models, all breathe that national fpirit. The characters, indeed, in thefe dramas, are magnanimous and grand ; but, at the fame time, impetuous and inhuman. To move a people, accuftomed to horror, it was the bufinefs of tragedy to adopt fables, full of the moft atrocious and difaftrous events, or little attention or fuccefs could be expected from their reprefentation. But modern tra-

(s) *Dell'Opera in Mufica Trattato.* Napoli. 1772. 8vo.

gedy, cultivated by a people many ages civilized, friends to commerce, hofpitable to
ftrangers, and profeffing a religion which
infpires charity, mildnefs, peace, compaffion,
and beneficence, if it did not diminifh atro-
city, would difguft, beyond the power of
poetry and mufic to fupprefs."

Metaftafio certainly meant this *Eftratto*
and commentary as an apology for deviating
from the Stagirite in his own practice,
though he had not the courage to publifh it.
But in writing for modern mufic, he furely
had powerful reafons for extending the fubjects of his dramas beyond mere terror and
compaffion, to which Ariftotle, and his implicit followers, think all tragedy fhould be
confined. Our poet has, indeed, fuccef-
fully violated this canon of the ancient dramatic legiflator, by exciting an intereft in
the fufferings and rewards of every public
and focial virtue : fubjects more appropriated
to mufical expreffion, than the terrors excited by atrocious crimes and dire calamities.
This is ftill adhering to another affertion of
Ariftotle : that the chief end of tragedy is
*to purge the paffions.* The mental cathartics
indeed of the modern lyric bard are not
violent, but rather lenient and anodyne, than

cauftics

caustics or stimulants. The ridicule frequently thrown upon singing in pain, dif-
tress, and misery, by persons ignorant that
ancient tragedies, with all their terrors,
were constantly *sung*, was a sufficient motive to Metastasio to try to enlighten the
public, by his remarks on particular doctrines of Aristotle. Indeed, those who either hear or peruse the dramas of Metastasio, with a determination to allow him no
merit, but that to which he is intitled by
his implicit obedience to the decrees of Aristotle and of French critics, or the servile
imitation of the ancient Greek poets, rob
him of much just praise, and themselves of
pleasure, in not giving way to their own
reason and feeling, instead of judging by
line and rule. The delight which he has
excited on the stage, with the assistance of
music, and in the closet, with that of un-
biassed taste and sensibility, seems justly to
intitle him to more praise as an *original* writer, than *could* be due to him for mere clas-
sical larceny or imitation. What but oblivion, did his learned preceptor Gravina acquire by his tragedies, written exactly on
the Greek model? Our countryman, Mr.
Mason's tragedies on that plan, will ever be
admired

admired, in perufal, for the exquifite beauty of the poetry; but it is yet a doubt, whether they will ever have due juftice done them on. the ftage, for which, indeed, he never intended them, nor did he expect they could fucceed in reprefentation, as originally written.

It has been faid, that Mr. Gray ufed to difpute the merit of Metaftafio; and would not allow his dramas to be legitimate tragedies, or any thing more than mere fketches, or outlines of tragedy, compared with the expanded dramas of his favourites, Racine and Voltaire. His friend, Mr. Mafon, has lately been more liberal, in acknowledging the merit of the Italian lyric poet, in a note (p. 102) of his ingenious *Effays on Englifh Church Mufic.* " How great a dramatic writer (fays he) would Metaftafio have been, if not compelled, in fubferviency to his mufical compofers, to furnifh them only with *Libretti!* It muft, however, be allowed, that his lyrical dramas, as originally written, in refpect to theatrical contrivance, and judicious developement of the ftory, infinitely excel 'the generality of our modern tragedies."

But befides the merit allowed him by Mr. Mafon, the beauty of Metaftafio's fentiments and poetry, have been the admiration of all Europe, for more than fifty years.

Modern mufic is, perhaps, too florid for narrative poetry. The airs certainly impede the bufinefs of the drama, and ufurp an attention of another kind. It is doubtlefs true, that if mufic had been out of the queftion, Metaftafio's dramas might have been eafily more expanded, and rendered fitter for declamation, and, perhaps, perufal. But one of the greateft difficulties which Metaftafio had to encounter, and for the vanquifhing of which he has been the moft admired by thofe who have ftudied the mufical drama, was the compreffing the fables he chofe, into fo fmall a compafs, yet rendering all his plots clear, his principal characters ftrongly marked and confiftent, and his fentiments tender, nervous, or philofophical, as occafion required.

If Metaftafio, in writing for mufic, had expanded fentiment in fuch long fpeeches, as thofe of which Mr. Gray has left us examples, in the Fragment of his *Agrippina*, his dramas might have been called *fine tragedies*, but would never have fucceeded as *operas*, in which fentiment is expanded by
*vocal*

*vocal expreſſion,* ariſing from ſituation, more than by *verbal articulation* (*t*).

Regarded as pieces for *declamation,* the characters and ſentiments are not ſufficiently expanded; but, as *muſical dramas,* they are in all reſpects the moſt perfect that have ever been produced.

(*t*) *Giulio Strozzi,* one of the early lyric poets of Venice, in his *Delia,* an opera performed in that city, 1639, entirely in recitative, ten years before any thing like an *air* was attempted; after ſaying, in an adver-tiſement at the end of the *Libretto,* that he had cut out more than 300 verſes in the repreſentation of his opera, that he might not abuſe the patience of the audience, adds, that " it is the duty of a poet to relinquiſh his *flouriſhes* and *diviſions (ſue Gorghe)* which are his digreſ-ſions and epiſodes, to make room for the diviſions *(paſ-ſaggi)* of the ſingers." No time is kept in recitative; ſo that the ſinger was allowed to dilate and embelliſh ſentiment, *ad libitum.* A poet was then more at the mercy of the ſinger, than of the compoſer; and when vocal powers are great, and (as often happens) out-run propriety and diſcretion, the performer will not wait for moments of paſſion to diſplay his taſte, execution, and expreſſion, but will riot in *florid ſong,* whenever a liquid ſyllable or open vowel ſhall occur. Marcheſi has re-vived this primitive cuſtom of *gracing recitative,* not more to the ſatisfaction of the poet, or favourable to the buſineſs of the drama, perhaps, than *long introduc-tory ſymphonies,* or *aric di bravura,* of which the admirers of ſimplicity in the narrative muſic of the drama, ſo much complain.

" In

" In every work regard the writer's end,
Since none can compafs more than they intend."

Mr. Gray's feverity of decifion concerning the merit of Rouffeau's *Nouvelle Eloife*, is little lefs furprifing than his blindnefs to the merit of Metaftafio. Among all the citizen of Geneva's faults and fingularities, *infipidity* and want of intereft, we believe, has never been laid to his charge, by any other writer.

The reft of the chapters of Metaftafio's *Abftract*, which, in all, amount to twenty-nine, are replete with learning, ingenuity, good tafte, and, above all, with *good fenfe*; which, according to Horace, is the firft qualification of every writer :

*Scribendi recte, fapere eft et principium et fons.*
A. P. v. 309.

It was intended to have concluded thefe Memoirs, with a tranflation of the whole *Eftratto*, not only as a fpecimen of our author's ftyle in *profe*, but abilities in criticifm ; but the great number of his letters which have been inferted, will not allow fufficient fpace for a work of fo confiderable a length, in the prefent publication. And as for the additional

additional three volumes of his inedited works, mentioned in the Preface, and of which I was extremely ambitious of being the firſt to give a detailed account to the Engliſh admirers of·Metaſtaſio; after employing every probable means which my eagernefs to be in poffeffion of them, previous to the publication of thefe Memoirs could fuggeſt, I have, at length, had the mortification to hear from Vienna, that the printing the work which Mademoifelle Martines had reaſon to expect would be ready for publication in April laſt, has been impeded by the death of the Italian printer, *Alberti*. And now the fame Vienna correfpondent writes word, that on the 23d of laſt month (December) to his further enquiries, he had only received for anfwer, that " the work would be publiſhed early in the next month : the fame anfwer which had been given for feven months paſt." So that, for the prefent, I muſt content myfelf with giving my readers the opinion of an excellent Italian critic on the moſt interefting article among thefe poſthumous pieces, which he has feen in manufcript.

" Befides the *Abſtract* of the Poetics of Ariſtotle, another precious monument exiſts

of

of Metaftafio's profound ftudy of the Greek
dramatic writers. A manufcript is in the
poffeffion of his executors, fuperfcribed with
his own hand : *Efame di tutte le Tragedie e
Commedie Greche per foccorfo della mia memoria, e non per pubblicarfi.* By the friendly
kindnefs of the learned counfellor Martinez,
I have been indulged with the perufal of this
MS. in which the remarks are extended to
the *terra incognita* of ordinary critics ; here
we fee reafons affigned for apparent defects,
which the practice of the times rendered neceffary ; and here we have a moft exact parallel of the whole pieces and their conftitu-
ent parts, drawn up with the moft captivat-
ing clearnefs and fagacity. And here we
may perceive, that it was not from the writings of Calderon (as has been carelefsly and
erroneoufly afferted) but from the Greek
poets, that he learned the art of weaving
his plots, and the exquifite reflexions, maxims, and political principles, with which
his dialogues are embellifhed, and which, to
common judges, feem fcattered at random ;
but which were drawn from the pureft and
deepeft fprings, and with a moft mafterly
œconomy,

œconomy, always appropriated to different
climates, ages, laws, and cuftoms (*u*)."

---

## TO THE SHADE OF METASTASIO.

IF ftill allow'd to liften, honour'd fhade !
And mortal forrows reach the happy dead,
Oh ! hear with fenfibility my ftrain,
Nor humble tears, nor heart-felt grief difdain !
No views finifter now fufpicions raife
That adulation minifters thy praife :
Thy worth and virtues precious to mankind,
Have long with veneration fill'd my mind.
　　Thy lenient ethics mitigate each fmart,
And, while they flatter, purify the heart.
The furious paffions are at thy controul,
And each emotion of the human foul.
Loft muft that mortal be, who hears in vain
Thy moral leffon, or thy pious ftrain !
To Love thy pen could dignity impart,
Devoid of vice and each infidious art ;
Nor haft thou ever deign'd *his* caufe to plead,
Unlefs when worth and honour claim'd the meed,
　　The friend of virtue in a gay difguife,
Which captivates alike the weak and wife ;
The diffolute and lawlefs patient hear
Thy tale of woe, and drop a pitying tear.

(*u*) *Offervazioni fopra Metaftafio dell' Abate Bertola.*
Baffano, 1784. 8vo.

　　　　　　　The

The fons of Epicurus learn to feel,
The wounds óf fuff'ring worth, and wifh to heal;
Infenfibly the hardeft hearts dilate
At noble deeds, and fain would imitate.
   Benignant pow'r ! humanity to charm,
And all its vile propenfities difarm ;
Not by harfh rules, which ne'er convince the
      mind,
Nor pious cant, of more infipid kind :
More fweet thy moral fong, in virtue's praife,
Than fporting firens could to pleafure raife ;
Nor for the ftage, was virtue ever dreft,
In fuch a pleafing, fuch alluring veft.
   Long may thy precepts regulate the heart,
And joy feraphic to mankind impart !
Long may thy dulcet meafuresMufic guide,
And tafte and feeling over art prefide !
While intellectual radiance beams around,
And to the heart points each impaffion'd found !

APPENDIX.

# APPENDIX.

---

AFTER the preceding sheets were printed, and the press was closed, I accidentally
heard, that previous to the publication of
the *Three Volumes of Metastasio's Posthumous
Works*, at Vienna, an itinerant German
*Colporteur*, or book pedlar, hearing of the
solicitude with which these books had been
sought by the English, in that city, during
many months, contrived to get the start of
the trade by procuring, by some unknown
means, the possession of seven or eight copies
of each impression of the work, with which
he arrived in England a fortnight ago; during
which time he had been hawking his *inesti-
mable* little bale of Metastasian goods, without

out fuccefs; owing to the price he fet upon it being fo enormous, that no importer of foreign books would venture to deal with him; nor would he part with a *fingle* fet, on any terms. However, by the favour of a perfon in whofe hands they were left for a day or two, I obtained a fight of them for juft three hours; during which fhort period, I made the following hafty remarks, with which I prefent my readers, as *addenda* to the Memoirs of the Poet's Life and Writings.

The firft volume contains his Obfervations on the Greek Dramatifts, to which there is no other preface or introduction, than the following:

*Nota di alcuni offervazioni da me fatte fopra tutte le Tragedie e Commedie Greche che ci ri-mangono, per foccorfo della mia memoria.* " Mi-nutes of fome obfervations which I have made on all the Greek Tragedies and Come-dies that are come down to us, to affift my memory."

He begins with the Tragedies of Æschy-lus; feven of which only have been pre-ferved, out of ninety-feven which he is faid to have written. Metaftafio's analyfis of *Prometheus chained,* the firft of Æfchylus's dramas, was the only one of thefe fhort
articles

articles which I had time to read. Of this he fays :

" It is difficult to characterize this drama, it is fo extravagant and fantaftical. The fcene is a *horrid rock*. *Force* and *Violence*, perfonified, order Vulcan, in the name of Jupiter, to chain Prometheus to this rock, for having too much favoured human kind. Vulcan executes the command, though with much reluctance ; and not only binds every part of the culprit's body to the rock with iron chains, but faftens his breaft to it with adamantine nails. Prometheus, after this, is left alone to curfe the tyranny of Jupiter. In the mean time, the daughters of Thetis arrive on the wings of the winds, to form the chorus. They tell him, that they had heard the ftrokes of the hammer in their grotto at the bottom of the fea, and were come to confole him, and to learn the occafion of his difgrace. Prometheus, in the dreadful ftate in which they found him, relates in a circumftantial manner, the benefits which he had conferred on mankind. Saying, that Jupiter, the ufurper of Saturn's kingdom, was a tyrant, and would be dethroned by another, whom he (Prometheus) knew, but whofe name he would not reveal.

The

The chorus counfels him to fubmiffion ; but he refufes to comply. At length *Oceanus* arrives on a winged monfter, neither defcribed nor named, on a vifit to the fufferer: pities him, and offers his interpofition : it is rejected, and after a long debate, he departs to the found of Triton's trumpet. The chorus weeps, and advifes him to be calm and fubmiffive ; but all in vain. They are interrupted by the arrival of a furious cow; that is, by the daughter of the river Inachus. Prometheus, in fpite of the nails in his breaft, manifefts much curiofity to know the hiftory of this cow. She, with great eloquence, fatisfies him ; and he, in correfpondent terms, tells her her fortune. A fit of madnefs agitates the cow, and fhe quits the ftage. Prometheus, ftill obftinate, continues his imprecations. Mercury enters, and by command of Jove, orders him to declare who it is that will dethrone him, on pain of a violent encreafe of his torments. Prometheus laughs at his threats; infults Jupiter and his meffenger, when the heavens grow dark, and a furious ftorm of wind, thunder, and lightning, enfues. Prometheus cries out, invoking Themis (or Juftice) to terminate the tragedy.

" Father Brumoy will not abfolutely
allow,

allow, that Io appears in the form of a cow; but the author, at verſe 590, calls her Βȣκεϱω, *bubulis prædita cornibus*: and at verſe 675, Κεϱαςις, *cornuta*; and the ſcholiaſt explains Ἰης εἰς βȣν μεταβληϑεισης.

" There being only a ſingle character chained to a rock, who receives a few viſits, it would have been difficult not to preſerve the *unity* of place. But Pere Brumoy thinks Æſchylus wonderful in having invented this unity."

Being, at length, in poſſeſſion of a copy of this poſthumous publication, over which my power is unlimited, I ſhall extend my extracts of the poet's remarks on the Greek dramatiſts, and give a ſhort account of the reſt of the contents of theſe volumes.

" *The ſeven chiefs againſt Thebes.* This tragedy can hardly be called a drama, conſiſting only of extreme long choral odes, and a ſhort narrative. The ſtyle is extremely lyrical ; full of metaphor and imagery, particularly in the choruſes. The fable finiſhes at the 823d verſe, with the death of the two hoſtile brothers. The reſt of the play conſiſts of weeping and wailing, and a decree of the people concerning the funeral rites of the ſlain, granted to Eteocles, and denied to Polynices. Antigone wiſhes to bury the latter ;

latter; but is oppofed by the herald, and the tragedy ends, without the audience knowing how it will be determined. So that the unity of action is violated, and the fable left unfinifhed. There is a fcene between Eteocles and the chorus, againft the importunity of fearful women, which is long, ufelefs, and comic.

" *The Perfians.* It is difficult to fay what is the real fubject of this tragedy. The repetition of the narrative of the defeat of the Perfians at the battle of Salamis, and the perpetual lamentations of the chorus of aged Satraps, compofe the whole drama. Atoffa, the mother of Xerxes, by a kind of magical incantation, evokes the fhade of Darius her hufband, to give her counfel and news of her fon Xerxes. The ghoft knows nothing of what has happened, and has it to learn. But afterwards tells her, that Xerxes was illadvifed to contend with Greece. And ere he difappears, gives the following advice to the old men.

' My ancient friends, farewel: and 'midft thefe ills
' Each day in pleafure bathe your drooping fpirits,
' For treafured riches nought avail the dead.'

POTTER.

" Atoffa

" Atoffa hearing of the great flaughter of
the Perfians, and the fhameful flight of her
fon, fays:

   ' Unhappy fortune, what a tide of ills
   ' Burfts o'er me ! Chief this foul difgrace, which fhews
   ' My fon divefted of his *rich attire,*
   ' His royal robes all rent, diftra&ts my thoughts.
   ' But I will go, chufe the moft gorgeous veft,
   ' And hafte to meet my fon.'

POTTER.

" At length, Xerxes appears with a lift of
the flain ; exhorts the chorus to tear his hair,
beat his breaft, rend his garments, and join
with him in loud lamentations. And with
this alternate fymphony, the tragedy ends.

" *Agamemnon.* This is unanimoufly allowed by the literary world, to be the moft
difficult and obfcure of the tragedies of
Æfchylus, abounding with diftorted and
daring metaphors, with figures and ideas that
only belong to lyric poetry. The plot is
the affaffination of Agamemnon, by Clytemneftra and Ægifthus. The perfon of Agamemnon is little feen ; he only appears once,
and what he fays, is not fufficient to furnifh
an idea of his chara&ter. That of the falfe,
perfidious, and cruel Clytemneftra, is well
drawn. The chorus is animated, obfcure,
and

and lyrical : the enthufiaftic predictions of Caffandra are of the fame kind. The tragedy begins with a watchman, or fentinel, who fpeaks from the top of the royal palace. Clytemneftra having placed him there to difcover when a lighted flambeau was to be feen, which would difcover the ruin of Troy. And this was to be communicated by perfons placed at equal diftances from mount Ida and Argos. The flambeau is feen, and foon after a meffenger arrives, as fwift as lightning, with the news of the taking of Troy.

" In this, as well as in other Greek tragedies, at the opening of a door in the fcene, the dead body of the perfon flain is difcovered, and often of many perfons, not very eafy to comprehend. In like manner, the words and cries of perfons are heard in the ftreet or fquare, who are killed in the interior palace. In this tragedy, the murderers remain unpunifhed.

" The *Choephoræ*, or *Bearers of Libations*. The fubject of this tragedy is the fame as that to which Sophocles and Euripides have given the title of Electra. Æfchylus ftyles thofe damfels *Choephoræ* who were in the fervice of Clytemneftra, but partial to

I

Electra,

Electra, and who follow her with the libations to be made to the tomb of Agamemnon. The ftyle, as ufual, is tumid and figurative to excefs; but the conduct, in general, fimple and natural.

" In all the three Electras, probability feems wanting for the fuccefs of Oreftes's enterprife; but in this, more than in the others. Oreftes, alone, unknown in the royal palace of his enemy, kills his mother, and the tyrant, without a fingle guard, domeftic, or any one crying out or oppofing him. The fcene in which Oreftes barbaroufly obliges his mother to enter the palace for him to murder her on the dead body of Ægifthus, is fuch an atrocious act of inhumanity, that Pere Brumoy himfelf, who ufed to be tranfported with every thing concerning the golden age of Athens, is obliged to confefs this tranfaction to be infupportable.

" Clytemneftra, at verfe 893, in order to move her fon to compaffion, that he might not kill her, opens her breaft, and reminds him of the milk which he had fucked from it. And a little before, verfe 754, the nurfe of Oreftes, having thought him dead, weeps over him, and reminds him of the fatigue which she had had in bringing him up; not forgetting to mention the inconvenience which he had put her to, during his little natural wants.

" To enjoy these beauties, we should be enabled to transport ourselves to those venerable ages, when such things were admired, as profane moderns are unable to comprehend.

" The *Eumenides*, or *Furies*. The action of this drama is the trial or absolution of Orestes. It begins in the temple of Apollo at Delphos. At the opening, the old Pythia appears, who makes a long invocation to all the presaging divinities, and retires to place herself on the tripod; but is seen no more throughout the tragedy, nor is it known why she appeared, nor why she did not return.

" At v. 93, Orestes, conducted by Mercury, quits the temple of Delphos, to go to that of Minerva at Athens.

" At v. 117, the Furies in a deep sleep in the temple of Delphos, answer, while they are snoring, the shade of Clytemnestra, who wishes to wake them, that they may pursue Orestes; and the ghost says : What! do you snore? So eager is the author that the audience should know and admire his invention.

3

" At

" At v. 235, Oreſtes appears in the temple of Minerva at Athens: and the Furies,
after a few verſes, join him. A manifeſt and
conſiderable breach of the unity of place.
For if this is not a change of ſcene, what is
it ? And yet Ariſtotle does not reſent the
ſacrilege. It is well for Æſchylus, that he
was born ſo many ages before M. d'Aubignac,
who, I know not how, has diſſembled this
enormity of the father of tragedy, or let it
eſcape his obſervation.

" At v. 663, Apollo ſays, that the ſon
owes not his corporal exiſtence to his
mother.

—— She but the nutrient ſoil
That gives the ſtranger growth.
*Procreat autem ille, qui inſilet* *.

" This is one of thoſe Grecian ſimplicities
which modern palates cannot taſte.

" *The Supplicants.* The conduct of this
fable has all the ſimplicity ſo much admired

* Euripides ſuſtains the ſame doctrine in Oreſtes :
My father was the author of my being :
Thy daughter brought me forth : he gave me life,
Which ſhe but foſter'd: to the higher cauſe
An higher reverence then I deemed was due.

POTTER.

by

by the fevere connoiffeurs of Grecian theatrical perfection. The fifty daughters of Danaus, to avoid being wedded to their fifty
coufins, the fons of Ægyptus, fly with their
father, to demand an afylum of Pelafgus,
king of Argos, and obtain it. The paucity
of events is fupplied by the extreme inactivity,
and prolixity, of the chorufes. The fcene is
near the fea fhore, where the images of the
gods are placed, who prefide at the Athletic
games, not far from the city of Argos.

" From v. 466, the Danaides, in order to
induce Pelafgus to afford the afylum which
he grants, carry on with him the following
ingenious dialogue :

*Chorus. (the daughters of Danaus).*
          Seeft thou thefe braided zones that bind our
            robes ?

*Pelafgus.* Ornaments thefe that fuit your female ftate
*Cho.*      Know then the honeft purpofe thefe fhall ferve
*Pelaf.*    What would thy words intend? Explain thyfelf
*Cho.*      If honour fhall not guard this female train—
*Pelaf.*    How can thefe binding zones fecure your fafety?
*Cho.*      Hanging new trophies on thefe images.
*Pelaf.*    Myfterious are thy words ; fpeak plainly to me.
*Cho.*      To tell thee plainly then, I mean ourfelves.
                                     Potter.

" The elegance of this little dialogue
needs no explanation, to thofe who by dint
of learning are become Athenians.

                                            " At

" At the fight of a fhip, which Danaus conjectures to be that which conducts the fifty fons of Ægyptus, he flies to the city to demand affiftance againft his perfecutors; without its being known, why he leaves his daughters, who being young and active, might have gone on this bufinefs much better than their aged father, and not have been expofed to the violence of their coufins. The father leaves them, and a fingle herald from their coufins comes to order them to embark with him. They refift. He offers to force them on board ; and they, though fifty in number, can only defend themfelves by their fcreams.

" But help arrives. Danaus has already been at Argos, and found Pelafgus; told him their danger, the foldiers are embodied, and have marched to the fea-fide in the time that a few lines have been uttered.

" The herald being departed, king Pelafgus invites Danaus and his daughters to come to Argos, affigns them habitations in the city, and departs. Danaus, before they fet out, gives his daughters fome wholefome admonition. But the thing which he recommends to them in the moft anxious and prolix manner, is, *that they do not difhonour him in a ftrange land ; that they afford no*

*opportunity*

*opportunity for scandal,* but remain modeſt, though young women *are much addicted to love.*

" Such an admonition in our times would be uſeleſs and injurious, ſuppoſing that royal princeſſes are incapable of failing in their duty; but in the time of Æſchylus, there were no ſuch ſuppoſitions; and ſimple nature was then repreſented, which is the delight of our literati."

After thus pointing out where the unities are violated, the plots imperfect, the perpetrators of horrid crimes unpuniſhed, and delicacy and propriety wounded, according to modern ideas; Metaſtaſio gives a ſketch of the life of Æſchylus, and apologizes, not only for his imperfections, but for being forced to point them out.

" Æſchylus (ſays he) was doubtleſs the father of tragedy. He firſt put narratives into action, invented the ſtage, tragic dreſſes and maſks; ſo that all the theatrical wonders in ſubſequent times are derived from his ſublime inventions. We therefore owe him infinite gratitude and reſpect, and ſhould exact them from others, if the envious impertinence of pedants, in order to depreciate their cotemporaries, did not ſtupidly and arrogantly

arrogantly exalt beyond meafure whatever was reprehenfible in him, which, however, ought to be refpectfully over-looked, in gratitude for the incomparable merit of a firft invention; and if proud of their lamentable obfervations, they did not erect themfelves into legiflators of an art of which they are wholly ignorant, and in which they have either had no experience, or when they have had the prefumption to attempt to acquire it, have become the objects of public derifion. Hence even refpectable men have been forced to reflect, and declare to the world how little is come down to us from our predeceffors that is valuable; not with a view to diminifh their fame, but merely to unmafk the livid and falfe oracles of the poor disfigured Parnaffus.

" The ftyle of Æfchylus is fublime, figurative, and metaphorical to excefs. Terror is always the object which he propofes: his fcholiaft afferts, that in the reprefentation of the Eumenides, many children died of fright, and many pregnant women mifcarried! *Credat Judæus Apella.*"

The remaining feven tragedies of So-phocles; the nineteen of Euripides; and
the

the eleven comedies of ARISTOPHANES, are analyzed in the fame concife and characteriftic manner as the dramas of Æfchylus.  Many of his reflexions on the Greek dramatifts have been inferted in the Abftract of the Poetics of Ariftotle.  Indeed more inftances feem to have been given by Metaftafio of the total inattention to any rule concerning the *unities* in Sophocles, Euripides, and Arifto-phanes, than in Æfchylus ; or rather more proofs that no fuch rule exifted, when thefe great fathers of theatrical excellence flourifh-ed,  For when any one of the unities has efcaped violation in their dramas, it feems more to have been by chance, than from any fixed rule or principle : as there is fcarce any one of their comedies or tragedies where they are entirely preferved ; though there are many which would have been much injured if they had efcaped violation.

The extreme difference in ancient and modern times, of manners, morals, religion, and even in the conftruction of theatres, renders clofe and fervile imitation of the Greek dramatifts now inadmiffible ; though the bold, fublime, and noble fentiments, the heroic virtues and characters, and the exquifite

quifite beauties of the conceptions and morality in the poetry of the choral odes, muft
always excite the wonder and rapture of men
of found learning and good tafte, in all ages
and countries, where the compofitions of the
ancient Greeks are underftood in the original, or their true fpirit is transfufed into
other languages by tranflation.

In the review of the Andromache of
EURIPIDES, Metaftafio has pointed out fuch
inftances in the language and fentiments of
that tragedy, as, if clofely imitated or tranflated, would be thought coarfe, indecorous,
and far from decent in a modern drama.

The ftrange events and feemingly abfurd
and impure language of the heroic characters,
would not be difficult for the moderns to
copy and adopt; but the fublime beauties of
the poetry, and fometimes of the fentiments,
will never be made common by theft or
open imitation in modern times.

So licentious, fcurrilous, and not only farcaftic, but malignant a dramatift as ARISTO-
PHANES, was not likely to be treated with
partiality by fo moral, benevolent, and decorous a writer, as Metaftafio; yet fo juft,
difcriminative, and candid are his reflexions

on

on the remains of this mercilefs enemy of
Socrates and Euripides, that his greateft admirers and imitators muft allow him to be
treated with that temper and fairnefs, with
which Ariftophanes never treated friends or
foes, or even the gods themfelves.

After indicating the defects in the plan
of his *Plutus*, Metaftafio fays: that " notwithftanding thefe cenfures, the dialogue of
this piece is fo natural, full of grace, and the
moft acute and poignant wit, that it manifefts the genius, and rich mine of ridicule
with which he was poffeffed. In the midft
of the moft indecent deformities with which
this comedy abounds, we fometimes meet
with traits of the moft folid morality;
particularly in the defence which *Poverty*
makes of herfelf, which is worthy of Plato.

" He regards the *Female Orators*, not like
Pere Brumoy, as a fevere fatire on women,
but rather as a fatire on the inconftancy and
folly of the Athenian people, in perpetually
reforming and changing their form of government ; adopting the vifions of the moft
extravagant projectors, provided they were
*new* ; and therefore the author recommends
that women fhould be placed at the head of
the

the ftate, as the only revolutionary project left untried. So that this is not the
moft indecent of his pieces, as has been
generally imagined, though certainly the moft
difgufting ; as he has not fcrupled to introduce a magiftrate eafing himfelf in the ftreet;
during which time he is extremely witty to
the fpectators, and gives them an ample dofe
of Attic falt and pleafantry.

" Ariftophanes (fays Metaftafio) was a
poet of an extraordinary imagination and
eloquence; daring, impudent, malicious, and
a contemner of all order, decency, humanity,
probability, and almoft common fenfe, in his
allegories and allufions ; provided they gratified his fpite and fpleen. Plutarch, among
the ancients, and Pere Brumoy, in modern
times, have declared this poet to be infuffer-
able among honeft and well educated men in
any civilized country. He delighted the Athenian mob, by ridiculing every thing that was
venerable, and which had long been thought
facred ; and his principal object was the
deftruction of religion and morality, by bur-
lefquing the reafoning of Socrates, as modern
philofophers do the facred writings and the
doctrines of the moft pious and profound
theologians."

Among

Among the *felect Letters* which occupy
the chief part of this publication, there are
feveral which were not inferted in the five
volumes of the Poet's correfpondence in the
*Nice* edition of his works; but thefe are
neither fo long, nor, feemingly, fo important,
as many that have been omitted. In looking
at the index of letters that appear in thefe
additional volumes, I perceived one to the
Emprefs Queen; feveral to the Princefs di
Belmonte; three to Goldoni; three or four
to Calfabigi; two to the celebrated chief of
the Bologna fchool of finging, Bernacchi;
two to Diodati; two to Captain Benincafa;
one to Father Bofcovich; one to Mr. Hoole,
and one to Cahufac, that are not in the Nice
edition.

Of three notes written in French, by the
Emprefs Queen, to the imperial laureat, two
have already been inferted in thefe Memoirs.
The inedited poetry is very inconfiderable;
and the fketch of his life is chiefly taken
from Rezer's epitome.

His WILL, made in 1765, and the CODI-
CIL, dated 1780, inferted at the end of the
third volume, caught my attention; and I
was very glad to find in them a clear and fatisfactory refutation of the want of affection
for

for his family, which has been unjuftly laid
to his charge *; and which, if true, would
have confiderably diminifhed the excellence
of his moral character.

It appears in his *Teftament*, made 1765,
that he bequeaths to his brother LEOPOLD
(whom he calls his *amabiliffimo fratello*) 500
Roman crowns a year (the intereft of 30,000
crowns) and the fame to his fifter BARBARA.
To Mademoifelle Marianna Martinez, he
leaves 12,000 florins, with his harpfichord,
clavichord, mufic-books, and book-cafe; and
appoints her refiduary legatee, in cafe fhe
furvived her brother Giufeppe.

In the *Codicil*, dated 1780, *his brother and
fifter being dead*, he made a new and more
confiderable difpofition of his effects in favour of the Martinez family, with whom
he had lived in uninterrupted friendfhip and
affection, upwards of fifty years; and to
whofe care and kindnefs, during a long
feries of ill health, he afcribed his longe-
vity.

Another draw-back from his fortitude
and philofophy, which has been triumphantly
made by thofe who, unfoundedly, accufed

* See Vol. I. of thefe Memoirs, p. 112.

2

him

him of an invincible repugnance to speaking of old age, and death, is taken off; not only by his frequently mentioning both in his letters, with no more horror than other mortals; but by the following passage in his last will:

"Having been afflicted with a very precarious state of health during forty years, which often rendered life insufferable, it is my wish, after my decease, to have my body opened by a skilful surgeon, in hopes that some discovery will be made, that may be of use to my survivors." Envy itself could fasten no *vice* upon him; and the *frailties* and *infirmities* that have been laid to his charge, seem very easy for candour to invalidate.

END OF THE THIRD AND LAST VOLUME.

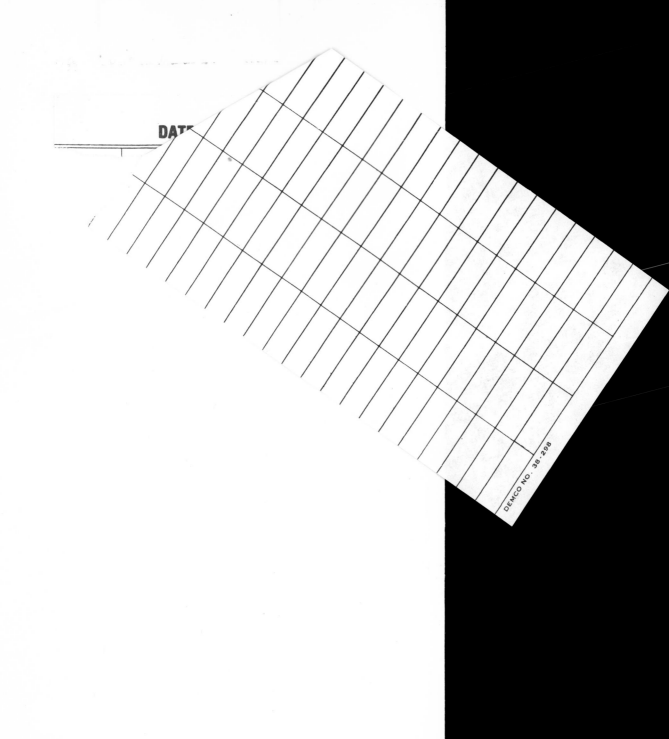

DATE

DEMCO NO. 38-298